THE

# DUKES OF NORMANDY,

FROM THE

## TIME OF ROLLO

TO

## THE EXPULSION OF KING JOHN

BY

PHILIP AUGUSTUS OF FRANCE.

---

BY

### JONATHAN DUNCAN, ESQ. B. A.

AUTHOR OF

" The Religions of Profane Antiquity,"

---

LONDON:

JOSEPH RICKERBY, SHERBOURN LANE;

AND

HARVEY AND DARTON,

GRACECHURCH STREET.

1839.

# PREFACE.

THE object of this work is an attempt to supply
a deficiency in the historical literature of England. The popular abridgment of Goldsmith
conveys but scanty information of our earlier
annals, nor have his successors in the same department added much to our stock of knowledge.
We are not indeed aware of any publication
adapted for the use of schools, and young readers
of both sexes, which treats of that portion of
history which forms the subject of this volume.
It would have been an useless undertaking to have
narrated the lives of the Norman and Plantagenet
princes, in their character of kings of England,
that task having already been so frequently and
fully accomplished; our endeavour has been to
portray them as DUKES of NORMANDY, merely
introducing such slight allusions to England as
were necessary to preserve the harmony and con-
nection of the narrative.

In collecting our materials, we have diligently consulted the old chroniclers, that our facts might be based on authentic testimony; and where the early writers contradict each other, we have carefully balanced their respective evidence, and drawn our conclusions without prejudice or bias.

The most ancient of the Norman historians is Dudon, dean of Saint-Quentin. He owed his preferment to Duke Richard the First, to whom he had been sent on a deputation by Albert, Count of Vermandois. Conciliating the favour of Richard, Dudon received from him the most flattering marks of his approbation, and shared largely in the ducal patronage. He composed a work in Latin, divided into three books, on the origin, customs, and exploits of the Normans, from their first irruptions into France, down to the close of the reign of Richard the First. The authenticity of this work has been called in question by some writers, and Lobineau, in his HISTOIRE DE BRETAGNE, pronounces it to be a tissue of fables; but the Abbé de Vertot and and the Abbé de Moulinet speak of it in the highest praise in their dissertations SUR LA MOUVANCE DE BRETAGNE. The censures of Lobineau, who was wedded to a ridiculous hypothesis, which at once crumbled into dust, if Dudon was to be credited, are now disproved. Dudon has been followed

by Robert Wace, William of Jumièges, and Dumoulin.

Wace was a native of the island of Jersey.
He was born at the commencement of the twelfth
century, and died in England about the year
1184. He is the author of several poems, but
his most celebrated production is the " Roman de
Rou," which contains an account of the first incursions of the Northmen into England and
France, and the history of Rollo and his successors, down to A. D. 1106, being the sixth year
of the reign of Henry the First. This poem contains 16,547 verses, partly in octo-syllabic, partly
in Alexandrine metre. We have made use of
the beautiful edition, published at Rouen, in two
octavo volumes, with the notes and comments of its
learned editor, M. Frederick Pluquet, of Rouen,
who received much valuable assistance from the
excellent annotations of M. Auguste Le Prevost,
and other Norman antiquarians.[1]

[1] The other works of Wace are, " Le Brut d'Angleterre."
It contains eighteen hundred lines of octo-syllabic verse, and
is curious as the first authentic work which contains a history
of the origin of Arthur's Round Table ;—" Chronique Ascen-
dante des Ducs de Normandie," commencing with Henry the
Second and retrograding to Rollo ; it contains hree hundred and
fourteen Alexandrine verses ;—" L'Establissement de la Feste
de la Conception, dicte le Feste as Normands." It is written in
the vulgar idiom, or patois of the country ;—" La Vie de Saint
Nicolas," a poem in octo-syllabic verse. These are his recog-
nised works, but others have been erroneously attributed to him

William Calculus, a monk of Jumièges, usually called William of Jumièges from the monastery of which he was a member, flourished in the thirteenth century, and has left six books, " De Gestis Normannorum," which are collected in the "Bibliotheque des Historiens Français," of André Duchéne.

William of Poitiers wrote the Life of William the Conqueror, and those who wish to read minute details of all his battles, may consult that author.

The most interesting, the most instructive, and the most veracious of all the old Norman historians, is Ordericus Vitalis. He was born in England in 1075, and died in 1141, or 1142. He entitled his work " Historia Ecclesiastica," and he ranges through the whole history of the church, from the death of Christ down to the times in which he himself lived. His thirteen books are full of sudden transitions from one subject to another, between which there is no connexion, and this repulses the reader; but when the thread of the narrative is seized, and the several facts are classified, each under its proper head, the labour of the task is amply repaid. The literary world are indebted to M. Guizot, for a French translation of

as the " Roman du Chevalier au Lion," which was written by Chrestien du Troyes, and the "Roman d'Alexandrie," composed in the twelfth century, by Alexandre de Bernays.

Ordericus, executed in a masterly style by M. Louis Du Bois, of Lisieux, who has carefully collated all the Latin editions, and corrected many errors by the aid of original manuscripts.

The work of Dumoulin is a dry folio, but valuable for its facts. It commences with the first irruptions of the Northmen, and terminates with the expulsion of King John.

Among modern writers, M. Depping has thrown considerable light on the early history of Norway and Denmark, and the first piratical adventures of the people of those countries, in his " Histoire des Expeditions Maritimes des Normands." This work merits the attention of historical students.

The "Histoire de la Conquête de l'Angleterre par les Normands," by Augustin Thierry, is, without doubt, the most valuable addition to the early annals of the British monarchy that has been published in our times. The deep research, the profound reflections, the impartial spirit, and the even-handed justice of this accomplished scholar, recommend his volumes to readers of every class ; and we have often been surprised that they have not been honoured with an English translation. We have largely availed ourselves of the erudition of M. Thierry, particularly in the sketch we have drawn of the reign of Henry the Second.

From the various scources enumerated, and many others which are incidentally cited in the text and notes, the materials of this volume have been collected. It was originally twice its present size, including an account of the Norman conquests in Italy, Sicily, and Apulia; and a general review of the administration of justice throughout the duchy. We have omitted the first, because the expeditions of the Tancreds of Hauteville strictly relate to the exploits of individual adventurers, who received no assistance from the Dukes of Normandy; we have suppressed the latter, because, on the best reflection we could give to the subject, it appeared to assume rather stiffly the character of a treatise on jurisprudence.

We have confined ourselves, therefore, to one single point,—a simple and popular narrative of the History of the Northmen, from their first establishment in Neustria, including their conquest of England, and their acquisitions on the Continent. Care has been taken to bring prominently forward all the leading facts, while the narrative has been disentangled of all insignificant details.

J. D.

GUERNSEY, 1839.

# CONTENTS.

## APPENDIX.

THE

# DUKES OF NORMANDY.

## INTRODUCTION.

THE western part of France, called in modern times
Normandy, formed a portion of Celtic Gaul, when that
province, after a resistance of nine years, was reduced
under the dominion of the Romans. It was named
by Julius Cæsar, Lugdunensis Secunda, the Second
Lyonnese, and ranked the second of the seventeen
departments of ancient Gaul. On the south it was
bounded by the third and fourth Lyonnese; on the
north and east by the second Belgic; and on the north
and west by the ocean.

After its conquest by the Franks, and shortly before
the death of Clovis, this territory was comprised within
the kingdom of Neustria; which, from the mouths of
the Scheldt in the north, stretched in a southerly
direction to the confluence of the Allier with the Loire,
following the course of this latter river to its junction
with the sea below Nantes.

Under the empire of Charlemagne, Neustria was
confined within the limits of the Seine and the Loire;
but shortly afterwards it resumed the old boundaries
which it had when forming the second Lyonnese,
being nearly the same as those of modern times,

B

bounded on the west by Brittany, on the east by
Picardy and the Isle of France, and on the south by
Perche and Maine.

The second Lyonnese was inhabited, on the right
bank of the Seine, by the Veliocassians, from whom
the modern name Vexin is derived. Rouen (Rothomagus) was the capital.

The country of the Veliocassians, which was the
most populous, extended to the river Oise, on which
was built the Celtic town of Briva Isara, now called
Pontoise.

The Caletians dwelt on the sea-coast ; their territory
was the modern Pays de Caux, (Pagus Caleticus,) of
which Lillebonne (Julio Bona) was the capital. They
occupied the district from the margin of the ocean,
where Havre de Grace stands, to the castle of Eu, and
from the Seine to the Bresle. This extensive tract of
land was classed under the following divisions: Pagus
Augensis, the modern Pays d'Eu; Pagus Braicensis,
the Pays de Bray; and Pagus Tellogius, the Pays de
Tellau.

On the left bank of the Seine were the Eburovicians
and the Lexovians; Mediolanus and Noviomagus were
their respective capitals. These towns afterwards assumed the modern names of Evreux and Lizieux. In
a similar manner, Aragenus, the capital of the Bajo-
cassians, was converted into Bayeux.

The Unellians, dwelling on the western coast, had a
considerable city, called Crociatonum; on its ruins the
modern Valognes was erected.

Opposite Constantia were three small islands, dependencies on Gaul; Riduna, Sarnia, and Cesaræa, the
ancient names of Alderney, Guernsey, and Jersey.

The second Lyonnese contained only seven principal cities: Rothomagus Veliocassium, Rouen; Civitas Baiocassium, Bayeux; Ingenua Abricanorum, Avranches; Civitas Eburovicum, Evreux; Civitas Sesuviorum, Seéz; Civitas Lexoviorum, Lisieux; Constantia Castra, Coutances. There were, however, several small towns and villages in addition to these seven cities.

When the Roman empire was dismembered by the incursions of the northern barbarians, a mixed colony of Germans effected the conquest of Gaul. They were called Franks, because they had leagued themselves together to fight for freedom. The modern French are their descendants, and they took the name of their second conquerors, instead of the old appellation of Gauls.

The Franks had kings, but not one of them was a legislator. War was their sole occupation, and the science of government, or jurisprudence, was entirely neglected. The first attempt at civilization was made by Clovis, who established the seat of his monarchy at Soissons: he curbed his subjects under the yoke of laws, destroyed the last pretensions of the Romans to rule in Gaul, and embraced Christianity, which was also adopted by his people. Under the mild influence of the precepts of the Gospel the Franks quickly became refined, and the rights of person and property were respected.

On the death of Clovis his four sons divided his empire. Jealousies and rivalries broke out among them; war and murder disgrace this period of history. The dynasty of Clovis reigned three hundred and thirty-three years, under twenty-two kings, counting from Pharamond. This royal family is called the Merovingian race. To them succeeded Pepin, the founder of the Carlovingian line, father of the celebrated Charlemagne who consolidated the empire.

On the death of this enlightened sovereign, the unhappy divisions among his sons spread anarchy and discord in all directions; his defensive policy was abandoned, and the northern pirates, who had invaded Belgic Gaul so early as the year 286 of our era, but who had been held in check by the armed fleets stationed by Charlemagne at the mouths of rivers, again renewed their predatory incursions. Plunder alone was the object of the early adventurers, with which they returned to their native country. After the lapse of several centuries, Rollo, the most distinguished of the Scandinavian chiefs, subdued one of the finest provinces of Gaul, and acquired a permanent home and sovereignty, by founding the duchy of Normandy. The object of this introduction is briefly and rapidly to trace the character and conduct of his predecessors, before he obtained full and independent possession of Neustria.

The countries watered on one side by the Baltic, and on the other by the Northern ocean, and which stretch from the mouth of the Elbe to the middle of the frozen sea, remained for a long time unknown to other nations. The Romans had some faint knowledge of them, but when the intelligence which Rome had diffused was extinguished with the empire, the world, plunged again into darkness, became utterly ignorant of the people of the north. There were, indeed, no inducements to visit a country of so barren and inhospitable a character; its rocky coasts and severe climate, coupled with the absence of any wealth that might invite cupidity, were sufficient to repulse the most adventurous of the inhabitants of the south.

It is generally admitted that Norway and Denmark were densely populated to an extraordinary degree, and hence the old chroniclers speak of the north of Europe as the *officina gentium*, the workshop, or manufactory of nations. Modern writers, adopting this opinion, usually call it the " northern hive." Where population presses hard on the means of sub- sistence, as it did in those countries, one of the most obvious remedies is emigration, whereby the numbers of the inhabitants are brought down to the level of the supply of food. Although the most ancient written laws of Denmark date from the thirteenth century, and while those of Norway are posterior to the estab- lishment of Christianity in that nation, at both which periods emigration had ceased, yet the Norman writers, who lived among the posterity of the first invaders, affirm that the original emigrations were fixed by positive laws. They state that the law of primogeni- ture obtained in those countries, and that when the younger sons became of adult age, they were expelled not only from the paternal roof, but from the kingdom, the eldest brother alone remaining with his father.

National character and national habits will always be influenced to a great extent by geographical posi- tion. Norway and Denmark have a large range of sea-coast, with numerous isles, straits, bays, and rivers traversing lakes, and these afforded strong temptations to fishing. The people thus became expert sailors, and gradually ventured to greater distances from their own shores. The spirit of enterprise was naturally fomented

by the law of emigration, and the younger sons sought
fortune in piracy. Those who could not rule on land,
aspired to sovereignty on the ocean, and hence arose
the "sea-kings," so celebrated in the annals of the
northern countries.

The first descent of the Northmen on the coast of
Gaul, at least the first which has been recorded, took
place in the year 286. In the middle of the fifth century, the pirates, commanded by Odoacer, attacked
Orleans, and took possession of the islands at the mouth
of the Loire, which long continued to afford them a
safe retreat. About the same period, the Saxon adventurers formed establishments in Scotland and England, which constantly received fresh accessions of
their countrymen.

During the successive reigns of the Merovingian
princes, the incursions of the Northmen were constant
and regular, and those sovereigns, scarcely able to protect their coasts from insult, never attempted, by any
decisive policy, to strike terror into the adventurers.
But when Charlemagne obtained the throne of the
Franks, his vigorous administration not only repelled
the pirates, but constrained them to remain in their own
country. He erected forts which commanded the
most accessible bays and harbours, and wisely equipped
a naval armament to meet his enemies on their own
element. These prudent measures were neglected by
his successors. The vast empire that he founded,
crumbled to pieces in the feeble hands of his son Louis
Le Debonnaire. The resources of the nation,.devoted
by his father to its defence, were lavishly conferred on
the nobles and clergy, and the sinews of war were re-
laxed. The Northmen, in 830, landed on the isle of

Noirmoutier, burned the abbey of Saint Philibert, founded by Charlemagne, destroyed the convent of Notre Dame in the isle of Rhé, and extended their piracies into Aquitaine.

The disputes between the sons of Louis Le Debonnaire increased the feebleness of the empire, and the battle of Fontenay in Burgundy, fatal to the Carlovingian princes, who there met each other in mortal combat, reduced the power of resistance against the pirates. The carnage on both sides was so dreadful that the old chroniclers describe the field as the grave of the Frank chivalry, whose destruction opened a free passage to the Northmen.

> " Lá péri de France la flor
> E des Baronz tuit li meillor
> Ainsi troverent Paens terre
> Vuide de gent, bone à cunquerre." [1]

In 856, the most formidable of these freebooters made his appearance in the person of Hasting, or Hastenc. He ravaged Flanders and Vermandois, besieged Paris, burned the church of Sainte Genevieve, and received a considerable ransom to spare Saint Denis. His fleet sailed to the Norman islands of Jersey, Guernsey, Alderney, and Serk, which seem, even at that early date, to have been sufficiently important to invite cupidity.[2] He next invaded Touraine, putting every thing to fire and sword. After continuing his ravages for two years, he embraced Christianity, and received from Charles the Bald of France the province of Chartres, as the price of his submission.

This adventurer was followed by another piratical chief, named Regnier, who, accompanied by his principal officers, had an interview with Charles the Bald

---

[1] Roman de Rou, v. 316, 320.    [2] Roman de Rou, v. 425.

# ROLLO,

## FIRST DUKE OF NORMANDY.

——

THE earliest records of Norway describe that country
as divided into twenty small principalities. Halfdan,
the Black, sovereign of Nordenfeldt, subjugated all
his rivals, and raised himself to undivided sovereignty on
the ruin of the thrones of his competitors. His son,
Harold, surnamed Harfagre, from the beauty of his
hair, succeeded him in 863, and possessing the talents
and ambition of his father, extended and consolidated
his empire by conquering all the neighbouring states.
After ten years of war, the terror of his arms secured
him against foreign aggression, and he then devoted
his attention to the internal government of his possessions. He issued an order commanding all the pirates
of Norway, under the severest penalties, to abstain from
plundering their own countrymen; but, notwithstanding this prohibition, a Norwegian chief, named Rhólf,
or Rollo, made a descent on the province of Viken,
from which he carried away considerable booty.
Harold, enraged to the last degree at this daring act
of disobedience, cited Rollo before his council, who
condemned him to perpetual banishment.

The cluster of islands, on the coast of Scotland,

called the Hebrides, had afforded refuge to many Norwegians, who had either been exiled by Harold Harfagre, or who, disdaining to submit to his authority,
had there sought a voluntary retreat.  Thither Rollo
directed his course with a small fleet of six vessels,
accompanied by some friends, eager for new adventures under his auspices.

The old chroniclers, Dudon of Saint Quentin and
William of Jumièges, whose statements have been
copied by Robert Wace, affirm that Rollo sailed from
the Hebrides to England,—that he landed on the
coast,—attacked the natives, and repulsed them with
great slaughter, making several prisoners.  Little credit, however, can be given to this expedition, for the
forces of Rollo were too feeble for such an expedition, and the improbability of the whole narrative
becomes the greater, when it is known that the celebrated Alfred was then King of England.

After describing this successful attack on the English
coast, the Norman annalists represent the Norwegian
adventurer doubting what course to pursue,—whether
to return to Denmark and avenge himself on the king,
or to try his fortune in France, or form a permanent settlement in England.  From this state of uncertainty
and vacillation he is relieved by a dream.  Rollo
fancied himself on a mountain in France, so lofty that
he could survey the whole country from the summit,
and on which there was a stream of purest water.  He
imagined himself covered with leprosy, and that he was
cleansed after having bathed in the water.  The mountain was covered with birds, all of which, in succession, dipped their wings in the stream, and when Rollo
raised his hand, they flew to him, and perched on his

head and shoulders. The plumage of the birds was of
a red colour. In the morning, the chieftain related
his dream to his companions, and by their advice, he
sent for a Christian interpreter, who gave the following explanation of his nocturnal vision. " The mountain of France," said he, " is a symbol of holy church ;
the fountain of water denotes baptism; the leprosy is
an emblem of original sin. No king or emperor, however extended his dominions, or however brave his
troops, can find any medicine, by force of arms, to cure
this leprosy ; but you, Rollo, will be cleansed from the
taint by baptism. The birds, which dipped their wings
in the water, are your companions, who will abandon
paganism, and embrace Christianity. Their red wings
are emblems of the red shields of the Northmen." [1]
This interpretation of his dream induced Rollo to quit
the shores of England.

The fleet of the adventurers immediately set sail for
the coast of France, but contrary winds drove them on
the isle of Walcheren. Their landing was opposed by
the " Wacfreiz," the inhabitants of West Friezeland.
The Northmen were victorious, and plundered and devastated the country to so fearful an extent, that a famine
ensued. The people, however, rallied, and Rembaut,
Duke of Friezeland, and Regnier, Count of Hainault,
united their forces and attacked the invaders ; but fortune still favoured Rollo, who repulsed his opponents,
notwithstanding the desperate courage and unflinching
resolution of Rembaut, who declared that he would
die by the sword or be drowned, rather than accept
terms of arrangement from the Norwegian leader.
Rollo advanced from conquest to conquest, and after

[1] Roman de Rou, v. 915 to 1018.

having overrun all the intermediate country, he arrived at the banks of the Scheldt.  The Count of
Hainault was made prisoner ; the terms of his ransom
were the liberation of twelve Norman chiefs, then in
his power, and the payment of all the gold and silver
that could be gathered from the churches.  Peace was
then concluded, and Rollo steered for France. [1]

The piratical fleet arrived safely at the mouth of the
Seine ; the adventurers followed the course of the
river, and made their first landing at Jumièges, where
Rollo was joined by several parties of Danes and Norwegians, who gladly followed the banner of so renowned a leader.   From Jumièges he advanced to
Rouen, the capital of Neustria, anchoring at Saint
Morin, anciently called Saint Martin-de-la-Roquette.[2]
The terror inspired by preceding invaders had damped
the courage of the Rouennais, who dared not offer any
resistance to this new enemy ; their city had been frequently pillaged by the Northmen on former occasions,
and dreading the recurrence of a similar calamity, they
received Rollo as a conqueror and a master.   He pru-
dently pledged himself that no violence should be offered to the property or the persons of the inhabitants,

---

[1] In the Roman de Rou, Wace declares that Rollo had pity on Regnier, restoring him to his wife with great courtesy :—

> " Rou fu mult débonaire, de Regnier out pitié,
>   D'aler quite à sa fame, il dona plain congié."  v. 1136.

But Dudon of Saint Quentin and William of Jumièges give a very different account
of these transactions.  According to their statement, Rollo threatens to cut off the
head of Regnier, unless his twelve companions are given up, and then he exacts all
the gold and silver of the province.  " Tunc uxor Raineri flens et ejulans super eo,
convocatis principibus suis misit ad Rollonem, ut pro duodecim comitibus captis
redderet sibi suum seniorem.  Ilicó Rollo, susceptâ legatione, remisit ad eam dicens ; non reddetur Rainerus tibi, sed decollabitur, nisi reddideris prius meos comi-
tes, mihi insuper dederis quicquid auri est et argenti sui ducaminis."

[2] " Rotomo venit, portæque cui innexa est ecclesia Sancti Martini naves plurimo
milite fœcundas adhæsit." Dud. apud Duchesne, ii. p. 76.

and then made his peaceable and triumphant entry into Rouen.

The personal views of Rollo were widely different from those which had influenced any of the numerous freebooters who had invaded Gaul. These latter sought only plunder, with which to return to their native land, but Rollo desired a permanent establishment in a foreign country. These sentiments were shared by his principal officers, most of whom had been expelled by Harold Harfagre, and they had no prospect of improving their fortunes in Norway. The fine locality of Rouen, and the beauty and fertility of the surrounding country, induced them to select it as their headquarters; and from the year 876, till he assumed the ducal sceptre, Rollo continued *de facto* sovereign of the capital and of almost the whole province.

At this period, Charles the Simple reigned in France. That monarch marched against the Northmen, but he was defeated, and Rollo, profiting by this first victory, plundered Meulan, and pushed on to Paris. While hovering round the capital, into the suburbs of which he made frequent incursions, he dispatched small parties to Bayeux, Evreux, and Lisieux, with others to survey the state of the country, and ascertain the means of defence collected in the different towns. The intelligence received induced him to assault Bayeux, which he captured, and took the daughter of Berengier, Count of Bayeux, for his mistress. Her name was Papia, and she became the mother of William Longsword, second Duke of Normandy.

Quitting Bayeux, Rollo led his victorious army against Evreux, which fell under his power, and he again menaced Paris. The French king was filled with alarm, believing this formidable warrior to be invincible, and summoned Franco, archbishop of Rouen, to his capital, there to meet his assembled nobles, that they might devise some plan to conciliate their restless enemy. . It was resolved to request an armistice for three months, which Rollo granted, though many of the French barons reproached Charles with pusillanimity and cowardice, in thus soliciting a favour from the Northern freebooter, and the Norwegian chief became the object of their jests and ribaldry. Rollo smothered his resentment till the stipulated period had elapsed, for his sense of honour kept him faithful to his engagements; but as soon as the truce had expired, he took a signal revenge, slaughtering the inhabitants and devastating the land. He penetrated into the interior of France, up to Sens-sur-Yonne,—ravaged the Gatinais,—destroyed Etampes,—pillaged Villemeux near Dreux, and then bent his steps towards Paris. The whole population rose in mass to arrest his destructive attacks, but they were defeated, after which the conqueror plundered Dunois and the country round Chartres, an ancient city of great wealth, and in which the chemise of the Virgin Mary was consecrated. [1]

The inhabitants of Chartres, aware that Rollo would attempt to plunder their property, made active preparations for resistance. The bishop, Gocelmes, displayed great energy and spirit, and all the clergy were employed in preaching and singing psalms to rouse the courage of the people. Many powerful barons marched to the relief of the city, among whom were the

---

[1] " De la Saincte Virge Marie Mere de Dé
I esteit la kemise, tenue en grant chierté."
*Roman de Rou*, v. 1570, 1.

Duke of Burgundy and the Count of Paris. The
French fought bravely, but the fury of the assailants,
and their military renown, at last created a panic
among the defenders. Then the bishop, taking the
holy relics and the blessed chemise, issued forth from
the gates, accompanied by the clergy and the men-at-
arms, chanting hymns and imploring the protection
of the Virgin. When the Northmen saw the solemn
procession, their courage quailed; they fled, and encamped on a neighbouring height.

The French, now fully satisfied that a miracle had
been wrought in their favour, vigorously pursued the
enemy, being led to the charge by the Duke of Burgundy and the Count of Paris. According to the
French chroniclers, the Northmen lost six thousand
eight hundred men, but the Norman annalists reduce
the number to eighteen hundred. However this may
be, it is certain that Rollo was repulsed with great
slaughter, though his troops fought with their accustomed bravery, nor did the battle terminate till the
approach of night.[1]

The Northmen were reduced to a fearful extremity,
knowing that the engagement would be renewed in the
morning. One of Rollo's favourite chiefs advised him
to cut his way through the hostile army under cover
of the darkness, and this recommendation was carried
into effect with complete success. And here they
did an act peculiar to the manners of that remote
age. They slaughtered all the horses and oxen they
could collect, flayed them, and formed an intrenchment
with their skins. When the dawn broke, and the

---

[1] The battle of Chartres was fought on the 20th of July, 911. *Recueil des
Historiens de France*, t. 8.

French saw this singular fortification, they desisted
from further pursuit, being shocked at the unusual
sight.  The horror they felt arose out of the superstition of those days, for it was universally believed that
the skins of recently slaughtered animals possessed extraordinary virtues; and as the courage of the defenders
of Chartres was animated by the confidence they reposed in the chemise of the virgin, so were their fears
excited at beholding this palladium of the Northmen.
Even to this day the peasantry of the Bessin, where
ancient usages are better preserved than in any other
part of Normandy, repose unbounded faith in the
medicinal properties of the blood of animals.  They
bathe themselves with bullocks' blood to alleviate
pains in the limbs, and plunge their naked arms into
the warm entrails of a dying ox as a cure for atrophy
and rheumatic affections.

Escaping from the danger that threatened him before the walls of Chartres, Rollo laid waste the whole
country from Blois to Senlis, massacring young and
old, and violating wives and maidens.  The nobles
assembled in a body, and formally laid their complaints
before Charles the Simple, beseeching him to adopt
such measures as would protect his Christian subjects
against the pagan pirates.  They stated that not an
acre of land was cultivated from Blois to Senlis; that
no one dared move from his castle, or stir out of a
town; that the farmers could not till their land, nor
cultivate the vine; and that universal famine would
ensue, unless Rollo was arrested in his desolating
career.[1]

1  "Veient lor félonie, veient lor crualté
    De Bleis tres k' a Sainlis n's un arpent de blé !

In reply to this application, the king expressed deep sympathy with the sufferings of his people, but defended himself against any reproach of indifference by remarking, that he was only one man, and that his barons had not rallied round his standard as their honour, their interest, and their fealty demanded. To prove his personal anxiety to terminate this war of extermination, he offered, on condition that Rollo and his companions would renounce paganism, and be baptized in the Christian faith, to give him his daughter Gisele in marriage, and all the maritime district between the river Eure and Mount Saint Michael.[1]

This proposition being approved of by the French barons, Archbishop Franco was dispatched on an embassy to the Norman chief, and he eloquently pointed out the advantages of this alliance, the honour of being husband of the king's daughter, and the happiness he would enjoy in holding in peace a rich and spacious kingdom. Rollo submitted these proposals to his companions, and with their concurrence, he adopted them.

Charles the Simple, attended by his principal barons, met the Norwegian adventurer at St. Clair-sur-Epte, a

Marchans n'osent aler n'à chastel n'à cité ;
Vilains n'osent en vigne laborer ne en pré."
                    *Roman de Rou*, v. 1823, et seq.

[1] "Gille, une moie fille, li donrai à molllier,
E la terre marine, s'il s'i vout otrier,
Desû Oure curt tresk' al Mont Saint Michel."
                    *Roman de Rou*, v. 1850.

William of Jumièges fixes the limits from the river Epte to the borders of Brittany. "Mandans si Christianus efficeretur, terram maritimam ab Eptæ flumine usque ad Britannicos limites, cum suâ filiâ nomine Gislâ, se ei daturum fore."

The river Coesnon separates Normandy from Brittany, emptying itself into the sea at Mount Saint Michael, which it leaves in Normandy, by the sinuosities of its stream, a circumstance which has given rise to the distich,
            " Coesnon par sa folie
            A mis le mont en Normandie."

town three leagues distant from Gisors, and two from
Magny. The conditions of the treaty having been
duly explained, and accepted by both parties, Rollo
stretched out his hand to the king in token of homage,
but this was not deemed sufficient, the solemnity requiring that he should kiss the royal foot. To this
humiliation he resolutely refused to descend, and the
French consented that it should be done by proxy.
Charles raised his foot, when the Northman appointed
to act for Rollo threw the king to the ground,[1] a gross
act of rudeness, scarcely credible even in those rough
times, but one related by the old chroniclers of both
nations with as much unanimity as merriment.

The unfortunate Charles was not in a position to
resent this affront, but gave his daughter to Rollo in
presence of the spectators, offering to add Flanders to
Normandy, in augmentation of her dower; but this
the Norwegian refused. In lieu of Flanders he insisted
on having Brittany, declaring that Normandy alone
was so unfruitful a country that it would not subsist
his followers. It had, indeed, been reduced to sterility
by his continued ravages and those of his predecessors,
though it is now one of the most fertile and best cultivated provinces in France. The demand of Rollo was
conceded, and Juhael Berengier, Earl of Rennes, the
capital of Brittany, was compelled to do him homage.
Rollo was forthwith invested with the ducal authority,

---

[1] " Rou devint hom li Roiz è sis mainz li livra;
    Quant dut li pié beisier, baisier ne se daingna;
    La main tendi aval, li pié el Rei leva,
    A sa buche le traist è li Rei enversa;
    Asez en ristrent tuit è li Rei se drescha."
                                Roman de Rou, v. 1901, et seq.
  In this passage Wace attributes the act to Rollo himself; but the older writers
say it was done by proxy.

and baptized by archbishop Franco, when he received
the name of Robert, and was married to Gisele.[1]

Many French writers, whose judgment has been
warped by national vanity, harshly condemn Charles
for thus surrendering one of the finest provinces of his
kingdom, but these censures are undeserved.  Before
the treaty of Clair-sur-Epte was formally executed,
Rollo had been really master of Neustria for twenty-six
years, Charles having only the nominal title of king ;
and the people of Rouen preferred the rule of a foreigner
who protected them, to the dominion of a native prince
who was powerless to defend their rights.  In ceding
to Rollo a territory from which experience had shown
that he could not be expelled by force, Charles converted an enemy into a friend, and by creating him
one of the chief vassals of the crown he secured his
other provinces against his aggressions.  He experienced, indeed, still greater benefits by this prudent
policy, for it became the personal interest of Rollo to
oppose any future invasion of the Northmen ; and thus
Neustria was interposed between the pirates and the
frontier of France, and any fresh adventurers would
have united themselves to their countrymen rather than
devastate lands and cities of which they were possessed.
In addition to these advantages, the conversion of the
pagans to Christianity was followed by the happiest
results, for as soon as they felt the influence of the
priests, their lawless habits were tamed, and they
advanced rapidly in civilization.

As soon as Rollo was seated on the ducal throne, he
rewarded the services of his companions in arms with
lands, villages, and cities, according to their rank and

[1] The treaty of Clair-sur-Epte was ratified in 912.

prowess. He established a rigorous police throughout the duchy, enacted salutary and impartial laws, protected the rights of person and property, and displayed the virtues of a legislator as brilliantly as he had done those of a warrior. One of the most remarkable of his laws was the " Clameur de Haro." The word *haro* is compounded of *ha!* the ejaculation of a person suffering or astonished, and *ro*, a contraction of Rollo. If a party were assaulted, or any trespass committed on his property, he thrice repeated aloud the word *haro*, and all who heard it were bound to come to his assistance. If the wrong-doer escaped, the cry was repeated from district to district, throughout the whole duchy, till he was apprehended, so that this system made every citizen a constable, and rendered escape almost impossible. This singular custom has still the force of law in the Channel Islands in matters of trespass, Guernsey, Jersey, Alderney, and Serk being the remnant of the ancient duchy of Normandy. So vigorous was the administration of Rollo that some of the old historians affirm that golden bracelets were exposed on trees in forests, and none dared touch them ; and though such a statement is not perhaps to be received in a literal sense, it sufficiently shows that the police and the law were remarkably efficient in repressing crime. In all cases of theft the criminal was hanged ; the accomplice shared the same fate as the principal, and those who knew of a robbery and did not disclose it were also capitally punished ; this system was undoubtedly severe, but the predatory character of his subjects, who had been habituated from boyhood to pillage, rendered this discipline indispensable. Wace thus describes Rollo in his legislative and judicial capacity :—

" Pais ama, è pais quist, è pais fist establir,
Par tote Normendie fist crier è banir
K'il n'i ait tant hardis ki ost altre assaillir,
Meson ni vile ardeir, ne rober ni tollir,
N' à home fere sanc, ne tuer, ne mulzrir,
En estant ne à terre, ne batre, ne ferir,
Par gait ne porpensé altre home traïr
Ne ait ki ost embler ne altre cunsentir."

*Roman de Rou,* v. 1950.

The ancient province of Neustria, now erected into
an independent duchy, lost its old appellation, and
received that of Normandy, the etymology of which
Wace derives from Northmen, the men of the North
of Europe.

" *Man* en Engleis et en Noreis
Senefie *hom* en Francheis ;
Justes ensemle North é Man,
Ensemle dites donc Northman,
Co est hom de North en Romans
De ço vint li nom as Normans.
Normanz solent estre apelé
E Normendie k'il ont poplé,
Por ço ke Normans la poplerent
Ki en la terre converserent."

*Roman de Rou,* v. 109 to 118.

Rollo is described both by the French and Norman
historians as a man of uncommon wisdom and energy
of character, generous, eloquent, just, indefatigable,
intrepid, of a noble figure, and majestic size.   He has,
however, been justly reproached with his cruelty to
Gisele, daughter of Charles the Simple, who pined to
death in consequence of his ill-treatment, and when
her father remonstrated against his behaviour to his
daughter, he beheaded the two noblemen who presented the letter of complaint.

On the death of Gisele, Rollo married his mistress,
Papia, and declared the child he had by her, afterwards called William Longsword, his heir and successor.   This nomination was ratified with great solemnity,

Berengier, Earl of Rennes, Alain, Count of Brittany, and all the Norman barons, swearing homage and fidelity to their future duke. The two most ancient chroniclers, Dudon of St. Quentin, and William of Jumièges, have not fixed the date of Rollo's death; they merely say that he lived five years after he had prevailed on his barons to recognize the right of his son to the dukedom. Ordericus Vitalis and Robert Wace have incorrectly counted these five years from the date of his baptism, which would place his death in 917; but in the chronicles of Flodoard, a French contemporary writer, he is frequently mentioned for ten years after that period. The truth is, that William Longsword was raised to the heritable ducal dignity in 926, and the death of Rollo belongs to the year 931.

faithful barons and three hundred horsemen, William
sallied forth from the gates of his capital, and gained a
decisive victory without the loss of a man.  Rioulf escaped into a thick wood, when pursuit was abandoned.
This success confirmed the authority of the prince, and
the courage he displayed in the unequal contest regained for him the lost esteem of his subjects.  Till
that period, he possessed rather the name than the authority of duke.

Immediately after this battle, William received intelligence that his mistress, Sprota, whom he had sent
to Fécamp during the siege of Rouen, had been delivered of a son, who afterwards became Duke Richard
the First.  These two events occurred in the year 933.

When Charles the Simple was expelled from the
throne of France, the sceptre was seized by Raoul, or
Rodolph, Duke of Burgundy.  The usurper died without issue, leaving a brother, Hugh, Count of Paris, the
most powerful baron of the realm, and called Hugh
the Great, on account of the extent of his possessions.
He might easily have seized the vacant throne, but
knowing the difficulty of retaining it in those turbulent times, he preferred securing the peaceable possession of Burgundy.  During the captivity of Charles
the Simple, his queen had sought refuge in England
with their young son Louis, known in history by the
title of " *Outremer*," or " Beyond the sea."  This
child, then sixteen years of age, Hugh determined to
proclaim King of France, and he dispatched the archbishop of Sens to London, to prevail on her majesty to
return with the youthful Louis, which, after some hesi-
tation she did, though entertaining great fears that
treachery was meditated against the last living scion of

the Carlovingian race. She was, however, inspired
with confidence by the promises of the Duke of Normandy, who offered his protection, agreeing to do
homage to Louis, as Rollo had done to his father ; and
she was still more encouraged by the pardon he extended to her friend, Alain, then a refugee in England,
to whom he generously restored the earldom of Nantes.
William Longsword also went to Boulogne, where
the queen and her son landed, and he then took the
oath of fealty with Count Hugh and the French
barons.

The authority of the young king, thus placed on the
throne by an exclusive party, and unsupported by the
national will, was but little respected.   He was soon
embroiled with his principal barons, who razed his
castles and conspired to deprive him of the crown.
Hugh gave him but doubtful assistance, husbanding
all his resources to retain Burgundy, and seeking to act
as umpire between the sovereign and the discontented
nobles.   Louis applied for aid to Otho, Emperor of
Germany, who refused to interfere unless with the approbation of William Longsword ; on which the king
of France went to Rouen, and after some interviews, a
triple alliance was concluded between the three monarchs.   Shortly after this transaction, the duke stood
godfather to the son of Louis, born at Laon in 941, who
was named Lothaire.

When William returned to Rouen he was received
by his subjects with the loudest demonstrations of joy.
The impressions of his early education soon rose again
in his mind, now unoccupied with foreign war or civil
commotion.   He rebuilt the Abbey of Jumiéges, and
expressed an anxious wish to pass the remainder of his

days in that sacred asylum. The abbot resolutely refused his request, on which the duke would neither eat
nor drink, and fell dangerously ill from exhaustion.
When reduced to this state, William summoned his
most attached barons, and repeated his desire to be admitted a monk in the abbey of Jumiéges, to which
they firmly objected ; but, at his request, they acknowledged his son Richard his successor, and swore
homage and fealty to the young prince.

We now come to those transactions which terminated
in the death of William Longsword. Herloin, the
second of that name, Earl of Ponthieu and Montreuil,
was brother-in-law of the Duke of Normandy, by his
marriage with Alice of Vermandois. Arnoul, the first
Earl of Flanders, was the bitter enemy of Herloin, and
had seized on the castle of Montreuil, in Picardy, near
the river Canche, distant eight miles from Boulogne.
Unable to recover this fortress from his too powerful
adversary with his own forces, Herloin applied for aid
to Hugh, Count of Paris, who was his suzerain, or
liege lord. It was refused, Arnoul being the friend
of Hugh, who, however, told Herloin that he would
not take any offence if he obtained assistance from
some other quarter. He then sought to interest the
king of France in his favour, from whom he received
precisely the same answer. Thus disappointed, he
next solicited the protection of the Duke of Normandy,
who, compassionating his misfortunes, summoned his
barons, and they resolved to lay seige to Montreuil.

The Flemings made every preparation to resist the
army of William, but the contest was short and decisive. The duke harangued the " Cotentinois," the
inhabitants of the district still called the Cotentin ; he

complimented them on their valour, and pronounced
them the bravest of his subjects. To them he assigned
the post of honour, and personally led them to the assault. Eager to merit the praise of their sovereign,
they rushed on the enemy with irresistible impetuosity,
and quickly obtained possession of the town and
castle. William generously offered to restore Montreuil without any indemnification, but Herloin begged the duke to retain it for himself, saying that he
was too feeble to defend it with his own troops; the
Norman prince, however, insisted on giving back
the place, and promised again to assist his friend,
should the Flemings venture to attack him. He
strengthened the fortifications, widened and deepened
the ditch, and erected a " *chevaux de frise*" round the
castle.[1] After having performed these friendly offices,
the duke returned to Normandy, and repeated his wish
to become a monk, and pass the remainder of his days
at Jumiéges; but his barons still refused their consent.

The Earl of Flanders breathed vengeance against
William for having aided Herloin in the recovery of
the castle of Montreuil, but being aware that he could
not sate his vengeance by an appeal to arms, he contrived a scheme for his assassination. Arnoul sent deputies to Rouen to solicit a treaty of perpetual peace,
and requested the duke to meet him at Amiens, there
to settle the terms, pretending that he was unable to
travel on account of the gout. To these overtures the
unsuspicious William consented, and repaired to the
appointed place. On his arrival at Amiens, he received

---

[1] The expression in the Roman de Rou, which we have rendered " *chevaux de
frise*" in the text, is " *de pel a herichon*," v. 2629, whence " *herisser*," to bristle.

a message from the perfidious Arnoul, stating that he
was at Pequigny, a small town on the river Somme,
distant three leagues from Amiens.   In the middle of
this river there is a small island, and thither the treacherous Fleming decoyed the confiding Norman.   The
duke landed on it, accompanied by twelve attendants.
He was received with every semblance of esteem by
the Earl of Flanders, who personally begged a treaty
of perpetual peace, which William granted.   He then
made the most solemn protestations of fidelity and
honour, after which he took his leave.   William was
about to embark in another boat, when one of the conspirators ran down to the shore, and pretending that
he had some important intelligence to communicate
privately, induced the duke to return alone.   No
sooner was he separated from his companions, than the
assassins rushed on their victim, and clove his head in
twain, on which the duke fell dead without uttering a
word. [1]

This assassination took place on the 20th of December, 943, according to Dudon of Saint Quentin ; on the
17th of the same month, according to William of
Jumièges; and on the 18th of December, 942, according to the second epitaph on the duke's tomb.   Fro-
doard, a contemporary historian, appears to decide the
date in favour of the two Norman chroniclers.

Alain and Berengier of Brittany, who had accompanied William on this fatal journey, saw the murder
perpetrated from the bank of the river, where they

[1] Among the four murderers Wace mentions Rioulf, the ancient Earl of the
Cotentin, vanquished by William under the walls of Rouen.  But Dudon and William of Jumièges, though they speak of a Ridulfus, or Rioulf, do not indentify him
with the early enemy of Longsword.  " Elricus, Balzoque, Rotbertus atque Ridulfus, perfidi." (*Dudon*, lib. iii. p. 105.)  " Henricus, necnon Balzo, Rotbertus quoque
atque Ridulfus." (*William. Gemmet*, lib. iii. c. 12.)

awaited the duke's return.  The murderers escaped on
the opposite shore, but the body of the prince was
recovered, taken to Rouen, and interred in the cathedral.

William Longsword reigned twenty-five years.   In
person he was tall and robust.  His countenance was
remarkable for mildness of expression.  Averse to a
military career, he showed courage and conduct, when
compelled to defend himself or his allies.  His piety
was sincere, and the assistance he rendered to the
monastic institutions of Normandy gained for him the
unbounded esteem of the clergy, who have honoured
his memory in the ancient chronicles with the highest
praise.

# RICHARD THE FIRST,

## THIRD DUKE OF NORMANDY,

### Surnamed Sans-Peur.

———

THE murder of William Longsword placed the independence of Normandy in imminent danger. Richard was a child, only ten years of age, unable to cope with Arnoul and the King of France, both of whom were suspected of entertaining designs against the ducal throne. In this critical situation the energy and prudence of the Norman barons saved the state. The Archbishop of Rouen invested Richard with the insignia of sovereignty, and a regency was appointed, composed of the most experienced warriors, presided over by Bernard, surnamed the Dane, who held the title and office of Viscount of Rouen.

Immediately after the acknowledgment of the young duke, Louis Outremer visited Rouen, offering his protection, and promising to punish Arnoul; but his real views were the reverse of his professions. Though he was materially indebted to William Longsword for his restoration to the throne of France, and also for the zeal that prince displayed in the treaty of alliance with the Emperor of Germany, ambition had driven from his heart every feeling of gratitude, and he now meditated the conquest of Normandy. Masking his real designs under specious promises, he persuaded the guardians of Richard to allow him to reside in the palace occupied by himself, during his residence at Rouen. Having thus far succeeded in his plot, his next object was to carry him off to France. Bernard, the Dane, and Osmond, his preceptor, having discovered this intended act of treachery, made known their suspicions to the people, who instantly rose in arms, and demanded the restoration of their prince. Louis intimidated, or seeing that the favourable opportunity had not arrived, not only released him, but solemnly guaranteed to him the quiet enjoyment of his dominions. By this apparently loyal conduct, he removed the distrust that had prevailed, and when he acknowledged his great obligations to William Longsword, and swore on the oath of a king that he would never injure his son, public confidence was entirely restored. Profiting by this change of opinion, he proposed to superintend the education of Richard, and bring him up with his own son, Lothaire, in which duplicity he was successful, and took his departure from Rouen, accompanied by the young duke, and his preceptor, Osmond.

The crafty Count of Flanders soon received intelligence of these events, and being uncertain whether Louis would attack him, or not, he determined to be on the safe side, and avert the threatened storm by bribes. He dispatched an embassy to the French king, with ten pounds weight of gold,[1] while his emissaries distributed considerable largesses among the royal favourites and the most influential nobles. His representatives declared that Arnoul would ever remain the

[1] Roman de Rou, v. 2922.

faithful ally of France; that he would have paid his
obeisance in person, had he not been confined by illness, and that he would justify himself against the
charge of having sanctioned the murder of William
Longsword. Having heard these statements, Louis
demanded the advice of his barons and chevaliers,
falsely pretending that his conscience must be fully
satisfied, and affirming that no one should be able to
accuse him of having participated in the crime im-
puted to Arnoul, by leaving it unpunished. The
French nobles, being all bribed, pleaded stoutly in
favour of the murderer. They insisted that mere
suspicion ought not to condemn him; that the king
would act partially and unjustly, unless he heard evidence; that Arnoul gave presumptive proof of his innocence by offering to stand his trial before Louis;
and, finally, they protested against any invasion of
his territories. These arguments, according with the
secret views and wishes of the faithless and ungrateful
Louis, were received by him with complacency.

The deputies of Arnoul, thus satisfied that their
master incurred no danger from the vengeance of
Louis, became more emboldened, and plainly told him
what line of policy the Count of Flanders recommended him to pursue. They advised the imprisonment of Richard and the seizure of Normandy. They
urged him to ham-string the young duke, a cruelty
often practised under the first and second races of the
French kings. They reminded him that Normandy
once belonged to his predecessors, and observed that
William Longsword, as the illegitimate son of Rollo,
had no valid title to the dukedom. They stimulated his avarice and ambition, by remarking that his

ancestors used to receive great assistance, in men and money, from the province over which he exercised neither power nor jurisdiction. Observing that these statements produced the desired effect, they dexterously hinted that, even if Arnoul had murdered Longsword, Louis was most benefited by his death, while no odium attached to him; and therefore that he ought to consider the Count of Flanders as a friend who had freed him from the presence of a powerful rival. The deputies completely gained their point.

The French king was then at Laon. After this last interview with the deputies of Arnoul, he ordered the young duke into his presence, and commanded him never to stir out of the town. He laid the same injunction on Osmond, his preceptor. Richard was handsome and amiable, and the gracefulness of his appearance and the mildness of his address had endeared him to all the attendants of the palace, by whom he was equally beloved and pitied. His popularity offended the queen, who was not only jealous that he shone to more advantage than her own son, but also because he stood between Lothaire and the Norman succession. Having discovered that the duke and his preceptor had amused themselves with hunting in the neighbouring forest, she denounced them to the king, who threatened, if they again went out of the town, to put out the eyes of Osmond, and to cauterize the feet of Richard.[1] This menace convinced Os-

---

[1] Dudon thus expresses the threat of Louis. "Senioris tui poplitibus coctis, privabo te oculis, si forsan eum quoquam amplius duxeris." In William of Jumiéges, the menaces of the king are addressed to Richard. He opprobriously calls him, "Meretricis filium, ultrò virum alienum rapientis." For particulars of these punishments, see "Notice sur les Tombeaux des Enervés de Jumiéges, par E. H Langlois."

mond of the vindictiveness, hatred, and treachery of Louis; and he contrived to send a messenger to Rouen, with intelligence of their being treated as prisoners, and daily exposed to mutilation or death. The news created universal consternation. The bishops and clergy offered up prayers in the churches for their deliverance, and the military vassals swore vengeance against France. A public fast was ordered to be held every month till Richard was liberated.[1]

In the mean time the faithful Osmond encouraged his young charge to hope for better days, and put his trust in God, cheering him up with the prospect of deliverance and revenge. He devised a stratagem for his escape, proposing that Richard should feign sickness, confine himself to his bed, and refuse either to eat or drink. He advised him to call for spiritual aid, and, after a few days, pretend to be dead. The young duke assented to this plan, and played his part to admiration. One night, when the king was at supper, the guards, who watched the apartment of Richard, hearing that he was dead, quitted their post. Osmond profited by their absence, roused the prince, concealed him in a bundle of straw, carried him into the court-yard, placed him before him on horseback, and escaped out of Laon. He had stationed another horse a short distance from the town: on arriving there, the duke mounted it, and they arrived in safety at Couci-le-Chatel, belonging to the Archbishop of Rheims, and where Bernard, Count of Senlis and Valois, received the fugitives with the utmost joy.

Bernard started that night for Paris, to solicit the

---

[1] Dudon affirms that this fast of three days was to be renewed every month till the prince was released from captivity. " Tridunum jéjunium in uno quoque mense populo indicentes."

protection of Hugh, the powerful Count of Paris; but he, being a vassal of Louis, refused to do any act that might involve his fealty; at the same time he promised to remain neuter, and abstain from injuring the pretensions of Richard to the dukedom. With this answer Bernard returned, and conducted the young prince from Couci to Senlis.

When Louis found that his prisoners had escaped, his rage was ungovernable, and he ordered the two captains of the guard to be hanged. Having thus sated the first impulses of his passion, he fell back on the craftiness of his mind; and determining to make another attempt to secure his prize by policy and negociation, he summoned Arnoul, Count of Flanders, to his assistance. That wily and unprincipled chieftain advised the king to win over the Count of Paris to his interests, by offering him one half of Normandy, as the reward of his co-operation. The bribe was tendered and accepted.

As soon as this compact was made known, Bernard of Senlis went to Paris, when he reproached Hugh with his breach of faith, prophesying that Louis would make a tool of him, while it suited his purpose, and expressing his conviction that he would not retain his share of the spoil for more than a twelvemonth. The Count of Paris replied, that he would fulfil his engagements with the French king, so long as the terms of the contract were respected; but that, if Louis made any attempt to overreach him, he would withdraw his forces.

Bernard of Senlis then consulted Bernard the Dane, Viscount of Rouen, who recommended submission, declaring that all defence would be useless against

such a coalition, and that resistance would only entail
the sacking of their towns and the devastation of their
fields. This answer astonished the protector of Richard, who did not penetrate the real policy of the governor of the capital. He left him disheartened and
mortified.

Having completed their preparations, the confederates invaded Normandy. The people, acting under
the advice of Bernard the Dane, laid down their
arms, and Louis entered Rouen in triumph. The inhabitants, however, were amazed at this tame surrender, and more particularly at the marked respect
paid by Bernard to the king. The Dane soon wormed
himself into the royal confidence, and when he felt his
power, he began to exert it. He persuaded Louis
that he had taken no part in the escape from Laon,
that the blame rested solely with Osmond, and he
solemnly protested that he did not know where the
young duke was concealed. He acknowledged his
obligations to William Longsword, and said that he
would certainly have protected Richard, had he given
any promise of emulating the virtues of his father; but
that, for the sake of his countrymen, he was disposed
to do homage to a wise king, and reject a wrong-
headed boy. With this discourse Louis was delighted,
and he swore, by the oath of a Christian, that he
never intended to hurt a hair of Richard's head, an
attestation which Bernard appreciated at its true
value.

Having thus ingratiated himself with Louis, Bernard told him that the terms of his treaty with Hugh
were bruited abroad, and beseeched him to say if he
had really conceded the whole of Lower Normandy to

the Count of Paris. On being answered in the
affirmative, he expressed the greatest astonishment
and indignation; he reminded Louis that Hugh and
his brother had conspired to expel Charles the Simple,
and deprive him of his inheritance; that he had only
been induced to restore him by the persuasion of William Longsword; and he then nettled his pride by re-
peating many of the contumelious jests which Hugh
had been wont to apply to him before his accession.
Having thus worked on his passions, Bernard told
the king that Lower Normandy contained the most
fertile land, that the inhabitants were the bravest of
the Normans, that the district could raise ten thousand horsemen, and that the agricultural villains
were the most skilful and industrious of the whole
population. He cautioned him against the ulterior
designs of Hugh, who, he said, would seize the whole
province, and then drive Louis himself out of France.
" Will you, then," exclaimed Bernard, " deprive a
little boy of his inheritance, and give it to such a traitor, felon, and tyrant as Hugh?"

Irritated and alarmed at this speech, Louis declared
that he had been totally ignorant of the immense advantages he had placed in jeopardy. He promised
to break his treaty, and he kept his word; for he immediately sent an order to Hugh, commanding him to
evacuate Lower Normandy. The messenger reached
him at Bayeux, which he was besieging. His rage
was excessive; but he was compelled to submit, and,
on his departure, Louis took possession of the whole
province.

While Bernard, the Dane, had been thus scheming
to dissolve the alliance between the King of France

and the Count of Paris, he had secretly sent to Harold, King of Denmark, requesting his armed assistance on behalf of the youthful Richard. Harold was a warlike and noble prince, and making common cause with his countrymen, he equipped a formidable body of troops, and landed safely at Cherbourg, where he was quickly joined by the inhabitants of Lower Normandy. Bernard dissembled his joy at the arrival of these succours, and sent the King of France word of the invasion. Louis assembled his army, and marched against Harold. Before the sword was drawn, Bernard recommended an interview between the two monarchs, which took place. Among the French negociators present was Herloin, Earl of Montreuil, who had been protected by Longsword, but who deserted the child of his benefactor, and became the friend of his enemy. At the sight of this traitor the indignation of a Norman was so excited that he rushed on Herloin, and slew him. A general battle ensued, in which the French were completely defeated. Louis endeavoured to escape, but he was not so fortunate. His bridle-rein had been cut, and his horse became restive. Some Norman cavaliers seized him, but he succeeded in bribing one of them, and lay concealed for some days in one of the small islands with which the Seine is studded. Bernard found out his retreat, and conducted him prisoner to Rouen.[1] Louis obtained his liberty through the intercession of Hugh, Count of Paris; but the conditions were severe. The Normans insisted on retaining his

[1] The circumstances attending this intervention of Harold are variously related by the Norman chroniclers, and the whole subject is very obscure. The curious reader is referred to the supplemental notes appended to M. Depping's "Histoire des Expeditions Maritimes des Normans."

two sons, as hostages; but their mother would only
part with Carloman, the younger. As substitutes for
the elder, the bishops of Soissons and Beauvais were
accepted. They were not released before Louis had
recognized the title of Richard, and solemnly abandoned all pretensions to Normandy, simply reserving
the formality of homage from the duke. Henry of
Huntingdon says, he was obliged to submit to the
most humiliating terms, as we learn from the speech
that chronicler attributes to William the Conqueror,
addressed to his army before the battle of Hastings :
" Did not your ancestors capture the King of the
French, and imprison him at Rouen, till he restored
Normandy to the boy Richard, your duke, on the
express condition, that in every interview between the
King of France and the Duke of Normandy, the latter should be girded with a sword, and the former
present himself without a sword, or even a dagger." [1]

. After these arrangements had been completed, Richard quitted Senlis, where he had remained under the
protection of Count Bernard, and made his triumphal
entry into Rouen, where he was received with accla-
mation by all the inhabitants. This restoration to the
ducal throne took place in 945.

The defeat of Louis, and his surrender of all claims
to Normandy, produced a remarkable change in the
policy of Hugh, Count of Paris. He resolved to form
a permanent alliance with Richard, and, to this end,
the duke was affianced to the count's daughter, then a
child; but proper pledges were given that the mar-

---

[1] " Nonne patres vestri regem Francorum in Rotomago ceperunt et tenuerunt,
donec Ricardo puero duci vestro Normanniam reddidit, eo pacto quod in omni col-
lucotione regis Franciæ et ducis Normanniæ gladio dux accingeretur, regem verò
nec gladium, nec etiam cultellum, ferre liceret."

riage should be consummated, when the bride had attained to a suitable age. Hugh invested Richard with the order of knighthood, and the very best understanding prevailed between them. By this alliance, offensive and defensive, they felt themselves in a condition to retain their respective dominions in security, and bid defiance to their external enemies. They were soon put to the test by Louis and Arnoul, who had persuaded Otho, Emperor of Germany, to declare war against Hugh and Richard, and the confederates opened the campaign in 946. Repulsed from the Isle of France, on which ancient Paris stood, the hostile forces suddenly advanced against Rouen, from which Richard marched out at the head of his Normans and Bretons. Though still very young, he showed himself worthy of his heroic ancestors, and displayed the prudence of a general, combined with the valour of a soldier. Being anxious to detach the Germans from a strong position, which they occupied, he pretended to fly in disorder, and thus dexterously decoyed the advanced guard of the enemy between the mountain Beauvoisin and the capital, when he returned to the charge, slew the nephew of Otho with his own hand, and totally routed the hostile army.

Enraged at the discomfiture of his troops and the loss of his nephew, Otho advanced in person with the whole of his forces, and laid siege to Rouen. The Normans, undaunted at this formidable attack, prepared for a vigorous resistance. The resources of Richard seemed to increase in proportion to the dangers by which he was menaced. The most prudent in . counsel, and the most intrepid in action, providing for all public wants, and guarding against all contin-

gencies, the young duke inspired his followers with
fortitude, courage, and confidence; and the Emperor
of Germany was repulsed in all his attacks, and finally
driven from his entrenchments.

Despairing of success in this expedition, Otho convened his barons, and pointed out the difficulties of
carrying on the siege. His principal officers advised
him to demand a truce of three months with Richard.
Otho a second time assembled his barons, and convinced that he had embarked in an unprofitable and
inglorious quarrel, he broke out in bitter reproaches
against Arnoul, whom he threatened to deliver into
the hands of Richard; but his barons opposed him,
pointing out the dishonour of placing any man in the
power of an enemy who would assuredly put him to
death,[1]—a just, humane, and noble sentiment. After
some further deliberation Otho determined to retreat;
and Arnoul, having heard that the emperor meditated
purchasing his own security, by giving him up to the
Normans, fled the camp with his troops. The noise of
this movement alarmed the French and Germans, who
mistook it for an attack by Richard: they retreated
in disorder, and were pursued up to the gates of
Amiens, suffering great slaughter. This decisive victory was followed by peace and the dissolution of the
triple alliance.

Louis and Otho were more incensed against Hugh
than Richard, and applied to the pope to excommunicate the Count of Paris. Their request was granted,
but Hugh derided the thunders of the Vatican. In
954, the King of France died, in consequence of an

---

[1] " L' en ne deibt mie rendre ostage ne prison
A home ki l'ocie, pois qu'est sun compaingnon."
*Roman de Rou,* v. 4185.

injury he had received when hunting, and was succeeded by his son Lothaire.  The Count of Paris, now
old and infirm, showed the high esteem he entertained
for the duke of Normandy, by appointing him guardian to his son, known in history as Hugh Capet,
who seized on the throne of France, after the death of
Lothaire, and founded the Capetian dynasty.  It was
in 955 that Richard received this flattering mark of
confidence.  According to the old chroniclers, Hugh
thus addressed his family:—" I desire, my dear children, that you will endeavour to model your characters after the example of Richard, your guardian, and
that you will take his good counsel as the rule of prudence.  You know that I have affianced your sister
to him, and that they will be married, as soon as she
has attained to a proper age.  These are the most
sacred wishes of my heart, which fervently implores
the blessing of Heaven on the full accomplishment
of these my desires."  In the following year Hugh
died.

Peace was preserved during six years, but in 961, a
new opponent to the Duke of Normandy appeared on
the stage.  Theobald, surnamed the " Trickster,"
Count of Chartress, Blois, and Tours, had married the
Duchess Leutegarde, mother-in-law of Richard, and,
in right of his wife, he claimed certain lands which the
duke refused to surrender.  Theobald formed an alliance with Lothaire, King of France, and ravaged the
open country.  The Norman historians relate various
stratagems by which it was attempted to secure the
person of Richard, and describe Theobald as a second
Arnoul.  But these statements are in most respects
void of truth, and in others, too highly coloured by

national prejudices. The French and Normans met on the banks of the river Deppe, where a sanguinary battle was fought, in which Richard greatly distinguished himself, by personally rescuing Walter, his grand falconer, whose horse had stumbled with him in the river. The army of Lothaire was defeated with severe loss, and the victorious Richard returned triumphantly to Rouen.

His stay in the capital was short, for hearing that Theobald had gained possession of Evreux, Richard desolated the whole territory of Chartres. After horrible depredations on both sides, the hostile princes encountered each other, when fortune again favoured the arms of Normandy. The city of Chartres was burned, and Theobald with great difficulty escaped with life. These continued successes roused the jealousy of the neighbouring potentates, and raised up an armed confederacy, consisting of Lothaire, King of France, Theobald, Earl of Chartres, Geoffrey, Earl of Anjou, the Count of Maine, and the Earl of Belesme, whose united armies wasted the lands, and depopulated the cities of Normandy. [1] The duke felt himself unable to resist this formidable combination, and dispatched messengers to Denmark to solicit the aid of Harold. That chivalrous prince, whose chief delight was war, quickly responded to the call, and the Danish fleet anchored safely at Gefosse, on the Seine. The auxiliaries and the Normans first marched against Theobald, carrying fire and

---

[1] Flodoard, a French historian, states that this combined attack on Normandy was to punish Richard for having disturbed an assembly held at Soissons, when he seduced some of the king's vassals from their allegiance. " Placitum regale, diversorumque conventus principum Susessionis habetur, ad quod impediendum, si fieri posset, Ricardus filius Willelmi Nordmanni accedens, à fidelibus regis quibusdam persuasus, et interemptis suorum nonnullis in fugam versus est." (Anno 961.)

sword into every district, destroying churches and
houses, corn and cattle. They next invaded the territories of Lothaire, where their ravages were equally
exterminating. Consternation seized on all, and the
cries of the people were responded to by the clergy and
barons. Remonstrances were presented to the King
of France, bitterly reproaching him for drawing down
such misery on the nation to indulge his personal hatred
against the Duke of Normandy.

Lothaire, unable to turn a deaf ear to the complaints
of his subjects, which were energetically supported by
the chief men in the realm, selected Vulfaldus, bishop
of Chartres, as ambassador to Richard, and he immediately repaired to Rouen. At his first interview, the
prelate reproached the duke with introducing a horde
of pagans into the country, who had destroyed so
many Christian churches, and expressed his astonishment that a prince, so renowned for the excellence of
his character and the goodness of his heart, could permit them to slay men, women, and children, in cold
blood. " By my honour," replied Richard, " I have
acted with propriety ; and if the land be ravaged, it is
no reproach to me. I am resolved to punish Theobald,
and humble the pride of the French King. They have
attacked me without provocation, and with the aid of
God, I will have revenge. My friend," continued the
duke, " I will not impose a lie upon you; I would
rather see all the churches razed to the ground, than
live dishonoured; and more freely would I abandon
Normandy to the pagans, than be expelled from it by
the King of France. Had I fallen within his power,
I know he would have murdered me. He incited
Theobald to carry war into my kingdom. Neither

truce nor peace will I grant, until my city of Evreux is restored." [1]

The bishop, nothing disconcerted, used all his spiritual eloquence to shake the resolution of Richard, and appease his anger : he implored him not to incur the vengeance of Heaven, by maintaining his league with the pagans, the enemies of the holy faith. He beseeched him to grant an armistice, and pledged his sacerdotal word that Lothaire should give him a pacific and honourable meeting at Saint-Clair-sur-Epte. The reluctance of Richard was at last subdued : the proposed interview took place, and a definitive treaty of peace was ratified between France and Normandy. As soon as Theobald heard of this reconciliation, he hastened to obtain terms for himself, which the duke generously granted. Richard found it no easy task to satisfy his Danish allies; their restless character fitted them alone for war, and they saw all prospect of future plunder vanish from their grasp by these pacific arrangements. The duke offered lands and the rights of citizenship to those who would remain in Normandy, receive baptism, and embrace the Christian doctrine. Some consented, but the great majority sailed for the coast of Spain, where they disembarked, and pillaged eighteen cities. The war between France and Normandy terminated in 969.

Shortly after the peace the Duchess of Normandy died, without leaving children. All her personal effects were divided between the poor and the monasteries. Richard then determined to marry his mistress Gonnor, for which purpose he convened his barons, who readily gave their consent to the proposed union. All

[1] Roman de Rou, v. 5020, et seq.

the Norman chroniclers represent her as a lady of high
birth and breeding, but, in truth, her father was one
of the duke's foresters. She was a great favourite with
the clergy, having made large presents to the churches,
particularly to Notre-Dame-de-Rouen, on which she
bestowed some curious and beautiful embroidery,
worked by herself and her maidens. She also
caused precious cloths to be worked with silk, illus-
trating the history of the Virgin Mary and the saints. [1]
The six children of this connexion were Richard, who
succeeded to the dukedom; Robert, archbishop of
Rouen; Mauger, Earl of Corbeil; Emma, married to
Ethelred, King of England ; Hadwige, who espoused
Geoffrey, Duke of Brittany ; and Matilda, who was
united to Odo, Earl of Chartres.

During this reign, war raged for twenty-five years,
but when peace was established, the people felt the
benefits of the wise system of policy which Richard had
adopted in the internal administration of his government. He was sincerely beloved by his subjects, who
acknowledged with gratitude the equity and mildness
of his sceptre. He was remarkable for his bounty to
the clergy, and the zeal he displayed to propagate the
Christian religion. He built the cathedral at Rouen,—
the church of the Benedictines at Saint Ouen,—that
of the Holy Trinity of Fécamp, near to his palace,
and the abbey of Saint Wandrille. He also constructed his own tomb at Fécamp; not inside the
church, but outside the gate under a gutter, in order,
as he said, " That the rains might wash his body clear
of his numerous sins." [2] This royal sarcophagus being
finished, Richard ordered that during the remainder

1 Chronique de Normandie.          2 Roman de Rou, v. 5881.

of his life, it should be filled every Friday with corn,
which was to be distributed to the poor, with five sous
of the currency of Rouen. It may here be remarked,
as a curious fact, that the dukes of Normandy scarcely
coined any money up to this period, and somewhat
later, though the coined money of Mans, Anjou, and
Poitou was very common.

Richard fell sick at Bayeux, in the environs of which
city the dukes of Normandy had a palace. The Abbé
De La Rue fixes the locality at Balleroy, [1] and M.
Pluquet at Nôron, where the ruins may still be seen. [2]
Finding his strength fail, the duke desired to be removed to Fécamp with his children, and his half-bro-
ther, Raoul, Count of Ivry, son of Sprota and Asper-
leng, superintendent of the mills at Vaudreuil. He
then delivered up the ducal authority to his eldest son,
and in the presence of his prelates and barons, received
the sacrament, and died universally regretted by his
subjects in 996. [3]

Firm in adversity, intrepid in war, mild and merci-
ful in prosperity, this illustrious prince, during a
chequered and eventful reign of fifty-five years, never
once belied his character. Every day of his life was
marked by the faithful discharge of those duties which
best ennoble monarchs. He has been named Sans-
Peur; to that title may be added Sans-Reproche,
for his memory deserves undivided homage and respect.

Essais Historiques sur la Ville de Caen et son Arrondissement.
Note to Roman de Rou, v. 5888.
Dudon fixes his death in 1002, but it is a gross error.

D

# RICHARD THE SECOND,

## FOURTH DUKE OF NORMANDY,

### Surnamed The Good.

———

RICHARD the Second succeeded his father, Richard
Sans Peur, in the ducal throne of Normandy, in 996.
His first policy was to obtain the zealous support of the
church, in which view he gave very considerable sums
of money to the monks, and completed the monastery
of Fontenelles, which his father had commenced.   He
also prevailed on William of Dijon, called the " Blessed,"
on account of his piety, to establish himself at Fécamp,
which abbey the duke endowed with extensive lands.
During a reign of thirty years, he displayed justice,
benevolence, courage, and religion, and the happiness
enjoyed by his subjects entitled him to the glorious
title of " The Good," conferred upon him by his contemporaries, and confirmed by posterity.

At the commencement of this reign, a rebellion
broke out among the peasantry, and as they had common grievances, they united together, and bound themselves by an oath not to separate before they had obtained redress.   This revolt originated in the rigorous
exaction of the barons, who harassed the peasantry
with vexatious services ; but the chief cause of discon-

tent was the establishment of a game law, by which
the villains were interdicted from hunting in the woods,
lest they should kill deer.　The insurrection was soon
quelled by the vigour of the Count of Ivry, uncle to
the duke, who, however, tarnished his fame by the per-
petration of the most horrible cruelties.　Some of the
rebels were impaled, others had their eyes put out,
many had their right hands amputated, while the principal leaders of the sedition were burnt alive.　Those
who held property were punished by the confiscation
of their estates. [1]

[1] From the subjoined passage, extracted from the Roman de Rou, the vexations
of the people seem to have multiplied to a fearful extent :—

> " Ne poent une heure aveir paix
> Tuz en jur sunt sémuns de plaiz.
> Plaiz de forez, plaiz de moneies,
> Plaiz de purprises, plaiz de veies,
> Plaiz de biés, plaiz de moutes,
> Plaiz de fautés, plaiz de toutes." v. 6008, et seq.

Wace then states that the villains " *oumune fuscint.*"　On this very remarkable
expression we are induced to offer some extended remarks, as we here detect the infant
form of municipal corporations.　The phrases, " faire cumune : la cumune re-
mest à tant," admit of a much more copious signification than has generally been
suspected, applying to the organized associations of the poorer classes against the
usurpations of the higher classes, both among the inhabitants of towns and the ru-
ral population.　We must not, however, conclude that the idea inferrible from
" *faire cumune,*" to establish corporations, was popularly entertained before the end
of the tenth century ; for Wace, by an anachronism very common in the middle
ages, has antedated these institutions, and given them a colouring which belongs to
later times.

We agree with Bamage that towns, boroughs, and even villages existed in Normandy before the reign of Richard the Second, which possessed independent rights
and privileges, and which gave birth to allodial and burgage tenure, as it is explained in the " Viel Coutumier," titles 28 and 31, and in the amended " Coutumier," articles 102 and 138.　We shall pause to explain the signification of the terms
allodial and burgage tenure.

" Allodium," in a strict legal sense, is the opposite to " feodum."　The former denoted property in the highest degree, free from any rent, servitude, drawback, or
contingency whatever ; the owner was said to have *plenum et directum dominium,*
full and immediate ownership.　Such was the law in England among the Anglo Saxons, but after the conquest the feudal tenure was introduced, which abolished allodial
proprietorship, and by a fiction of law, vested all the land of the country in the king.
From that time, no subject, not even the first baron in the realm, held independent
property ; he had only the usufruct, not the absolute possession ; or, as Sir Edward

Fearing lest this intestine discord might have been secretly fomented by some of the great vassals of the duchy, the duke commanded all his earls and barons to renew their homage, and repeat the oath of fidelity. The Earl of Hyèmes alone refused, in consequence of which his territory was attacked, and himself made

Coke says, he had *dominium utile*, but not *dominium directum*; i. e. the useful, but not the direct, occupancy.

Burgage tenure, according to Blackstone, is where houses, or lands which were formerly the site of houses, in an ancient borough, are held of some lord in common socage, by a certain established rent. Glanvil and Littleton identify tenure in bur_gage with tenure in socage; which, they say, exists where the king, or other person, is lord of an ancient borough, in which the tenements are held by a rent certain. The essential character of this holding, therefore, is the *certainty* of the conditions of the tenure, the rent being defined, and not subject to fluctuation.

With reference to Normandy, Basnage is of opinion that allodial tenures obtained before Charles the Simple ceded Neustria to the Northmen, and that they derive their privilege from agreed compositions, paid by several of the old towns. He thinks that such towns had ransomed themselves from any contingency of being pillaged, by the payment of money, and that they were thus guaranteed in the secure possession of their houses *proprietarily*, in contradistinction to *beneficially*, because benefices were confined to landed estates. The burgage tenure in Normandy, as well as in England, differed from allodial tenure, inasmuch as the former recognized dependence on a superior; nor was property situate on such lands deemed immoveable. "In tenuris autem per Borgagium sciendum est, quod possunt vendi et emi, ut mobile." (*Vetus Consuetudo*, title 31.) Consequently, burgage-tenure estates were not liable to the "treixiéme," which succeeded the "congé," or licence of the lord to alienate, nor to reliefs, nor to wardships, nor homage, &c., but simply to the payment of a rent, fixed and certain, as acknowledgment of tenancy. Brothers and sisters shared alike, and wives had one half of that species of property called "Conquêts," acquired during marriage by their husbands. Jumièges, in Normandy, affords a proof of the existence of allodial tenure at an early date, for William Longsword purchased it with gold, and then gave it to the monks, thus admitting that he had no ducal claims on it. This is attested by William of Jumièges, c. viii. b. 3, and by Walsingham, in his Ypodigma Neustriæ: "*Abbati locum tradidit cum tota villa quam a lodariis auro redemit.*"

It has been asked, were the charters, which established corporate privileges in the twelfth century, a new right, granted by the sovereign? Or, did they merely ratify and recognize an old right? We read in all of them: "*Major et Scabini habebunt placita de hæreditatibus atque catallis.*" If they had complete jurisdiction over the heritable and moveable property situate within their towns, why does the charter of the town and liberties of Rouen contain the following reservations?—"*Salvo jure, salvis curiis dominorum qui ibi terras habuerint ?*" Why do all these charters terminate with these words—"*Salvo jure nostro et alieno et salvo jure ecclesiarum nostrarum ?*" These reservations would be idle words, unless we conclude that the sovereign never intended to invade rights precedently acquired, but simply to grant to persons holding property on allodial district, the means of preserving and transmitting such property, without having recourse to the arm of the feudal law.

prisoner. He was confined in the tower of Rouen, from which he escaped after a detention of five years; but being totally destitute, and fearing to be re-captured, he resolved to throw himself at the feet of the duke, and supplicate his pardon. Richard, touched with his misfortunes, received him again into his favour, generously gave him the province of Eu, and married him to the Countess Esseline, the wealthy sister of Amschetil, Baron of Harcourt.

Before the establishment of " tabellions," or notaries, which does not date earlier than the thirteenth century, various modes existed for the transmission of immoveable property. Richard the Second made use of the transfer by the verge, or rod, of which the Salic law speaks, title 49; and also André Duchesne, in the Additamenta ad Hist. Norman. page 317. Written deeds were frequent, particularly when property was conveyed to churches and other religious houses, for to legalize such transactions the consent of the sovereign and the lords was required. Ordericus Vitalis mentions numerous examples of this usage, which prevailed in his time, and his statements prove the existence of the feudal system, and the indispensable necessity of obtaining the licence, or " congé," of the lord of the fief to sell, or alienate. We may remark in the written deeds of the sovereigns, collected by Mabillon, Martène, Dacheri, Dumoustier, and others, a great variety of properties acquired by no other solemnity than the " congé" of the lords of the fief. In them we see that William the Bastard, after the conquest of England, gave away immense demesnes by very different forms of title. " Conferebantur etiam primó multa prædia nudo verbo, atque scripto, vel cartâ, tantum cum domini gladio, vel galeâ, vel cornù, vel craterâ, et plurima tenementa cum calcari, cum strigili, cum arcu, et nonnulla cum sagittâ; sed hæc initio regni sui, posterioribus annis immutatus iste modus." (Ingulfi Historia.) We read in Bracton, lib. iv. c. 8 and 14, that when a vassal rendered back to his lord lands which he had received, but which were to be conveyed to another party, he gave back the verge or stick presented to him, when first put into possession. If the vassal, for any crime or dereliction of homage, were deprived of his estate, the Salic law, titles 48, 61, 63, required that the stick should be broken publicly before the court, in proof that the contract was cancelled. This form of law was rendered by the Latin word, exfustucare, or exfustigare, from fistuca, which signifies a small twig, or from fustic, a stick; whence is derived the French proverb, applied to a termination of intimacy between two friends: " Ils ont rompu leur paille," because from festuca is formed fétu, which signifies a rush, or straw. We may detect the same tradionary mode of parlance in the homely English phrase, " He has cut his stick."

In reference to the revolt of the people, mentioned at the commencement of this note, William of Jumièges thus expresses himself: " Contigit quoddam pestiferi oriri seminarium dissidii. Nam rustici unanimes per diversos totius Normannicæ patriæ comitatus, plurima agentes conventicula, juxtà suos libitus vivere decernebant. Quatenus tam in sylvarum compendiis, quàm in aquarum commerciis, nullo obsistente ante statuti juris obice, legibus uterentur suis. Quæ ut rata manerent, ab uno quoque cætu furentis vulgi duo eliguntur legati, qui de creta ad Mediterraneum roboranda ferrent conventum."

Ethelred, King of England, had married a sister of the Duke of Normandy, who received intelligence of that monarch's being plunged in excesses, while his wife was treated with contumely, and the affairs of the nation were shamefully neglected. Richard remonstrated with him on the impropriety of his conduct, which so exasperated Ethelred that he assembled an army for the invasion of Normandy, charging his general to bring the duke prisoner to London. The expedition embarked at Portsmouth and landed at Barfleur. Néel of Saint Sauveur, now called Saint Sauveur-le-Vicomte, in the department of La Manche, commanded in this district, and collected his forces to repel the invaders; even the women joined his standard.[1] On their first landing, the English committed dreadful ravages, but they were speedily attacked and routed, and so exterminating was the slaughter, that very few fugitives reached the fleet to announce the discomfiture of the army. Ethelred vowed vengeance, but Pope John the Sixteenth interposed, and reconciled the two brothers-in-law.

Shortly after these events, Richard married Judith, daughter of the Duke of Brittany, by whom he had six children: Richard, his successor in the dukedom; Robert, who succeeded his elder brother; William, who became a monk in the abbey of Fécamp, and died very young in 1025; Alice, married to Renauld, Earl of Burgundy; Eleonora, to Baldwin, Earl of Flanders, and Papia, to Guilbert, of Saint Valery. The duchess Judith founded the magnificent abbey of Bernay, in which she was buried.

[1] Both Wace and William of Jumièges speak of these female warriors. " Sed et fœminæ pugnatrices, robustissimos quosque hostium vectibus hydriarum suarum excerebrantes."

While Normandy enjoyed the happiness of a wise administration, England groaned under the tyranny of Ethelred, who massacred all the Danes within his kingdom. When intelligence of this treacherous barbarity was communicated to Sweyn, King of Denmark, he levied an army, and landed his forces in the north of England. He quickly marched on to York, when the barons, disgusted with Ethelred, and alarmed at the sight of this formidable expedition, submitted to the invader, who hastened on to London, which capitulated. Sweyn soon completed the conquest of the whole kingdom, which, at that time, had no fortresses or strong-holds, and Ethelred, with his wife and son, took refuge in Normandy, abandoning the crown to the King of Denmark. Richard received them with all the courtesy which a generous prince owes to a monarch in distress, and they continued to enjoy his protection and hospitality, till the people of England, groaning under the tyranny of Sweyn and his successor Canute, invited the exiled princes to return to their native country. Several battles were fought with the Danes, but the death of Ethelred, [1] and the assassination of his son, Edmund Ironside, gave undivided sovereignty to Canute.

The Danish prince now sought the alliance of the Duke of Normandy, proposing to marry the widow of Ethelred, and offering his sister Estrita to Richard, who was free to contract a new marriage, in consequence of the death of Judith of Brittany. This negociation, after some reluctance on the part of Emma, who regarded Canute as the despoiler of the inheritance of her children, was carried into effect, with the complete

[1] Ethelred died in 1016.

approbation of the English and Normans; and it was
expressly stipulated that, on the death of Canute, the
kingdom of England should devolve on the children
of Ethelred and Emma, failing issue from Emma and
Canute. [1]

Odo, Earl of Chartres, had married a sister of Richard, and as she died without offspring, the duke
claimed back her dowry, which Odo refused to restore.
A war ensued, and Odo was signally defeated, at the
battle of Tilliéres, a strong fortification erected by the
Normans to defend their frontier. The campaign, however, was continued with vigour on both sides, and
Normandy and the Chartrain were desolated by fire
and sword. Richard summoned to his aid two of the
Scandinavian princes, Olaf Tryggveson, and Swend,
his brother-in-law. A violent tempest drove the fleet
of these two princes on the coast of Brittany. Fearing to be attacked by superior numbers in a hostile
country, they dug deep trenches in front of their encampment, and filled them up with loose earth. When
the Bretons came to the charge, horses and men were
engulphed in these pits, and easily slaughtered. This
stratagem seems to have been a favourite with the
warriors of former times. It is mentioned by the old
annalists to have been adopted on three occasions; in
992, at the battle of Conquereuil, between Conan,
Duke of Brittany, and Fulk, Earl of Anjou; secondly, at the conflict just mentioned ; and thirdly,
in an invasion of Aquitaine, by the Scandinavians.

After having repulsed the Bretons, the auxiliaries
reached Normandy without further interruption, and

[1] The marriage of Canute and Emma took place in 1017, in which year Judith
of Brittany died.

united their forces with those of the Duke of Normandy. The Earl of Chartres was alarmed at this powerful confederacy, and solicited the King of France to avert the storm that menaced him with ruin. Through the intercession of that monarch, the hostile parties were conciliated, and hostilities terminated, Odo restoring the disputed dower, except the town and castle of Dreux. On this occasion, the Scandinavian prince, Olaf, was converted to Christianity, and received the rites of baptism, after which he returned to his own country. [1]

In 1019, Robert, King of France, demanded assistance from the Duke of Normandy to besiege Melun, which had been fraudulently sold to the Earl of Chartres and Blois, by one Walter, the vassal of Bouchard, Count of Melun, while the latter was assisting his majesty in his wars. The duke granted the succours required, and a simultaneous attack was directed against the town, the French assaulting it on one bank of the Seine, the Normans on the other. All resistance was fruitless, and some of the principal inhabitants dispatched an emissary to the duke, acquainting him with their intention of opening a gate, leading into the fortress, at a given hour. Richard availed himself of this offer, and entered Melun a conqueror. He spared the lives of the garrison, but delivered up the treacherous Walter to the King of France, by whose orders he was hanged at the gate of the castle. Melun was restored to Bouchard.

After this exploit, the duke returned to Rouen,

---

[1] This was the last expedition of the Scandinavian princes to Normandy. The names of these two chiefs are variously given by the Norman historians, but we have followed the opinion of M. Depping.

where he remained six months in tranquillity, when he
was solicited by the King of France to assist him in
the reduction of Burgundy.   Henry, Duke of Burgundy, was uncle to the King of France, and died
without issue, having adopted as his successor, Otho
William, Count of Dijon.   This choice displeased the
people, and a strong party invited Landry, Count of
Nevers, to seize the dukedom.   This he did, but others
applied to Robert, King of France, offering Burgundy
to him, as the nephew of the late duke, and his nearest
of kin.   This prospect of aggrandizement was too al-
luring to be slighted, and to succeed in the enterprize,
the Norman alliance was requested.   The Count of
Nevers had obtained possession of Auxerre, into which
he had thrown a strong garrison, when the French troops
and thirty thousand of their allies arrived before that
city.   The blockade was so strict and efficient, that no
provisions could be introduced from the surrounding
country, and famine soon spread sickness among the
besieged.  To sally forth, and attack the combined army,
was an experiment which prudence did not sanction
against superior numbers.    Aware of the desperate
situation of the inhabitants, the King of France summoned the garrison to surrender at discretion, and deliver up the Count of Nevers, under pain of being put
to the sword.   This menace opened the gates, but Robert pardone  the count.

The surrender of Auxerre was followed by that of
Sens and other towns; but the castle and town of Ava-
lon made a determined resistance, the siege lasting
three months.   When it surrendered, Robert dis-
graced his victory by massacring most of the inhabitants, an act unworthy of a soldier, who ought to re-

spect the courage of a vanquished enemy.   The entire
conquest of Burgundy now followed, which the King
of France bestowed on his son Henry, who, on succeeding to the throne of his father, yielded the province to
his younger brother, from whom the first race of the
dukes of Burgundy, of the blood royal, descended,
which family continued during three hundred and
sixty years.   Robert expressed his gratitude to Richard in presence of the two armies, and the Normans
returned to their country, covered with laurels and
loaded with spoil.

   The King of France and the Duke of Normandy had
scarcely separated, when a new enemy called them to
the field.   Their assistance was claimed by Baldwin,
Count of Flanders, to support his title to the duchy of
Lorraine, which Otho the Third, Emperor of Germany,
had guaranteed to Godfrey, Earl of Ardennes, Bouillon, and Verdun.   This war was protracted during
two years, and was terminated by a compromise, Lorraine being surrendered to Godfrey, while Valencien-
nes was transferred to Baldwin.

   At the termination of this campaign, the Duke of
Normandy put away Estrita, sister of Canute, and
married Papia, a Danish lady, by whom he had two
sons, Mauger, Archbishop of Rouen, and William,
Count of Arques.

   Richard the Second reigned during thirty years, and
by his valour, prudence, and magnanimity conciliated
the confidence and friendship of the King of France,
winning the esteem of cotemporary princes and of his
own barons and subjects.   He was as much beloved as
respected by his own people, and their attachment to
his person was manifested on all occasions.   Richard en-

dowed several monasteries, and particularly that of Jumièges. In him the unfortunate always found a friend; he had the happy talent of anticipating the public wants, and flatterers found no favour at his court. If the least injustice, committed under the sanction of his authority, came to his ears, he instantly made reparation, and he used to repeat as a golden maxim, "The injustice of princes honours their victims."

Under his government agriculture was protected, commerce encouraged; and general prosperity pervaded all classes, and the laws were impartially administered. He fell sick at Rouen, and feeling that the hour of his death was fast approaching, desired to be removed to Fécamp. There he repented of his sins, took the sacrament, and received absolution. He gave a third of his moveable property to the poor, and divided the remainder among his sons. He appointed his eldest son, Richard, his successor to the ducal throne, and bestowed the province of Hyèmes on his second son, Robert, on the express condition that he should owe homage and fealty to his elder brother. Shortly after these arrangements were completed, Richard died at Fécamp, on the 23d of August, 1026, where he was buried in a tomb adjoining that of his father.

# RICHARD THE THIRD,

## FIFTH DUKE OF NORMANDY.

———

RICHARD the Third inherited the virtues of his father; but scarcely had he girded on the ducal sword, than he was compelled to draw it against his brother, who, discontented with the limited province of Hyèmes, seized on the town of Falaise, towards the close of December, 1027. He was quickly dispossessed of his conquest; for the duke, collecting a small portion of his troops, attacked Falaise, which Robert, after a vigorous resistance, was compelled to abandon. He was pursued to the walls of Hyèmes, and taken prisoner. Repenting of his rashness, he threw himself on the generous clemency of his victorious brother, obtained his pardon, took the oath of homage and fealty, and was reinstated in his authority. Tranquillity being thus restored, the duke disbanded his army, and returned to Rouen. He died suddenly, after an entertainment given to his barons, many of whom shared the same fate, which excited suspicions of poison. Some historians have accused Robert of this crime, because he had to humble himself to his brother, but cotemporary writers have done him more justice. Robert had recognized his error; he had made every reparation in his power, and given the strongest proofs of his sincere reconciliation; while all his actions, during his subsequent reign, disprove the accusation, and justify him in the eyes of posterity.

The death of Richard the Third was equally lamented by the nobles and the people. His courteous manners, his prudence and courage, had won the hearts of all his subjects; they saw with satisfaction the virtues of his father revived in him, and anticipated similar benefits from his reign. He was buried near the great altar of the church of St. Ouen.

Richard died without lawful issue, and was succeeded by his brother Robert. He left three illegitimate children. The eldest became a monk at Saint Ouen, of which he was elected abbot, and over which he presided during fifty years: the other two were daughters, one of whom married Walter of Saint Valery, and the other the Viscount of Bayeux.

# ROBERT THE FIRST,

## SIXTH DUKE OF NORMANDY,

#### Surnamed The Magnificent, and by others, The Devil.

———

ROBERT, second son of Richard the Good, succeeded his brother with the unanimous assent of all the vassals of the duchy. His great uncle, Robert, Count of Evreux and Archbishop of Rouen, performed the ceremonies of his coronation, placing the ducal tiara on his brow, the mantle on his shoulders, and the sword in his hand ; after which he administered the customary oath, by which the duke swore to maintain the liberties of the church, to defend his people, and cause justice to be impartially administered.

The first public act of his reign was to build the abbey of Cerisy, near to the town of St. Lo, which he amply endowed, and there established a community of monks. He was particularly attached to the church, regular in his devotions, and carried his piety to the extent of feeding and washing the poor with his own hands,—acts of humility attested and glorified by the monkish chroniclers.

At the commencement of his reign Robert was the dupe of an intrigue, of which the Archbishop of Rouen

ing an armed force from various quarters, the duke laid
siege to that fortress, which at once surrendered, the
garrison obtaining permission to retire with their effects; but Hugh never dared again to appear before
Robert.

These intestine feuds being quelled, the duke returned to Rouen, where he received an embassy from
Baldwin, Earl of Flanders, who entreated his support
against his own son, Baldwin of Lille, surnamed the
Pious. This latter had espoused Adele, daughter of
Robert, King of France; and impatient of dependency
on his father, he determined to strip him of his dignity and territories, and had already, by force of arms,
subdued a large portion of his dominions.

In so legitimate a cause the Duke of Normandy
readily drew his sword, and entering Flanders with a
considerable army, he took possession of Cassel and
Terouane, devastating the country, and slaughtering
the inhabitants. The fierceness of his attacks and the
terror of his name quickly reduced the rebels to submission, who returned to their allegiance, giving hostages to Robert for their continued fidelity. The next
object of the duke was to reconcile the father and son,
in which he was perfectly successful.

Towards the close of July, 1051, the duke received
intelligence of the death of Robert, King of France, to
whom he was sincerely attached. This event was followed by circumstances which again involved the
Normans in war. Constance, widow of the King of
France, was a woman of depraved heart and infamous
character; but such was her ascendancy over her husband, that she committed crimes of the blackest dye
with impunity. Two sons were the fruit of their

union, between whom this unnatural mother artfully
fomented discord, and she resolved to place the
younger brother on the throne to the exclusion of the
elder. To carry this project into effect she declared
that such was the will of the late king, and secured
the armed assistance of the Earl of Champagne, to
break the hereditary succession to the throne. Her
adherents rapidly increased, when her eldest son,
Henry, seeing the storm ready to burst on his head,
repaired to Fécamp, imploring succour from the Duke
of Normandy, and offering him, as an indemnification for his expenses, Chaumont, Pontoise, and the
French Vexin. He remained eight days with the
duke, who loaded him with presents and courtesy, at
the expiration of which time, he accompanied him to
France, at the head of a formidable army. The Normans ravaged the territory of the rebels with unre-
lenting fury, carrying on a war of complete extermination; for it was a maxim with the duke, that the
greater the carnage, the shorter the conflict; and it
was this terrible policy which gained him the sur-
name of " the Devil."

Already had the Normans reduced Senlis, Beauvais, Amiens, Laon, Reims, Noyon, Arras, Peronne,
Melun, and Sens. The hostile armies now approached
each other, and a decisive action seemed inevitable,
when the opportune death of Constance saved the
effusion of blood. Henry took peaceable possession
of the throne of France, and bestowed on his brother
the duchy of Burgundy. He gratefully acknowledged
the services of the Duke of Normandy, pledged inviolable friendship to his powerful ally, and conferred
on him the territories he had promised.

While Robert was absent on this expedition, Alain,
Duke of Brittany, deemed the opportunity favourable
to assert his independence, and renounce his homage
to Normandy.  As soon as the duke returned from
France, he took measures to quell the insubordination
of his refractory vassal; and first constructed a strong
fortification at Carrouges, on the frontier, which he
confided to the Viscount of Saint-Sauveur: he then
led his troops into Brittany; taking Dol by assault,
which he pillaged.  Alain, approaching his opponent
by a circuitous route, fell upon the rear of the Norman army, which he attacked with success; but the
governor of Carrouges, having been apprized of this
movement, had marched out of that fortress, and arriving, at the critical moment, on the field of battle,
the Bretons were placed between the two hostile
forces, and slaughtered without mercy.  The duke of
Brittany fled to Rennes, whence he dispatched an embassy to the Archbishop of Rouen, entreating his
friendly interposition to procure peace, and promising
to return to his allegiance.  The prelate, accordingly,
repaired to Brittany, and conducted Alain to Mont
Saint Michel, where he swore homage and fealty to
Robert, 'who then withdrew his forces from the territories of his vassal.

The Norman barons had frequently urged on Robert
the policy of marriage, but he constantly and firmly
resisted their frequent entreaties.  He was warmly
attached to a country girl of Falaise; and if this il-
licit intimacy were criminal, his fidelity to his mistress
did him honour.  As a prince, he deemed it improper
to raise a woman of the lowest birth to the ducal
throne; for had he chosen to have made that proposal

to his nobles, no doubt they would have given their
consent; but as a man, his excellent feelings would
not allow him to abandon a confiding female, or de-
sert her offspring. Robert understood the point of
honour in a different sense from princes who have
flourished in ages of more refined civilization; and his
son William, born in 1027, and afterwards the conqueror of England, received so careful an education,
that in his youth he displayed the brightest promise of
future greatness. When the boy had attained to his
eighth year, his father determined to visit Jerusalem
and the Holy Land. Having announced this intention to his barons, they strenuously opposed his departure, pointing out the dangers of so perilous an
expedition, and particularly insisting on the necessity
of his marrying, that there might be a direct heir to
the throne, without which it was feared that the numerous collateral branches of his family would each
advance their pretensions, and involve the kingdom
in anarchy and civil war.

To these remonstrances Robert replied that he did
not intend to leave them without a chief. "You
know," said he, "that I have a child by Harletta,
and I am satisfied that he is really my son; therefore
I conjure you, by the love and obedience you owe
me, to accept him as your prince. I now give him
seisin of the duchy, and constitute him my sole heir.
I appoint my cousin, the duke of Brittany, governor
of Normandy during my absence; and till the child is
of sufficiently mature age to rule in person, I confide him to the guardianship of Henry, King of
France."[1]

[1] Roman de Rou, v. 8107, et seq.

Having made this declaration to his council, the
duke convened the states-general, when the prelates
and barons again attempted to shake his resolution,
but in vain. Thus finding all opposition fruitless,
they received and recognized the young William as
their lawful sovereign, and took the oaths of homage
and fealty to his person. An instrument to this effect
was drawn up, with all the requisite formalities, and
being duly authenticated, it was deposited in the
exchequer of Rouen, after which Robert took his son
to Paris, and gave him in charge to King Henry the
First, who, flattered by the confidence reposed in him,
and glad of the opportunity of testifying his gratitude
for the signal services he had received from the Duke
of Normandy, vowed to treat the boy as his own child.

Robert now departed for Palestine, a journey which
he conceived to be the most certain mode of securing
his salvation. He visited Rome on his way, and received from Pope Benedict IX. the pilgrim's staff.
But though he nominally assumed the character of a
pilgrim, he displayed a royal magnificence during his
travels. The mule on which he rode was shod with gold.
When at Constantinople, he complied with the ori-
ental custom of dropping his mantle on the floor, when
introduced to the emperor of the east. A chamberlain
picked it up, and returned it to the duke, who refused
to wear it again, saying that a mantle which had
touched the ground was unfit to cover the shoulders
of a Norman. Falling sick at Jerusalem, he was carried on a litter by four Moors, and being accosted by
a pilgrim about to return to Normandy, who desired
to carry home some intelligence of his sovereign, the
duke told him to report that he had seen four devils

carrying him on their shoulders to Paradise, alluding
to the dark countenances of those infidels.

Having visited the Holy Sepulchre, Robert departed from Palestine; but a sudden fever terminated
his days, towards the end of June, 1035, after he had
reigned seven years. He was buried at the church of
Notre Dame at Nice, in Bithynia, on the second of
July following.

Duke Robert possessed in an eminent degree all the
great qualities which characterise a hero: he was
brave, liberal, generous, and just. Firm and steadfast
in his friendship, he disdained to take any mean advantage over those who stood in need of his support,
but perilled his life and fortunes with the pure dis-
interestedness of the best days of chivalry. If he indulged in war, it was not with any mercenary motive, nor from views of personal aggrandizement:
he fought for glory in the spirit of his age. Nor
would he suffer his rightful authority to be trifled
with, but resented any attempt to limit his prerogative with.marked severity; yet he never abused his
conquests, but pardoned his enemies, when he had
sheathed his sword.

# WILLIAM THE CONQUEROR,

## SEVENTH DUKE OF NORMANDY.

From his Accession in 1035 to the Death of Edward the Confessor.

---

## SECTION I.

THE old chroniclers were fond of mixing up fable with fact, and as they lived in superstitious times, their fictions were usually of a supernatural character. The conqueror of England was too illustrious a personage to be overlooked by the compilers of historical romance, and we accordingly find several prodigies accompanying his birth, which deserve to be recorded, as showing the spirit of the age. Of these we shall select a few of the most ingenious and striking.

During her pregnancy, his mother had two remarkable dreams, both predicting the future greatness of her son. She imagined that a lofty tree issued from her loins, the branches of which overshadowed the whole of Normandy; and on another occasion, she fancied that her intestines were stretched over the whole of Normandy and England, both of which dreams received their solution when William was firmly seated on the ducal throne and had reaped the fruits of the victory at Hastings. Immediately after birth, the child was placed on a small heap of straw, which he clutched with his hands, on which the nurse observed, " This infant begins so early to collect and amass, that I know not what large possessions he will acquire, when arrived at manhood." When yet a child in the castle of Falaise, he was visited by William Talvas, Count of Bellesme, Alençon, and Sees, who, judging from his features that he would quell the ambition of his house, exclaimed, " May the curse of Heaven light on you, since through you and your race my power will be laid low, and the fame of my posterity be obscured." [1]

William was eight years of age when his father died, having succeeded to the duchy in 1035. His youth offered no curb to the lawless and predatory barons, and though the mass of the people and the majority of the nobles recognized his title, yet the illegitimacy of his birth afforded a pretext for several of the crown vassals to break out into open insurrection, some desirous of gratifying their private resentments, others wishing to overthrow the authority of William. Thus the duchy was convulsed with anarchy and civil war, and it became the more difficult to quell the rebellion, since the adherents of the duke, instead of rallying round the throne, were engaged in devastating the lands of each other. The whole province was a scene of confusion, and as Dumoulin forcibly observes, " treason, perfidy, and impiety were arrayed in court robes, while justice was dressed in crape." [2]

William promulgated an edict, commanding all his

---

[1] These anecdotes are recorded by Dumoulin, p. 120, folio.
[2] In the seventh book of William of Jumiéges, the reader will find full particulars of these insurrections.

E

subjects to lay down their arms, but it was treated
with ridicule; on which his counsellors wrote to Alain,
Duke of Brittany, who had been appointed governor
of Normandy by Robert, inviting him to interpose,
and reduce the rebels by force of arms. He at first
adopted pacific measures, reminding the barons of their
oaths, and appealing to their sense of honour, but this
conciliatory advice being utterly disregarded, he
marched his troops into the duchy, and severely punished several of the malcontents. The intentions of
Alain were misrepresented to the people, and he was
accused of meditating the usurpation of the duchy,—
a charge entirely without foundation. But unfortunately the rumour was believed, and Alain was poisoned
at Vimoutiers. His body was removed to Fécamp,
and deposited in a tomb adjoining those of the two
Richards.

The death of the Breton prince was followed by the
murder of Turoldus, the preceptor of William, a man
of superior knowledge and exemplary virtue, who had
discharged his important trust with a diligence and
fidelity that merited public esteem. To attempt the
life of the duke himself was the next measure resolved
upon by the rebels, and this audacious enterprise was
undertaken by William Montgommeri, Viscount of
Hyèmes, who entered the castle of Vaudreuil during
the night, penetrated into the chamber of William, and
slew the Lord of Crespon, senechal of Normandy, who
slept in the apartment; but the noise awakening
the lieutenant of the senechal, he rushed on Montgommeri, and stretched him dead on the floor.

Thus surrounded by dangers which menaced both his
throne and his personal safety, the youthful sovereign

convened those barons who had been unflinching in
their attachment, and requested their advice to aid his
inexperience. The first measure adopted by this assembly, was to appoint Raoul-de-Gacé, constable of
Normandy, guardian to William; they then passed an
edict, commanding all persons to desist from carrying
arms without a special licence from the duke; and au-
thorized the constable to attack the castles of all who
refused obedience to this mandate. These proceedings
united the rebels, who were menaced by a common
danger; but it also drew all the faithful and peaceable
vassals to the ducal standard. A decisive battle terminated the hopes and schemes of the malcontents, and restored the duke to the full exercise of his prerogative.

An interval of repose succeeded these disturbances,
which the counsellors of William devoted to the cultivation of his mind. The duke had received from nature a vigorous and penetrating intellect, and inherited all the martial virtues of his ancestors. These
advantages were happily matured, and the Norman
prince became the most prudent and enlightened monarch of the age. In 1046, being then nineteen years
of age, he took into his own hands the reins of government. He selected his confidential friends and advisers
among the most upright and intelligent of his subjects,
banishing from his presence all whose characters were
stained with vice. He disarmed those vassals who had
taken part in the revolts which had troubled the commencement of his reign; enacted severe laws against
murderers and incendiaries, and summoned his barons to
repeat their oaths of allegiance. All the well disposed
cheerfully obeyed this command, and the people at
large rejoiced at the promulgation of the edicts which

guaranteed them against loss of life and property; but those to whom restraint was irksome, and to whom rapine had become habitual, again raised the standard of rebellion.

Guy, son of Raymond, Count of Burgundy, and Alice of Normandy, daughter of Duke Richard the Second, claimed the duchy by right of his maternal descent. He had been brought up with William from infancy, and was indebted to his liberality for the provinces of Vernon and Briosne, but now fired by ambition, he contended that the illegitimacy of his benefactor excluded him from the throne. Guy found supporters among the discontented Normans, and many of the principal barons ranged themselves under his banners, among whom were Néel, of St. Sauveur, Viscount of Cotentin, and Raymond, Viscount of Bayeux.

William, more astonished at the ingratitude of Guy than alarmed at his threats, consulted Mauger, Archbishop of Rouen, who recommended him to secure the alliance, or at least the neutrality, of the King of France, and the duke accordingly repaired to Poissy, where the king was then residing. Henry received him with friendship, promising armed assistance, which he engaged to lead in person. Having concluded this negociation, William returned to his capital, assembled his troops, and marched to Argentan; he was shortly afterwards joined by the French auxiliaries at Hyèmes.

The combined forces advanced on Caen, where they received intelligence that the enemy were encamped at Val-des-Dunes. The royal army, commanded by Henry, and the ducal army, under the orders of William, hastened forward in two divisions, simultaneously

attacked the malcontents, and gained a complete victory.   William performed prodigies of valour, and
Henry, stimulated by a generous rivalry, nearly fell a
victim to his impetuous courage, having been unhorsed by the lance of a Norman knight, named Con-
stantin, afterwards slain by the Count of St. Pol, who
sought him in the crowd, eager to avenge the affront
received by his sovereign.   The battle of Val-des-
Dunes was fought in 1047.

The rebels having been thus dispersed, the Count
of Burgundy retreated with the remnant of his cavalry
to Briosne.   This town was protected on the west by the
river Rille, which bathes its walls, and on the east by
a strong fortress, which commanded the valley and all
the approaches.   William, foreseeing that Briosne
would be the refuge of the vanquished, rapidly pursued Guy, to prevent his victualling the place, and
occupied all the neighbouring heights so securely that
it became impossible to throw any succour into the
town.   Guy was thus forced to surrender.   William
spared his life, but deprived him of Vernon and
Briosne, refusing henceforward to acknowledge him as
one of his vassals.   He commanded him to retire forthwith to Burgundy, where he was treated with contempt for his ingratitude to his relative and benefactor.

The duke, having quelled this rebellion, in which
many of the chiefs were either killed or taken prisoners, proceeded to confiscate the estates of those who
had escaped, and ordered all the fortresses erected
during the troubles to be razed.   William was grateful
to the King of France for the assistance he had ren-

dered, and he soon had an opportunity of testifying his sincerity, by repaying the services he had received.

In the spring of the following year, 1048, Geoffrey Martel, Count of Anjou, proud of the advantages he had gained over the Counts of Champagne and Chartres, refused to do homage to the King of France : he even aspired to the throne of that kingdom, and commenced hostilities by attacking the Counts of Guienne and Poitiers, both of whom he defeated and made prisoners. Henry, in his turn, now solicited aid from William to subdue this refractory vassal, who selected his most able officers and best disciplined troops, and hastened without delay to join his ally. The combined armies entered Anjou together, and laid siege to the castle of Meulan, which they carried by assault. The duke displayed such feats of heroism that he excited the jealousy of the French nobles, and particularly that of Henry, who envied the continually rising fame of the Norman prince, to whom, however, he loudly expressed his thanks for the victory achieved. The reputation of William now spread far and wide, and the Counts of Gascony and Guienne, as well as some of the petty kings of Spain, sent him presents of valuable horses, to testify their admiration of his valour.

This war being concluded, Henry and William returned to their respective dominions. The firm and equitable administration of the duke, and the glory he had acquired, had tamed the insolence of the most refractory of his nobles, and internal peace was established. He was soon, however, compelled to buckle on his armour to repel a foreign enemy. Geoffrey

Martel,[1] detesting William for having aided Henry,
invaded Normandy without any declaration of hostilities, seizing the town of Alençon and the castle of
Domfront.  He placed a strong garrison in both, and
returned home in triumph.  The duke soon arrived before Domfront, and established so effectual a blockade
that no supplies could be furnished to the besieged ;
yet they found means to apprize Martel of their situation, imploring him to march to their relief, otherwise
famine would compel them to surrender.  The Count
of Anjou accordingly put his troops in motion, but
fearing to hazard an engagement, he never approached
in sight of Domfront.

During this campaign, Néel of Saint Sauveur, Viscount of Cotentin, who had joined the rebellious
standard of Guy, Count of Burgundy, and concealed
himself in Brittany after the battle of Val-des-Dunes,
repented of his treason, and anxiously desired a reconciliation with William.  In order to obtain his
pardon, he prevailed on Odo, of Penthievre, to furnish
him with some squadrons of cavalry.  These he led
into Anjou, and by his skill and courage defeated the
Angevins in several encounters, thus materially thwart-
ing the designs of Martel.  For these signal and unexpected services, which proved his repentance and
renewed fidelity, he was again received into the ducal
favour, and reinstated in all his possessions.

The reluctance of Martel to advance to the relief of
Domfront, and the victories of the Viscount of Cotentin, discouraged all who had followed the banners of
the Count of Anjou.  William, having left some troops

---

[1] This Geoffrey was born in 1006, and died in 1060.  His wars with William
are fully narrated by William of Poitiers.

to keep that castle in check, laid siege to Alençon, but the inhabitants, confiding in the strength of their walls, not only set him at defiance, but insulted him with reflections on his birth. They hung skins over the battlements, to remind the duke that his mother was the daughter of a furrier at Falaise. Incensed at these reproaches, William swore by the *splendour of God,* his customary oath, that he would cut off the hands and feet of those who had been guilty of this insolence: his soldiers shared his indignation, and rushed furiously to the attack; the besieged fought valiantly, but William having slain the governor with his own hand, their courage failed, and the victory of the Normans was complete. The lives of the garrison were spared, but thirty-two persons had their limbs amputated, to satisfy the oath of the duke. [1]

William then returned to Domfront, which at once surrendered. He stripped it of all that could be serviceable in war, built a strong fortress at Hambrieres, on the frontier of Maine, to keep the Count of Anjou in check, and entrusted the command of it to Robert Giroye.

The counsellors of William had long and anxiously urged the necessity of his marriage, and the duke himself, having experienced in his own person the numerous dangers which beset illegitimate princes, readily yielded to the wishes of his barons. Matilda, daughter of Baldwin the Pious, Count of Flanders, was the princess selected to share the ducal throne. Negociations to this effect were commenced in 1048, but at a

---

[1] " Illusores veró, coram omnibus infra Alentium consistentibus, manibus privari jussit et pedibus. Nec mora; sicut jusserat, triginta duo debilitati sunt." *(Willelm. Gemmet,* lib. vii. c. 18.)

council held at Rheims, in 1049, Baldwin was prohibited from granting his daughter to William, and William was commanded not to receive her hand. The canonical objection to this union did not arise from consanguinity, but from affinity, Adèle of France, mother of Matilda, having first been married to Richard the Third of Normandy, uncle to William. This marriage, however, never appears have been consummated; but, at this period, the court of Rome seized hold of the most trifling pretext to extend canonical impediments, by which its authority was strengthened. At length the pope granted a dispensation, and Baldwin conducted his daughter to the castle of Eu, where the marriage was solemnized in 1053. [1]

This happy event was celebrated throughout Normandy with great rejoicing, and the general satisfaction would have been complete, had not Mauger, Archbishop of Rouen, hurled the thunders of the church against this auspicious union. Although the pope had granted a dispensation, this audacious prelate excommunicated the duke and duchess, not from any religious scruples, for he was a most immoral character, but because the children of this marriage would exclude from the dukedom his brother William, Count of Arques. The insolence of Mauger was, however, summarily punished. A legate was dispatched from Rome to Normandy, who assembled the prelates of the duchy at Lisieux; he pointed out the double crime of Mauger, his treason to his sovereign, and his disobedience of the papal mandate, insisting on his deposi-

[1] None of the Norman historians fix the date of the marriage, but the Chronique de Tours places it in 1053. The scruples of the church were not fully satisfied till 1059, when they were fully quieted by Lanfranc, afterwards archbishop of Canterbury.

tion. The primate of Normandy was accordingly deprived of the archiepiscopal throne, and banished to the island of Guernsey; in attempting to reach Cherbourg, he was drowned, but his body having been cast on shore and recognized, he was buried at Cherbourg. The deposition of Mauger took place in 1055.

When William, Count of Arques, saw that the duke, so far from heeding the excommunication of the archbishop, had taken prompt and effectual measures to deprive him of the primacy, he began secretly to foment a rebellion, and taking advantage of the absence of his sovereign, whose presence in the Cotentin was called for by measures of state, the count assumed the title of Duke of Normandy, fortified his castles, corrupted the fidelity of the governor of the castle of Arques, and then ravaged the province of Caux with his troops. Henry, King of France, now jealous of William, perfidiously aided the rebels with money, awaiting the opportunity to assist them with his forces. When the duke received intelligence of this revolt, he summoned his refractory vassal to do him homage, who, so far from submitting, sent back word that he would soon strip the usurper of his duchy.

So outrageous a menace rendered William furious. His impatience to punish this insolence prompted him to depart from the Cotentin with only a few attendants, after having ordered his army to follow him to the walls of Arques. On the road he received numerous complaints from the farmers and peasantry, who had been reduced to the most wretched condition by the ravages of the count. In crossing the province of Caux, he met three hundred horsemen, who had armed themselves to resist the rebels; he placed himself at

their head, and with this small band attacked and defeated several marauding parties, whom he compelled
to take shelter in the castle of Arques. This fortress
was very strong, being built on an abruptly precipitous
rock, which commanded all the subjacent country,
and the only mode of reducing it was by famine.
William dug entrenchments round the castle, and
charged Giffard, Count of Longueville, to prevent any
succours being thrown into the fortress.   He then returned to the Cotentin, to terminate the arrangements
suspended by this revolt.

During the blockade, the Count of Arques, whom
the scarcity of provisions soon began to inconvenience,
contrived to send an emissary to the King of France, to
whom he represented the deplorable situation of the garrison of Arques. Henry, glad to seize this opportunity
of injuring his former friend, assembled his troops,
and marched to the succour of the count.   Giffard, apprized of the approach of the royal army, and hearing
that it would remain a night at Saint-Aubin-sur-Scie,
ambushed the choicest of his soldiers in a wood, and
when the king, on the following morning, renewed his
march, a detachment of forty Norman horsemen presented themselves to dispute his passage. The French,
provoked at this bravado, rushed from their ranks ;
the Normans fled from them, and were pursued ; but
when they reached the ambuscade, the fugitives
wheeled about, and being supported by their comrades,
who suddenly darted from the woods, the enemy,
taken by surprise, were repulsed with great slaughter.
Among the slain was the Count of Abbeville, brother-
in-law to the Count of Arques, and many others of
rank.   Nevertheless, Henry succeeded in throwing

provisions into Arques: he even attacked the entrenchments of Longueville, but they were so courageously
defended, that the king, despairing of success, and
fearing a second discomfiture, sounded a retreat, and
returned to France.

The same courier brought intelligence to the duke of the
arrival, the attack, the defeat, and the retreat of the king;
but he was displeased that the castle of Arques had been
revictualled. He arrived shortly at the scene of action,
seconded the gallant Count of Longueville, and vowed
that he would not quit the spot, till the count and the
castle were in his power. If the presence of William
encouraged his own troops, it equally dispirited the
rebels, who again being pressed by famine, renewed
their applications for succour to the King of France,
but Henry refused, not daring to hazard a second enterprise of that character.

Thus disappointed in his expectations, the Count
of Arques, all whose resources were exhausted, was
compelled to throw himself on the generosity of his
nephew, and he sent a messenger offering to surrender
the fortress, on condition that his life, and the lives of
his adherents, were spared. The demand was granted,
but the miserable appearance of the garrison, who resembled spectres rather than men, so affected William
that he pardoned his uncle, and treated him with the
affection of a relative. All the vassals who had taken
part in the rebellion received the ducal clemency, excepting those whom fear induced to retire to France.

The submission of the Count of Arques, whom Henry
considered as an instrument to aid his own ambitious
views on Normandy, filled him with rage and mortification; he was jealous of the fame of William, and

determined to attempt the conquest of the duchy.
Having resolved on an invasion, the French monarch
summoned the crown vassals to assemble their troops,
and he soon collected a formidable army. It marched
in two divisions; the one commanded by Odo, brother
of the king, and the Counts of Chaumont, Montdidier,
and Ponthieu, entered Normandy through the province
of Bray; the other, under the orders of Henry, through
Evreux.

William made judicious preparations to oppose the
enemy, and followed their example of dividing his
troops. He confided a portion of them to his brother,
the Count of Eu, assisted by Hugh de Gournay, Hugh
de Montfort, the Count of Longueville, and William
Crespin. This force repaired to the Vexin to attack
the French division commanded by Odo. The duke,
at the head of his division, advanced to encounter
Henry, between Evreux and Louviers.

When the troops under Count Eu had reached the
banks of the river Andelle, they heard that the enemy
were encamped at Mortemer. A council of war decided
that they should march forward during the night, and
attempt to take the French by surprise. In this plan
the Normans completely succeeded, for they reached
the camp before daylight, when the troops of Odo were
buried in sleep. They set fire to the tents, and
slaughtered the enemy before they could form themselves in battle array. The French, however, fought
bravely, and victory was not decided till noon, when
the Count of Ponthieu being made prisoner, and ten
thousand men slain, Odo retreated in disorder. The
Count of Eu instantly dispatched a messenger to William, announcing his success.

separated by the river from those in advance, and
threw it into complete disorder. To increase the peril
of the fugitives, the bridge broke down, and all who
had not crossed over, were killed or taken prisoners.
The King of France was frantic with rage at this discomfiture, and soon afterwards died, whether from
grief and vexation, or from the injudicious use of
medicine, is uncertain. None of the Norman chroniclers fix.the date of the battle of Varaville, but as the
decease of the king certainly took place on the 14th of
August, 1060, it most probably happened in the spring
of that year.

The Duke of Normandy was now freed from one of
his most implacable and dangerous enemies, and as
Baldwin, Count of Flanders, father of the Duchess
Matilda, had been appointed regent of France, and
guardian of the young king Philip, by the will of
Henry, hostilities ceased, and a solid pacification ensued. William attended at the consecration of the
youthful monarch, displaying unusual pomp and magnificence.

The appointment of Baldwin to the regency was
only opposed by the Gascons. The Count of Flanders,
dissembling his resentment, equipped an army, under
the pretext of assisting the Spaniards against the Moors
and Saracens. He prevailed on Duke William to
unite his troops to the royal forces, and when they
were united in Gascony, Baldwin threw off the mask,
and crushed the rising rebellion. The Normans besieged and took Montauban, and by their repeated successes compelled the malcontents to do homage to the
youthful sovereign, to acknowledge Baldwin as regent,
and deliver hostages as guarantees of their fidelity.

On the return of the duke to Normandy, he convened the states of his duchy at Caen. The archbishop,
bishops, barons, and deputies from the third estate
composed this assembly; each delivered his opinion
with full freedom of speech. The objects of this meeting, which was held in 1061, were threefold; first, to
repress the licentiousness of the prelates and abbots;
secondly, to regulate the hour at which every citizen
should retire to his home in the evening, to prevent
nocturnal outrages, which were committed with impunity in the dark; thirdly to improve the civil and
ecclesiastical jurisdiction. The proceedings of this
assembly were marked by an order and regularity remarkable in such troubled times, and the rules they
established secured the internal peace of the duchy.

These arrangements having been completed to the
entire satisfaction of his subjects, with the exception
of some few discontented vassals, who were banished,
Normandy enjoyed repose till 1064, when the duke
was again called on to signalize his courage in the
field. Herbert the younger, Count of Maine, not
being able to resist the frequent attacks of surrounding
princes, acted on the advice of his mother, Bertha, by
throwing himself on the protection of the Duke of
Normandy, to whom he submitted himself as one of
his feudataries, and moreover declared him his heir, in
case of dying without issue. Herbert had only one
daughter, whom he survived, and on his death-bed he
implored his subjects to ratify his wishes, and accept
William as their chief, he alone being able to shield
them against their enemies. Scarcely had he paid the
debt of nature, ere Walter, Count of Mantes, Pontoise,
and Chaumont, prevailed on the Manceaux to acknow-

ledge him for their liege lord.   He was supported by
Geoffrey of Mayenne, and other powerful barons, but,
after a few actions, in which victory remained faithful
to the Norman banner, the Manceaux repented, and
carried the keys of Mans to William, who then invaded
Pontoise and Chaumont, and soon compelled Walter
to abandon his pretensions to the province of Maine.

This large accession to his dominions the duke resolved to secure as well by policy, as by force of arms.
Count Herbert had left a sister, who had retired into
Germany with her relatives.   William proposed to
affiance her to his son Robert, then a youth; this was
assented to, but as she died before Robert had arrived
at mature age, the marriage was never solemnized;
the alliance, however, secured the fidelity of the people
of Maine.

It was shortly after these events that William received intelligence of the death of Edward the Confessor, King of England, which happened on the 5th of
January, 1066.   A new career of glory was now
opened to him, and he was destined to unite the ducal
crown of his ancestors with the sceptre of England.

---

## SECTION II.

### FROM THE DEATH OF CANUTE, KING OF ENGLAND, TO THE BATTLE OF HASTINGS.

CANUTE died in the same year in which William,
seventh Duke of Normandy, succeeded to the ducal
crown, expiring on the 12th of November, 1035.   By
his mistress Alaine, daughter of the Earl of Hampton,
he left two sons Harold and Sweyn; by his wife Emma,

widow of Ethelred, King of England, and sister of
Richard the Second, fourth Duke of Normandy,
Hardi-Canute, and a daughter, named Gonilda, who
was married to the Emperor, Henry the Third.  Between these children, without distinction of legitimacy,
he divided his three kingdoms.  Sweyn received Norway, Hardi-Canute, Denmark, and Harold, England,
an arrangement directly violating his marriage-con-
tract with the widow of Ethelred, which stipulated that
his children by Emma, and her children by Ethelred,
should inherit his dominions, to the exclusion of his
offspring not born in wedlock.

Alfred and Edward, the sons of Ethelred and
Emma, resided in Normandy, and on the death of
Canute, the former, who was of a spirited character,
indignant at being despoiled of his inheritance by the
Danish princes, embarked at Barfleur for England,
where his mother still remained.  He was received on
his landing by Godwin, Earl of Kent, a wily and ambitious nobleman, who was suspected of having poisoned Canute.  By a treachery not uncommon in
those days, but which, in this instance, is not clearly
specified in the writings of the old chroniclers, Alfred
met an untimely death, and the assassins escaped
without detection.  There is, however, small room to
doubt that he was murdered by Godwin, or by his
orders.

Harold the First, King of England, died on the 14th
of April, 1089.  He was succeeded by his younger
brother, Hardi-Canute, King of Denmark, who died
in 1041.

The people of England were attached to the Saxon
line of princes, and Godwin, whose ambition was insa-

tiable, skilfully availed himself of the popular feeling,
to carry his own policy into effect. He convened the
principal nobility at London, and proposed that Edward, son of Emma and Ethelred, should succeed
to the vacant throne. This proposal exonerated
him from the suspicion generally entertained among
the leading men, of his having assassinated Alfred; it
was hailed with applause, and the same ambition
which murdered one brother, placed the crown on the
head of another.

Edward was a weak prince, and easy to be ruled.
Godwin knew his character, but fearful to seize the
throne for himself, he parted with the nominal sovereignty, more safely to exercise a secret, though absolute, dominion. To effect his purpose, he offered his
daughter Edith in marriage to Edward, not, as he artfully said, to confer glory on his family, but that he
might more efficiently combat the dangers which he
pretended to foresee. Edward received this proposal
with as much gratitude, as though Godwin, in giving
his daughter, had given him his crown. Edith was
an accomplished, beautiful, and discreet princess,
worthy of a better father and a better husband. Whether influenced by superstition or aversion, Edward
never used the privileges of a husband; on the contrary, he confined his wife in a nunnery, depriving
her of all the advantages due to her station. It thus
became certain that on the death of the king, there
would be no direct heir to the throne, and the ambitious sons of Godwin speculated on this contingency.

In 1051, William of Normandy passed over to England to visit Edward the Confessor, by whom he was
graciously received, and on this occasion the king de-

livered into his hands a nephew and a son of Godwin, to be by him retained as hostages for the future loyal conduct of that ambitious earl. Almost all historians, ancient and modern, have been silent respecting this journey, but it is particularly mentioned by Wace, whose father lived in those days and fought at the battle of Hastings. This interview between Edward and William had, no doubt, a great influence on future events, and it may reasonably be presumed that the Duke of Normandy was then promised the succession to the English throne, either by the reigning monarch himself, or indirectly through some of the Norman courtiers, who enjoyed the unreserved confidence of Edward. The hostages given from the family of Godwin render this supposition in the highest degree probable.

The duke remained but a short time in England, and very soon after his departure, Earl Godwin died, being choked, as Wace says, when dining with the king. The chronicle of Normandy thus relates the circumstances attending his death. Godwin asked his son Harold to fill him a cup of wine, which he did, but in the act of presenting it to his father, one foot slipped, and had he not recovered himself on the other foot, he would have fallen. Godwin, laughing, said to his son, " One brother helps the other:" king Edward observed, " If my brother were alive, he would serve me as well." Godwin, excited at this allusion, violently exclaimed, " May this morsel that I hold in my hand choke me, if I ever did the least injury to your brother." " So be it," replied Edward : Godwin then swallowed the morsel, which stuck in his throat, and killed him, and thus was the truth made known.

In 1065, Harold, son of Godwin, visited Normandy,

but with what intention is doubtful. The English chroniclers state that the object of this journey was to reclaim the hostages, whose detention could no longer be justified, after the death of Godwin; but the Norman chroniclers affirm that he was ordered to take the voyage by Edward, and declare William heir to the English throne. However this may be, it is certain that Harold was wrecked on the coast of Ponthieu, and seized by Guy, count of that province, who incarcerated him in the fortress of Beaurain sur la Canche. When William heard of his detention, he commanded Guy, who was his vassal, to release his prisoner, which he accordingly did, and personally conducted him to Eu, which is on the frontier between Ponthieu and Normandy, and there delivered up Harold to the duke.[1]

At this time William was engaged in a war with Brittany, against Conan, one of the petty counts of that province. In the campaign, he requested the assistance of Harold, who, in the chivalrous spirit of the age, cheerfully volunteered his services. The English prince commanded a detachment of the Norman troops, attacked Conan, who was besieging Dol, and compelled him to retire. He then pursued his victory by laying siege to Dinan, which soon surrendered. For these services William conferred the honour of knighthood on Harold.

The duke was well aware of the influence of Harold, and fearing that he would seize the English throne on the death of Edward, and thus deprive him of his promised succession, he determined to avail himself of the present favourable opportunity, not only to avert the

[1] " Ipse adducens apud Aucense castrum sibi presentavit." *Guielm. Poitiers.*

opposition, but secure the alliance, of the English prince. He therefore disclosed to him his expectations, affirming that the Confessor had constituted him his heir, and then offered him his daughter Adèle[1] in marriage, pledging himself to appoint Harold his lieutenant in England, and to provide munificently for all his relatives and adherents. Harold was not in a position to resist these overtures, for his personal liberty was at the disposal of William; he therefore agreed to all that was demanded. The duke, however, distrusting his sincerity, required the English prince to ratify his engagement by an oath, to which he also assented. This ceremony was performed by Odo, uterine brother of William, and bishop of Bayeux, in the cathedral[2] of that town. An artifice was employed on this occasion, which, while it denotes the superstitious character of the times, is not very creditable to the honour of the duke. The duke filled up a box with the most precious relics of the most eminent saints, which he covered over with an embroidered napkin, and on the top, visible, he placed an ordinary relic, the sanctity of which was not peculiarly remarkable. Harold took the oath in the usual form : so may God help me, and the Holy Gospels. William then removed the napkin, and exhibited the concealed relics, on which Harold had unwittingly sworn.

By this oath Harold engaged, if we are to believe

---

[1] Ordericus Vitalis says it was Agatha, another daughter of William's, and not Adèle, who was affianced to Harold. He adds, that this princess was so attached to her future husband, that she died of grief when, after his death, her father sent her to Galicia, to marry one of the sovereigns of that country.

[2] Almost all the old authors differ as to the place where this ceremony was performed. William of Poictiers fixes it at Bonneville, apud Bonam Villam ; Ordericus Vitalis, at Rouen ; the Chronique de Normandie, at Sainte Marguerite, near Jumièges. Wace declares that it took place at Bayeux, in which he agrees with the " Tapestry." See Appendix, No. 1.

William of Poitiers, who declares that he received his
information from many credible persons who were
present at the ceremony, to act as the vicar or attorney
of Duke William at the court of England, so long as
Edward the Confessor lived; that he would do all in
his power, both by recommendation, and bribes, to
guarantee and secure the sceptre of England to William after the death of the king ; and, moreover, that
he would not only give up Dover Castle, but such
other fortresses as the duke might wish to be garrisoned by Norman troops, and at the same time supply
them with provisions. The promise of surrendering
Dover Castle is also attested by William of Malmsbury, Eadmer, and his copyist Roger de Hoveden.
Ingulfus, Ordericus Vitalis, William of Jumièges, and
Matthew Paris are silent as to this part of the engagement of Harold ; they only agree in admitting
that he covenanted to accept William's daughter in
marriage.

Harold returned to England shortly after he had
concluded this agreement with William, and repaired
to the palace of Edward to give an account of his journey. Ordericus Vitalis says that, at this interview, he
disguised the facts, assuring the king, whose life
was daily despaired of, that William had promised
him his daughter in marriage, and having thus accepted
him as his son-in-law, had abandoned all pretensions
to England in his favour. Eadmer, on the contrary,
and his continuators, in order to preserve the honour
and sincerity of Harold, affirm that he gave a faithful statement of all that had happened to himself in
Normandy, and of the violent measures resorted to by
the duke to compel him to promise his co-operation in

attaching England to his duchy; and that Edward replied, that he had clearly foreseen what would happen,
and had expressly warned Harold of the consequences
of his journey, before he started. The historians of
the two countries give such versions of this fact as
suited their national prejudices.

On the 5th of January, 1066, Edward the Confessor
died, and was buried at Westminster. His piety had
prompted him to make a vow that he would undertake a pilgrimage to Rome, but his subjects opposed its
execution. The pope, receiving intelligence of their
reluctance to part with their sovereign, sent the king a
dispensation from his vow, on condition that he restored the abbey dedicated to St. Peter. Edward accordingly rebuilt the church, and the monastery attached to it, from the bottom to the top, and the dedi-
cation only took place eight days before he was interred
within its walls. The ancient name of Westminster
was Thorney. Wace, in the Roman de Rou, calls it·
Zonée, which he derives from Zon, a thorn, and Ee, an
island.[1]

Harold lost not a moment in seizing on the throne.
As soon as the king was buried, he caused himself to
be proclaimed his successor. He was crowned by
Stigand, Archbishop of Canterbury. Ingulphus and
his copyist, Florentin of Worcester, say that it was
Aldred, Archbishop of York, who crowned Harold;
William of Poitiers and Ordericus Vitalis, on the con-

---

[1] M. Auguste Le Prevost, in a note on this passage in the Roman de Rou,
quotes the following paragraph from an English chronicle, but he does not name
the author of the chronicle:—Circâ hæc tempora quidam civis Londoniensis con-
struxit ecclesiam i honore sancti Petri apostoli, in occidentali parte ejusdem urbis
in loco qui THORNIC tunc dicebatur et sonat quasi Spinarum insula ; nunc autem,
dicitur Westmosterium."

F

trary, assert that it was Stigand, Archbishop of Canterbury, although the other prelates had not given
their consent, and that this archbishop himself was
under an interdict pronounced against him by Pope
Alexander the Second, he having been accused of simony, and other breaches of ecclesiastical discipline.
The testimony of these two last historians is corroborated by the Bayeux tapestry, and receives additional
weight from the fact of William being highly incensed
against Stigand, after the battle of Hastings. He refused to be crowned by him, although that privilege
was part of his sacerdotal prerogative. as Ingulphus
remarks, but conferred that honour on Aldred, or Albert, archbishop of York. He did more to manifest
his displeasure, for he deposed Stigand, at a council
held at Westminster two years afterwards, in 1068,
and gave his diocese to Lanfranc, the first Abbot of
St. Stephen's, at Caen.

The coronation of Harold was followed by an event,
now too familiar to excite any wonder, but which, in
those superstitious times, was regarded with awe and
admiration : we allude to the comet which appeared in
the month of April, 1066. It was first seen in the
west, and travelled to the south. It is mentioned by
all the old chroniclers, but they differ as to the day of
its first appearance, and also as to the period of time
during which it was visible. The Saxon Chronicle
fixes it on the 18th of April; Florentin of Worcester
and Bertold of Coutances (the latter of whom continued the Chronicle of Hermannus Contractus up to the
year 1100, when he died) fix it on the 24th of April.
Labbe, the learned Jesuit, corrects Bertold, who is the
only author he quotes, and insists that the comet was

seen on the evening of the 23rd of the same month.
According to Florentin of Worcester, it was visible
during seven days; according to the Roman de Rou,
fourteen; according to Ordericus Vitalis and William
of Jumièges, fifteen; according to Bertold, and, after
him, Labbe, thirty.

After Harold was defeated and slain, his discomfiture was attributed to the celestial phenomenon. The
following verses, from an old chronicle published by
Labbe, commemorate the superstition of the times :—

> " Sexagenus erat sextus millesimus annus
> Cum pereunt Angli stellâ monstrante cometâ.

as well as these two leonine verses :—

> " Anno milleno sexageno quoque seno
> Anglorum metæ flammas sensere cometæ.

This comet is spoken of in the same spirit by Ingulphus, Ordericus Vitalis, Wace, and Matthew of West-
minister.

Tostic, the elder brother of Harold, jealous of his
ascendancy, endeavoured to foment civil discord, as-
piring to the vacant throne, by the right of primogeniture. He had enjoyed the county of Kent, since the
death of his father, Earl Godwin; but as soon as Harold discovered his machinations, he banished him from
England. Tostic had married a daughter of Baldwin,
Count of Flanders, and was therefore brother-in-law
to Duke William. He landed in Normandy with
his wife Judith, and encouraged the duke to attack his brother. He remained but a short time on
the continent, sailing to Norway to demand armed
assistance from the king of that country to invade
England.

When William first received intelligence of the success of Harold, he was amusing himself with archery in the park of Quevilly. He became thoughtful and gloomy; he spoke to none, and none dared to speak to him. This silence was at length interrupted by William de Crespon, Count of Breteuil, the duke's seneschal, who told him that the news was public, and could not be concealed from the Normans; while at the same time he exhorted him to assert his right by force of arms. This advice exactly accorded with the views and wishes of the duke, who dispatched a messenger to Harold, summoning him to observe the promise that he had made to him when in Normandy: but the English prince determined to hold what he had gained, and forthwith expelled all the Normans, who had enjoyed the protection of Edward, out of his dominions. He desired the messenger to tell William that he acknowledged having taken an oath to deliver up the English throne to him at the death of the Confessor, but that such an oath was not binding, having been extorted by force; that he, moreover, had promised to give what did not belong to him; that the crown was not his personal property, but belonged to the nation; that the people had chosen him for their sovereign, and that he could not transfer the sceptre to a foreigner without treason to his country.

The Duke of Normandy, though incensed at this answer, despatched a second envoy, with a more moderate demand, simply requiring Harold to marry his daughter. The English king replied, that he could not comply without the sanction of his council; and he quickly put an end to all further negociation by marrying the sister of Edwin and Morkar, the most pow-

erful barons of the North of England.  The hour for
parley or compromise was passed, and the sword became the sole arbiter of the dispute.

William now determined on the celebrated invasion,
and convened an assembly of his barons, to demand
their assistance.  This meeting was held at Lillebonne :  it was numerously attended by all the ducal
vassals; but the scheme met with decided opposition,
the duke being only supported by William de Breteuil
and his friends.  Those who condemned the policy of
this transmarine expedition, denied the right of the
duke to require their services beyond the sea, of which
element they seem to have been greatly afraid.  After
much dispute, the barons agreed to appoint William de
Breteuil their common representative and spokesman ;
and he, profiting by this confidence, at a second meeting made the most lavish offers of assistance in their
joint names, declaring that those who furnished twenty
men-at-arms for a continental campaign, would furnish forty for the English expedition.  The barons
were astonished and incensed at these liberal concessions, which they had not sanctioned, and openly protested against them.  The position of William was
critical, but he extricated himself with great dexterity.
Finding it impossible to carry his point, so long as
the barons deliberated in a public assembly, he had private interviews with each of them in turn, first address-
ing the most wealthy and influential, and accepted as
a favour what he could have neither claimed nor enforced as a right.  A record was drawn up of the free
gifts of each, and attested by the great seal of the
duchy :  the greatest possible publicity was given to
this instrument, and as those who did not follow the

example thus set, exposed themselves to the suspicion
of disloyalty, the list soon included all the barons of
Normandy.  An appeal was also made to the knights
of Poitou and Brittany to join the ducal standard,
and the prospect of sharing the plunder of England attracted adventurers from both those provinces.

The next measure of William was to secure the neutrality of France, then under the regency of Baldwin,
Count of Flanders, father of the Duchess of Normandy.  In this he was perfectly successful, for not
only did Baldwin promise not to invade the duchy,
but he allowed his son-in-law to levy troops in Flanders, and advanced him large sums of money.  As a
matter of sound policy, the regent committed an egre-
gious error, for the union of Normandy and England
raised up a power on the continent, which France only
subdued after centuries of war and immense losses.

The duke, however, did not limit his applications to
temporal princes.  The authority of the pope was
then all but omnipotent, and William sent ambassadors
to Rome to obtain the pontifical blessing on his arms,
promising to hold his conquest as a fief from St. Peter.
He justified his pretensions against Harold by four
pleas ; the murder of Alfred, by Earl Godwin ; the
expulsion of the Norman, Robert of Jumièges, from
the Archbishopric of Canterbury ; the promise made
by Edward the Confessor to declare him heir to the
English throne ; and finally, the oath of the Saxon
prince.  All these points were gravely discussed in a
conclave of cardinals, the duke pretending to plead
before a tribunal recognized by his adversary ; but
Harold had not sent any representative to Rome, too
proud to recognize a foreign jurisdiction, too patriotic

to compromise the independence of his country by
submitting to Italian dictation, or perhaps too clear-
sighted not to know that the judges had made up their
minds without intending to hear evidence.

The sentence of the church was entirely in favour of
William, who was declared the lawful heir of the Confessor, and Harold and his adherents were excommunicated. The duke completed his part of the engagement, by pledging himself to pay an annual tribute to Rome, which was the bribe he had offered to
his judges. It now became the interest of the pope to
give the expedition all the aid in his power, and a
legate was sent to Normandy, carrying with him a consecrated banner, and a ring containing a hair of St.
Peter's.

The papal bull, investing William with the title of
King of England, was read in all the churches throughout the duchy, and the enthusiasm of the people was
raised to the highest pitch. The news spread far
and wide that the expedition was blessed by the pope.
The duke published his declaration of war in all the
neighbouring countries: he offered pay and pillage to
every man who would serve him with lance, sword, or
cross-bow. Multitudes now flocked to his standard,
from far and near, from north and south; from Maine
and Anjou, from Poitou and Brittany, from France
and Flanders, from Aquitaine and Burgundy, from
Piedmont and the banks of the Rhine. Adventurers
of every grade and profession, all the lost characters of
Europe, rushed by various roads into Normandy.
Some stipulated for gold, others for land, while some
only asked for a free passage, and a chance of plunder.
The higher class of these auxiliaries bargained for a

of the army. When the duke stepped on shore he fell on his hands; but fearful that this accident might be construed into some bad omen, he, with admirable presence of mind, seized some of the sand, and holding up his arm, exclaimed, "Thus do I hold my lawful inheritance!" A camp was immediately formed, and fortified with timber.

When this invasion was effecting, Harold was in the north of England, opposing his brother Tostic, who, supported by a numerous fleet and army from Norway, had landed at the Humber, and defeated the Earls Edwin and Morkar, who had retreated to York. Harold came in sight of the invaders at Pontefract, and sent a friendly message to Tostic, offering to pardon his treason, and restore him to his estate and dignity. Tostic, in answer, asked what would be the fate of the King of Norway, his ally. "Seven feet of English ground," said the herald, "or perhaps more, for his stature exceeds that of other men." "Then," said Tostic, "let my brother prepare for battle: the son of Godwin will never abandon the son of Sigurd."

In the first shock of battle the king of Norway was slain by an arrow. Tostic then took the command, when Harold again repeated his offers of peace; they were again rejected. Victory rested with the English. Tostic and most of the Norwegian chiefs perished. The remnant of the army embarked on twenty-three vessels, after they had sworn not to return.

Harold received a wound in the battle of Pontefract, and was recruiting his strength at York, when a messenger arrived announcing that William of Normandy had planted his banner on the soil of England.

The king, thus taken at a disadvantage, deeply regretted that he had not been able to oppose the debarkation of the invaders, and he was the more unfortunate as the cruizers stationed off the coast to watch the movements of the hostile armament, had been compelled to run into port from a scarcity of provisions.  Harold, however, wasted no time in vain regrets, but at once led his victorious army towards the south, publishing, on his route, an order to all his barons to arm their vassals, and follow him to London. Had he waited in the capital till his troops could have been assembled, he must have secured an easy victory by dint of numbers; but his impatience conquered his prudence; he would not remain for the northern battalions of Edwin and Morkar, but marched rapidly to Hastings, his whole force being greatly inferior to that of the Duke of Normandy.

By this sudden movement Harold expected to attack the enemy by surprise, but the camp of William was vigilantly guarded.  Disappointed in this hope, he changed his tactics, and took up a position seven miles distant from the Normans.  He was advised by his principal officers to retreat to London, and ravage the country; for as the duke had burned his ships, in the heroic resolution to conquer or die, they argued that the Normans would soon suffer from scarcity of food, and, in the mean time, the whole country would be in arms.  " What," said Harold, " shall I desolate the fields that I have sworn to defend?  Shall I be a traitor to the people who have raised me to the throne?  Never: I will try the fate of arms with the few men I have, trusting to the goodness of my cause, rather than injure the meanest of my subjects."

William, whose policy it was not to hazard a battle, unless all negociation proved utterly fruitless, dispatched a monk, named Hugh Maigrot, to Harold, with three propositions for his acceptance :—to abandon the crown in his favour, or to abide by an appeal to the pope, or to decide their quarrel by single combat. The king at once rejected all these proposals.

The duke, notwithstanding this rejection, sent Maigrot a second time, with the following instructions :— " Tell Harold, that if he will fulfil his agreement with me, I will give him all the land north of the Humber, and yield to his brother Gurth the estates enjoyed by Earl Godwin : if he obstinately reject this offer, then you will tell him, before his officers, that he is perjured, and that he and all his adherents are now under papal excommunication."

Maigrot delivered this message with impressive solemnity, and when he pronounced the sentence of the church, the boldest were blanched with fear. Harold stood in no alarm of the sword of William, to whom he was fully equal in personal courage, but he dreaded the malediction of Heaven; and the soldiers, who would have intrepidly defied the blow of a battle-axe, trembled at the thunders of the Vatican. Gurth, however, had sufficient tact to neutralize the threat of his holiness; and the speech, attributed to him by Wace, is an excellent specimen of practical eloquence. " Fellow-countrymen," said the Saxon prince, " if the Duke of Normandy were not afraid of our swords, he would not seek to blunt them by a papal anathema; had he confidence in his knights and barons, he would not trouble us with messengers and negociators.

Would he offer us the land north of the Humber, if
he did not now tremble for the consequences of his
rash expedition? Would he parley, and offer a compromise, if he felt strong in the justice of his cause?
Let us not be the dupes of his artifice. Were we to
surrender all the land of England, except the country
north of the Humber, he would attack us at the first
convenient opportunity. He has already promised
your houses and estates to his followers; he will not
leave an inch of ground to you or your children :
every acre is pledged to his mercenaries. Will you
then beg your bread on a foreign shore, or 'defend
your rights with your sword?"[1]

This harangue had more effect than the menace of
excommunication, and the English swore to make
neither peace nor truce nor treaty with the invader;
but expel him from the territory, or die on the field
of battle.

It was on the eighteenth day after the victory at
Pontefract that the decisive engagement took place,
which terminated the Saxon dynasty, and transferred
the crown of England to the princes of Normandy.
Although this interval elapsed, the army of Harold had
received no effective reinforcements, only some few
stragglers having joined his standard. Among these,
the only persons above the common rank were Leofric,
Abbot of Peterborough, and the Abbot of the monastery
of Hida, near to Winchester, who was accompanied by
twelve of his monks and twenty men-at-arms. As the
hour of combat approached, Gurth requested his brother to retire from the field, and leave the command
with him. " Harold," said the young prince, " you

[1] Roman de Rou, v. 12, 363, et seq.

cannot deny that you took an oath to William, on
holy relics, whether of your own accord or by force
it matters not: why then hazard the fate of war with
perjury on your soul? I have not sworn to any thing,
nor has our brother Leofwin. It is a just war to us,
for we fight for our native land. Let us, then, alone
encounter the Normans: if we are repulsed, then you
can advance to our aid; if we fall, you can avenge
us." Harold was deeply affected with this generosity,
but his lofty spirit would not allow him to be a quiet
spectator, while his kinsmen exposed their lives.

The English front of battle stretched over a line of
hills, fortified on all sides with a rampart of stakes
and hurdles formed of osier. The position was judici-
ously selected to resist a superior force, supported by
a numerous body of cavalry. On the 14th of October
the Normans advanced in three columns. The first
was composed of the auxiliaries from Boulogne and
Ponthieu, with the different bands of mercenaries who
fought for a stipulated pay: the second consisted of
the adventurers from Brittany, Maine, and Poitou.
William in person commanded the third division,
wholly formed of his own countrymen. Before leading them to the attack, William thus addressed his
soldiers: " Fight bravely, and give no quarter. If
we conquer, we shall all be rich. Whatever I gain,
you will gain; if I succeed, you will succeed; if I
win the land, you will share it with me. Know,
however, that I have not come hither merely to
claim what is my due, but to avenge our whole
nation of the felonies, perjuries, and treacheries of
these English. They massacred the Danes in the
reign of Ethelred; they murdered my relation, Al-

fred. Advance then, and punish these crimes; and consider yourselves as men who, before this day closes, will either be dead or victorious."

At the given signal, Taillefer spurred his horse in front of the Norman line, and there shouted forth the war-song of Charlemagne and Roland, famous throughout all Gaul. The Norman archers attempted to drive the English from their intrenchments by repeated flights of arrows, but from this weapon they were securely sheltered by their rampart. This mode of attack proving fruitless, the infantry, armed with lances, and the cavalry, wielding long and heavy swords, boldly rushed on the gates of the redoubts; but the Saxon battle-axe cut through their coats-of-mail, and they were repulsed with disorder. The Duke of Normandy now changed his tactics : the archers had hitherto directed their arrows in horizontal lines; they were now ordered to throw them over the intrenchment, so that they might fall on the heads and faces of their enemies. Complete success attended this manœuvre, and it was then that Harold was wounded in the eye, yet he did not quit his post. The horse and foot again advanced against the intrenchment, but they were again driven back, and pursued to a ravine, the top of which was covered with brushwood ; into this they were precipitated, and many perished. A panic now seized the Normans. It was reported that the duke was slain, his horse having been killed under him : the invaders fled from the ground, but they were quickly rallied by William, who, uncovering his head, exclaimed to the fugitives, " Behold me! I still live, and, with the aid of God, I will conquer."

The presence of the duke, and the exhortations of

his brother Odo, the warlike Bishop of Bayeux, revived the drooping courage of the discomfited Normans, and they returned with fury to the charge. But
the firm and serried ranks of the English remained un-
broken, and William saw the impossibility of forcing
entrenchments defended with such obstinate gallantry.
He now had recourse to a stratagem, which changed
the fortunes of the day, and led to his complete triumph. He commanded his troops to retreat, which
they did in apparent confusion: the English, urged
to pursuit by a fatal impetuosity, abandoned their
impregnable position, rushed down into the plain, and
promised themselves an easy victory. The Norman
cavalry now wheeled about, and having all the advantage of the ground, broke through their opponents,
who had no weapon of defence but their heavy axes,
which it required both hands to wield: the sabres of
the horse, the lances of the infantry, the arrows of the
archers, spread death among the English ranks: they
retreated to the entrenchments they had so imprudently quitted, but the enemy entered along with
them, and though a stern resistance still was offered,
it was vain. Harold and his valiant brothers fell at
the foot of their standard, and at nine o'clock of the
evening of the 14th of October, the victory of Hastings
was complete.

The first recompense of the conquerors was to strip
the dead. In rifling the bodies of the slain, thirteen
were found wearing an ecclesiastical habit under their
military accoutrements. It was the Abbot of Hida
and his twelve companions. The name of their monastery was the first inscribed on the black-book of William for confiscation. Various accounts are recorded of

what became of the body of Harold.  If we are to
believe the Norman chroniclers, it was recognized
among the dead, not by its features, but by some
marks, and carried into the ducal tent.  William, according to their authority, refused to give it up to the
prayers of his mother, Ghita, or ransom it for its
weight in gold; but ordered William Mallet, one of
his barons, to bury it near the coast which Harold had
so bravely defended.

The statement of William of Malmsbury is very
different.  He says that the Conqueror, without wishing to accept any compensation from Ghita, immediately sent her the body of her son, and the unhappy
mother buried him at Waltham Abbey.

To these opposing versions we incline to prefer the
touching narrative contained in the manuscript of the
abbey of Waltham, the author of which lived at the
commencement of the twelfth century.  It is in substance as follows:—The monks of Waltham, seeing
with regret that Harold too rashly offered battle
against superior numbers, without waiting the arrival
of his reinforcements from the north, dispatched two
of their most eminent brethren, Osegod Cnoppe and
Alric, the schoolmaster, to watch the progress of events,
and render, in case of need, the last duties to their
protector.  The two monks stationed themselves so as
to be eye-witnesses of the battle, and presented themselves to William as soon as it had terminated, to
claim from him the body of Harold.  Their request
was granted.  They offered the conqueror ten marks
of gold, in token of their gratitude, and proceeded to
search for the mortal remains of the English monarch
among the slain, but they could not distinguish it.

Thus disappointed they had recourse to the mistress of Harold, the beautiful Edith, called the Swan-necked: they conducted her to the field of battle, and she discovered, by certain signs, the mangled body of her royal lover. The corpse was taken to Waltham Abbey, and many of the Norman barons followed the funeral procession.

On this important event, which terminated the line of Anglo-Saxon princes, a few remarks may be permitted. The pretensions of the rival princes to the throne have been variously defended and opposed by the chroniclers of the two nations, but, at this distance of time, their respective rights may be weighed without prejudice. That Edward the Confessor had promised the succession to William, and that Harold had sworn on holy relics to uphold the claims of the Duke of Normandy, may be admitted; but it is equally true that Edward had given a similar pledge to Harold, and that his oath had been extorted by force. The Confessor was a weak, superstitious, and incompetent prince, quite incapable, even if he had the right, to will away his kingdom; and in this view neither the title of William or Harold can be recognized. But it is certain that the people of England preferred Harold, who was the king of their choice, and who had signally evinced his patriotism during the reign of Edward, against the usurpations of his Norman favourites. He and his family had been banished through court-intrigue, and his sister, stripped of her regal dignity, had been imprisoned, and treated with every possible indignity. These hardships had been endured from the opposition offered by Earl Godwin and his sons to the Normans, who

had so ingratiated themselves with the Confessor, as
to have got possession of most of the chief offices of
the state; and thus Harold had powerful claims on
the gratitude of the Anglo-Saxon population, in whose
defence he had hazarded his life and fortunes, and
suffered exile.  Harold, therefore, had all the claims
and rights of a constitutional monarch, and as such
he was undoubtedly recognized by the people; while
William was regarded with distrust, and even hatred,
as the chief of a nation by whom they had been oppressed.  The evidence of this distinction may be
found in the constant rebellions that broke out during
the reign of the Norman line.

The loss of life at the battle of Hastings has been
variously computed.  De Thou reckons the number
of English slain at sixty-seven thousand six hundred
and fifty-four, and reduces that of the Normans to six
thousand and thirteen.  Ordericus Vitalis raises the
sacrifice of the Normans to fifteen thousand.  From
the Norman roll, drawn up at St. Valery, before the
expedition set sail, it appears that the army of the
invaders exceeded sixty thousand combatants, and it
is certain that the force which Harold brought into
the field was below twenty-five thousand, so that the
carnage of the English has been most grossly exaggerated.  In this battle Harold committed two grave
errors in strategy: he was wrong in not waiting for
Edwin and Morkar, who were marching to join his
ranks with all the militia of the north, and most imprudent in quitting his entrenchments without cavalry,
and thus exposing himself on the level plain to the
charge of the Norman horse.  But for these two capi-

tal mistakes, it is in the highest degree probable that the invading army would have been destroyed.

---

## SECTION III.

### FROM THE BATTLE OF HASTINGS TO HIS DEATH.

ʻThe death of Harold was followed by the submission of the powerful barons of England, and the people followed the example of their leaders. William was crowned on the 25th of December, being then forty-three years of age. He fulfilled his engagements to his followers, transferring the estates of the natives to the Normans, and introduced the feudal system of the continent. Some English jurisconsults have pretended that the duke simply *acquired*, but did not *conquer*, his new dominions, inheriting from Edward the Confessor, his relative, or by virtue of his promise ; but truth, unwarped by national pride, must acknowledge that William gained his empire by the edge of the sword, and reduced the aborigines to bondage.

The affairs of Normandy soon called him back to his own country. He appointed his uterine brother, Odo, Bishop of Bayeux, whom he had raised to the dignity of Earl of Kent, his viceroy ; and his faithful friend, William, Count of Breteuil, created Earl of Hereford, who had so warmly encouraged the invasion of England, was declared grand-senechal. William, knowing by what a precarious title he held his conquest, compelled Stigand, Archbishop of Canterbury, Edgar Atheling, the lawful heir to the throne, of Saxon descent, Edwin and Morkar, earls beyond the Humber, and others, to accompany him to Rouen, which he entered with splendour and magnificence. After he had satisfied that excusable vanity which prompted him to display his present grandeur before his subjects, he retired to Fécamp, living in privacy, and devoting himself with indefatigable industry to the better administration of the affairs of his duchy.

Having taken such precautionary measures as seemed best calculated to secure the peace of his hereditary dominions, he returned to England, where all his vigilance was required to curb the insurrectionary spirit which the rapine of his own barons had excited among the people. The details of these multiplied revolts belong to the history of England, and fall not within our province; suffice it to say that he was menaced by the two sons of Harold, who had taken refuge in Ireland, by the Danes, by Malcolm, King of Scotland, by the English, and even by some of the Normans. These conspiracies, however, he successively defeated, showing himself equal to the most arduous of positions.

In 1068 he sent for the Duchess Matilda, who was crowned Queen of England, and at the close of the same year his fourth son was born, afterwards King Henry the First.

In 1071, William appointed the Earl of Breteuil and Hereford, Governor of Normandy, though with limited powers, as he was ordered to act in concert with the Duchess Matilda. At that time great dissensions reigned in Flanders. Baldwin was dead; he had left a numerous family, and had disinherited his eldest son, Robert, on account of his disobedience, and appointed his second son, Arnoul, his successor. On the death of Baldwin, Arnoul took possession of the

duchy. He was attacked by his brother, who called
to his aid Philip, King of France, and that monarch
requested the personal assistance of the Governor of
Normandy, who cheerfully obeyed the summons, accompanied by only twelve of his followers. Robert
was supported in his pretensions by the Emperor of
Germany : a battle ensued, in which the French were
completely routed, and Arnoul and the generous Earl
of Breteuil and Hereford were slain. Robert was thus
reinstated in his hereditary dominions. The death of
the Governor of Normandy was deeply lamented by
the King of England ; in him he lost his truest friend,
and one of the most heroic of his barons; but he continued his support to his sons. William, the elder, received Breteuil, Pacy, and all his father's property on
the continent, and enjoyed his inheritance till his
death ; his younger brother, Roger, had the county of
Hereford, and all his father's English possessions, but
he shortly was deprived of them for his treason and
rebellion.

The absence of William in England emboldened the
Earl of Anjou and Geoffrey of Mayenne to attempt
the conquest of the province of Maine. They besieged
the castle of Mantes, and expelled the Norman garrison. The king soon marched against them, carried
the fortress of Fresnay, and summoned the town of
Silly, which at once submitted. He then led his army
to Mantes, threatening to put the soldiers and the inhabitants to the sword, unless they surrendered in
twenty-four hours. The rebels, appalled by a threat
which they knew would be carried into rigorous execution, delivered up the keys, and obtained their pardon. The Count of Anjou, however, aided by the

troops of the Duke of Brittany, advanced to meet William in the field, but when he found his adversary at the head of fifty thousand men, he offered terms of peace, which were accepted, and Robert, surnamed Courte-Heuse, eldest son of the Conqueror, received the investiture of Maine.

The life of William had been one continued scene of war and tumult, with scarcely any interval of repose; for so perilous had been his position, that even in peace he was constantly on his guard against foreign aggression or intestine revolt. He was now doomed to meet a new enemy in the person of his son Robert, to whom, after the death of the Earl of Breteuil and Hereford, he had given Normandy; but whether this donation was contingent or absolute, whether he had conceded the duchy in full sovereignty, or simply nominated Robert his lieutenant, or only declared him his successor after death, are points on which ancient writers are divided in opinion. However this may be, Robert determined to exercise an independent power, and his favourites, who wished to enrich themselves by his prodigality, urged him to insist on his father's abandoning some of his dominions in his favour. They dwelt on the avarice of the king, who kept his heir in poverty, and deprived him of the means of supporting his rank with becoming state. They reproached Robert with imbecility, in submitting to such thraldom. " Rouse yourself," they exclaimed, " and boldly demand a share of England, or at least the duchy of Normandy, so long promised to you in the presence of the nobles, who are ready to support you."

The young prince, inflamed with anger and goaded by cupidity, repaired to his father, and demanded to be

put into possession of the duchy. " My son," said
William, " your demand is unreasonable. I conquered England by Norman valour. I hold Normandy
by an hereditary title, and never shall the ducal crown
pass from my brow while I live." Robert answered :
" What shall I do? what can I bestow on my friends
and followers?" His father rejoined : " Obey me in
all things, as is your duty, and you shall have a fitting,
but subordinate command under me, as becomes the
relation of parent and child." Robert then said, " I
will no longer serve you as a mercenary. I must have
power and property of my own, that I may reward my
retainers. Give up to me, then, the duchy as you have
promised, and allow me to govern it, as you govern
England ; I shall still remain your subject and do you
homage." The king replied, " My son, your demand
is premature. You ought to feel shame at wishing to deprive me of dominions, which, if you are worthy of them,
you will receive in due time. Choose better counsellors, and distrust those rash young men who are constantly urging you to criminal enterprises. Be guided
by the bishops, William and Lanfranc, and other sages
whose wisdom is matured by age and experience." " I
came not to your presence," retorted Robert, " to listen to sermons, with which I have been nauseated by
my tutors. I am fixed in my resolution, nor will I
again fight for any one in Normandy in a subordinate
station." The king was violently incensed at the audacity of this speech and sternly answered, " I have
stated my intentions explicitly, and it is useless to
travel again over the same ground. So long as I live,
Normandy, my native land, shall never pass from my
possession. As to England, which I have conquered

with vast labour, I will not carve out of it any separate sovereignty; for, as Scripture says, 'a house
divided against itself cannot stand.' He who has permitted me to reign will dispose of my kingdom according to his pleasure. I wish all the world to be
well assured that, during my life, I will not part with
one iota of my prerogative, nor shall mortal man share
my authority. The pope placed the crown on my
head; to me alone he confided the sceptre of England.
It would, therefore, be disrespectful to his Holiness
were I to acknowledge an equal in my realms." [1]

Robert was now satisfied of the irrevocable decision of his father, and abruptly quitting him in violent rage, sought his advisers, when all resolved to
quit Normandy. The young prince was accompanied
by Robert de Bellesme, William de Breteuil, Robert
de Mowbray, and several other turbulent spirits, who
detested William because he curbed their lawless excesses. Robert travelled about from place to place
among his relations, vilifying the conduct of his father
in every quarter, and leading a life of the most repre-
hensible debauchery. His mother, Matilda, blinded
to his faults, and influenced by an excess of maternal
tenderness, remitted him large sums of money, without
the knowledge of her husband, who, when he discovered her weakness, was deeply afflicted, and reproached her in terms of bitterness. He commanded
her, under pain of his high displeasure, never again to
assist his undutiful son, but Matilda disobeyed his in-
junctions.

When William was assured of her conduct, he exclaimed, " Who in this world can expect to find a

[1] Ordericus Vitalis, liv. v. vol. ii. p. 369.

G

faithful and devoted consort? The wife whom I loved
as my soul, and to whom I entrusted my kingdom and
my treasures, supports my enemies: she enriches them
with my property; she secretly arms them against
my honour, perhaps my life." Matilda replied,
"Do not feel surprised, I pray you, if I love my
eldest born. Were Robert dead, and seven feet
below the sod, and my blood could raise him to
life, it should freely flow. How can I enjoy the luxu-
ries of opulence when my son groans in want? Far
from my heart be such hardness! your power cannot
deaden the feelings of a fond mother."[1] The king was
roused to fury by this firmness, but having no means
to punish the queen, he gave orders to arrest her secretary, Sanson, who conducted the correspondence with
Robert. The intended victim of royal vengeance was
apprized of his danger in time, and fled to the monastery of Ouche, where he saved his life by taking the
cowl.

In the mean time Robert had implored the aid of
Philip, King of France, by whom he was favourably
received, not as the French historians pretend, on account of their relationship, but because Philip, jealous
of the fame and power of the King of England, wished
to make his rebellious son an instrument to weaken his
formidable rival. Robert had fortified himself in the castle of Gerberoi, from which he plundered the surrounding country, and against this fortress his father marched.
This unnatural warfare was prosecuted with reckless
fury, but it happily terminated by a signal instance of
filial piety. In a sally from the castle the prince came
in personal collision with the king. The armour of

[1] Ord. Vital. liv. v. vol. ii. p. 373.

the combatants prevented recognition ; each thrust his
lance against the other: William was unhorsed, and
thrown violently on the ground.  A sudden cry from
the vanquished told the victor all the horrors of his
triumph: contrition and repentance struck to his soul ;
he rushed forward to raise up the author of his existence, seated him on his own horse, embraced his
knees, and supplicated for pardon.  The king loaded
him with reproaches, and was for some time inex-
orable, but he at length yielded to the prayers of Matilda, and the intercessions of the barons.  He gave
Robert the investiture of Normandy, and the homage
of Brittany, reserving to himself the right of sovereignty, making his son his lieutenant.

On the 2nd of November, 1083, Matilda, Queen of
England and Duchess of Normandy, departed this
life, to the poignant sorrow of her illustrious consort.
She was a princess of uncommon prudence, of rare virtue, and scrupulous, yet unaffected, piety ; nor can a
single reproach attach to her character, unless her
fondness for her son Robert was carried to a criminal
excess.  In 1066 she built the abbey of the Holy
Trinity, at Caen, for the Benedictines, at the time that
William erected the abbey of St. Stephen in the same
city.  In 1082 she endowed the Holy Trinity with
such munificence that William of Poitiers declares
her generosity to have exceeded that of any king or
emperor.  Rich and poor mourned her death, the
former, as a friend, the latter, as a benefactor.

This loss was soon followed by another.  Richard,
second son of the Conqueror, when hunting in the
New Forest, received so violent a blow on the temple,
by coming in contact with the stout branch of a tree,

G 2

that he was killed on the spot.  He was buried at
Winchester, with this simple epitaph on his tomb :—
" Here lies Richard, Duke of Biorne, son of King
William."

These domestic calamities were succeeded by an act
of presumption and ingratitude, which deeply wounded
the feelings of the king, and roused his sternest indignation.  He had loaded his uterine brother, Odo,
Bishop of Bayeux, with the highest honours.  After
the conquest of England he had created him Earl of
Kent ; and such was his esteem for his person and
confidence in his loyalty that, during his absence in
Normandy, he appointed him viceroy of the kingdom, and entrusted him with troops to quell the
insurrections in the north.  Odo had grossly abused
his trust, having almost exhausted the resources of
England by his rapacity and exactions, but the secret
motive of this conduct was yet unknown.  William
at length heard that this ambitious prelate aspired to
the pontifical throne, and that the monies raised in
England were transmitted to Italy to corrupt the nobles
and bribe the cardinals.  Odo had purchased a palace
at Rome, which already was furnished with every
magnificence ; he had equipped a fleet at the Isle of
Wight, and loaded the vessels with treasure ; the
barons who were to accompany him, had repaired to
the appointed rendezvous ; when suddenly, and to
the consternation of all, William arrived on the spot.
He immediately summoned a council, and thus addressed his barons :—

" Illustrious lords, listen attentively to what I am
about to say, and aid me with your advice.  Before I
crossed over to Normandy, I confided the government

of England to my brother, the Bishop of Bayeux.
Rebellion had reared its head in my hereditary dominions, and I was attacked both by my relatives and
by foreigners. By the protection of God, whose servant
I am, victory crowned my arms; and if I have remained long on the continent, it was to secure public
tranquillity. During my absence, my brother oppressed England; he despoiled the churches of their
lands and treasures; he took away the ornaments
which decorated them; he seduced from their allegiance my knights, whose duty it is to repulse the Danes,
the Irish, and other enemies, and has persuaded them
to follow him across the Alps. My heart sinks with
grief, more especially on account of the injuries inflicted on the church. Christian kings, who have pre-
ceded me, have always loved and cherished the church,
and enriched it with presents. Such were Ethelbert
and Edwin, the holy Oswald, Alfred, and my cousin
Edward the Confessor, who bestowed large donations
on the church, which we should regard as the spouse
of God. Nevertheless my brother, whom I appointed
viceroy of this kingdom, has seized the ecclesiastical
possessions by force; he has cruelly oppressed the
poor, and introduced disorder and rapine through the
realm. I now ask your advice; what course am
I to pursue to mark my displeasure, and prevent the
repetition of such abuses?"

Every one was convinced of the guilt of Odo, but
his rank, his lineage, and his authority, episcopal and
civil, imposed silence on all. The impatience of William soon vented itself in peremptory terms. "Whoever," said the king, " betrays his trust, and conspires
against the public weal, merits punishment. Seize this

man, who brings discord into the state, and guard him closely, that he may work no further injury to the nation."

The audience were struck with fear; all trembled to disobey the king, but none dared execute his order, for they dreaded the thunders of the church, if they laid hands on a bishop. Seeing their reluctance or timidity, William rose from his seat, advanced towards Odo, and seized him. The prisoner loudly protested against this violence, asserting his espiscopal prerogative. " I am a clerk," said Odo, " and a minister of the Most High: no bishop can be condemned without the judgment of the pope." The plea had its effect on the spectators, but it was adroitly parried by William. " I seize neither clerk nor prelate," said the king: " I seize the Earl of Kent, not the Bishop of Bayeux; I seize my temporal lieutenant, to account to me for his viceregal administration." [1]

The guards now did their duty; the ambitious Odo was arrested, conducted to Normandy, and imprisoned in the old tower of Rouen, for four years, that is to say, till the death of the Conqueror. This vigorous blow terrified the conspirators into submission, for none dared to provoke a vengeance which had not spared a brother.

William returned to Normandy, 1087, when a quarrel ensued between him and Philip, King of France. Various causes have been assigned for this rupture, some attributing it to private dissensions between the sons of the two monarchs, others affirming that it arose out of a demand on the part of the French king that William should do him homage for England. Ordericus

[1] Ord. Vitalis, liv. vii. vol. iii. p. 168.

Vitalis, the most exact and minute of the Norman historians, declares that the war was caused by the refusal
of Philip to surrender the province of Vexin, which
his father Henry had seized during the minority of
William, and which he was then unable to recover.

He now demanded the restitution of that province,
which was refused.   The duke was advanced in years
and corpulent, nor had he ever recovered from the fall
at Gerberoi, when unhorsed by his son Robert.   Some
coarse jokes are attributed to Philip against his rival,
but they are not mentioned by Ordericus Vitalis, and
are probably unfounded ; they are certainly unworthy
of historical notice.   At the close of July, 1087, William attacked Mantes, which he set on fire ; his
horse stumbled on some burning coal, and he was
thrown with violence.   The contusions he received
were so severe that he was compelled to return to
Rouen, where fever quickly announced the termination of his mortal career.   He prepared himself for
death with the firmness of a hero, arranged the affairs
of England and the duchy, drew up bequests for the
churches and the poor, and sent a sum of money to repair the sacred edifices he had so recently destroyed at
Mantes: he then summoned to his bed-side his two
younger sons, William Rufus and Henry, and invited
all the barons and knights to be seated.   Ordericus
Vitalis has preserved the following, as his genuine
dying speech:—

"My friends," said he, "sinking under the weight
of my numerous sins, I feel the liveliest apprehensions
at my approaching appearance before the final tribunal of God.   From earliest youth I was trained to
the use of arms, and I am soiled with blood : I cannot

enumerate the evils I have caused during the sixty
years I have passed in this world of bitterness; nevertheless I shall soon have to account for them before
the Eternal Judge. When my father, departing of his
own free will to foreign countries, delivered up to me
the duchy of Normandy, I was but a young infant,
being only eight years of age: from that period up to
the present time I have always supported the weight
of arms; during fifty-two years I have governed this
duchy amid the turmoils of war. My native subjects
have often conspired against me, and caused me serious grievances. They perfidiously murdered Turoldus,
my preceptor, Osbern, senechal of Normandy, the father
of his country, and many other faithful supporters of the
state. Nevertheless, in all these perilous circumstances
I was supported by the loyalty of the people. Frequently at night, owing to the fears of my relations, I
have been stealthily removed from my chamber, by my
uncle Walter,—and to escape from the villains who sought
to murder me, carried into the cottages of the poor. The
Normans are a generous people, if governed by firmness tempered with clemency; invincible in all great
difficulties, they excel all other nations, and being
more valiant than their enemies, they feel confident
of subduing them. If otherwise governed, they wage
war against each other, and consume the national
strength; fond of revolts, desirous of sedition, they
rush headlong into any rash enterprize. They must,
therefore, be led by equity, and forced by discipline to
walk in the paths of justice. If they are allowed, like
untamed horses, to run without a rein, they and their
princes will be overwhelmed with misery, shame, and
confusion. I have often experienced this to my cost.

My nearest relatives, who ought to have used all their
power to defend me against all the world, frequently
conspired against me, and sought to deprive me of my
inheritance.

" Guy, son of Raymond, Count of Burgundy, and
Alice of Normandy, my paternal aunt, returned me
evil for good. I had, however, received him with affection, when he returned from foreign parts; I had
treated him as an only brother; I gave him Vernon, Brionne, and large estates in Normandy. Nevertheless,
he outraged me by word and deed. He maliciously
stigmatized me as a bastard, as degenerate and unworthy of power. Traitor to his honour and duty, he revolted against me ; he seduced from their allegiance
several Norman barons, among others, Ranulph of
Bayeux, and Néel, Viscount of Cotentin. Forgetting
the homage and fidelity he had sworn to me, he endeavoured to deprive me of the whole of Normandy. Thus
then, when yet a beardless stripling, I was compelled to
take the field, and fight, at Val-des-Dunes, against
my vassals and my cousin. There, with the aid of
God, who is an equitable judge, I conquered my enemies between Caen and Argentan. I then laid siege
to the fortress of Brionne, in which I shut up Guy,
who had been wounded, and who had fled from the
field of battle. I retired from that place after having
driven the public enemy out of Normandy and recovered all my strong holds.

" Shortly afterwards I had to encounter misfortunes
still more severe. My paternal uncles, Mauger, Archbishop of Rouen, and his brother William, to whom I
had of my own free will given Arques and the pro-

vince of Talou, reproached me with being a bastard;
and they armed against me Henry, King of France,
and Enguerrand, Count of Ponthieu. When I heard
of this conspiracy I was in the Cotentin, and I
marched against them forthwith, though contrary to
the advice I received. I advanced against Arques with
a few knights, who displayed the utmost ardour to strike
the first blow, and soon, being strengthened by more
troops, I laid siege to that strong place. Before I
reached the plains which lie between the rivers Sie
and Garenne, my advanced-guard attacked Enguerrand, as he was attempting to enter the castle : he was
killed in a desperate conflict, for this knight was very
brave, and the troops he commanded were dispersed.
I pressed the garrison vigorously; I forced the perjured Count of Arques to retire from my dominions,
and never permitted him to enjoy the estates he had
forfeited by his treason. By a papal decree I deposed
from his archiepiscopal throne the insolent prelate,
Mauger, who was neither devoted to God nor faithful
to his prince, and I replaced him by the venerable
Maurilius, whom God had sent me from Florence, a
town in Italy.

"King Henry, confident in his power, boiling with
military zeal, and goaded on by my enemies, sought
to trample me under foot, as a man without defence.
He often invaded my territories with powerful armies;
but he never could boast of having collected much
plunder, or of having made many of my men prisoners.
Though he came with loud menaces and an imposing
array, he never returned very happy, or without having received some discomfiture. The bravest who

followed him in these expeditions were not the companions of his flight, for they perished under my sword and the sword of my barons and knights.

" Formerly King Henry, extremely irritated against me, levied a powerful army, which he arranged in two divisions, so as to crush Normandy by a double attack. He led one of these in person into the diocese of Evreux, to devastate the whole country up to the Seine; he confided the other to his brother Odo, to Raymond of Clermont, and the Counts Raoul de Mont Didier and Guy of Ponthieu, who entered Normandy by the fords of the Epte, to overrun the country of Bray, Talou, and the whole district of Rouen, and carry fire and sword down to the sea. At the news of this double invasion I marched without delay against the enemy; I stationed my troops along the bank of the Seine in front of the enemy, so that I was ready to repulse any hostile movement. Against Odo and his legions I sent Robert, Count of Eu, Roger de Mortemer, and other veteran knights. Having come up with the French at the castle of Mortemer, both parties prepared for battle. A fierce encounter followed, in which blood flowed in torrents. There were, indeed, brave men in both armies, who died rather than yield. The French fought for gain; the Normans, to repulse the invaders, and protect themselves and families. Finally, with the aid of God, the Normans triumphed, and the French took to flight. This battle was fought on the right bank of the Seine, during winter, before Lent, eight years after the battle of Val-des-Dunes. Guy, Count of Ponthieu, was taken prisoner; Odo, Raymond, and others fled, and owed their safety to the fleetness of their horses. Raoul, of Mont Didier,

would also have been made prisoner, had not Roger
de Mortemer, one of the chiefs of my army, assisted
him, for he owed him homage. In his peril, he rendered him a service as honourable as it was legitimate,
in guarding him three days in his castle, and then conducting him home in safety. For this conduct I banished Roger from Normandy; but being shortly afterwards reconciled to him, I restored his estates, except
the castle of Mortemer, in which he had secreted my
enemy, and which I was fully justified in taking from
him; but I did not keep it in my own hands, but
bestowed it on his cousin, William de Warenne, a
faithful vassal. I detained Guy, Count of Ponthieu,
in prison, as long as I pleased. After two years I received his homage; he was ever faithful, and served
me with a hundred men in any place I directed. I
loaded him with favours, and having thus honoured
him, dismissed him in peace. After the battle of
Mortemer, I ordered Raoul de Toëni to announce
what had happened to the King of France, who broke
up his camp in the night, and hastily retreated with
his whole army; since which time he never passed a
quiet night in my dominions.

" It was thus that, from infancy, surrounded on all
sides by adverse circumstances, I extricated myself
from them with honour, under the blessing of God. I
became in consequence an object of envy to my neighbours, but I was never conquered by them, for I
placed all my confidence in God, who supported me.
Of this the Bretons and Angevins can testify; the
French and Flemings can bear witness to it; and the
English and the Manceaux have bitterly experienced
it to their cost.

"Geoffrey Martel, Count of Anjou; Conan, petty Prince of the Bretons, and Robert the Friezelander, Count of the Flemings, undertook several perfidious enterprises against me; but as God protected me, they never succeeded in their views, however vigorous their efforts, however cunning their stratagems. I acquired the royal diadem, which none of my predecessors had worn; it was the mere effect of divine grace, and not the fruit of hereditary right. It would be most difficult for me to enumerate all my transmarine labours and dangers, and what desperate battles I had to fight with the people of Exeter, Chester, and Northumberland; with the Scotch, the Welch, the Norwegians, the Danes, and other enemies, who strove to deprive me of the kingdom of England; in all these perils I came off victorious. But though worldly ambition may exult at such triumphs, I am a prey to the terrors which fill me, when I reflect that, in all these actions, cruelty accompanied boldness. Wherefore, priests and ministers of Christ, I humbly beseech you to recommend me in your prayers to the omnipotent God, that he may pardon the sins which weigh so heavily upon me, and grant me salvation through his mercy. I desire that the treasure I have amassed be given to the poor and the churches, in order that what was the fruit of crime may be employed by the saints for saintly uses. Recollect how tenderly I have loved you, and how valiantly I have defended you against all rivals.

"I never violated the church of God, which is our mother; always and everywhere, so far as it was reasonable, I have profoundly reverenced it. I have never sold ecclesiastical dignities. Detesting simony, I have ever opposed it. In the election of dignitaries I have searched for men of moral conduct as well as of sound doctrine, and, as far as lay in my power, I have confided the government of the church to the most worthy. This I can truly prove by the instances of Lanfranc, Archbishop of Canterbury, Anselm, Abbot of Bec, Gerbert, Abbot of Fontenelles, Durand, Abbot of Troarn, and several other doctors of my kingdom, whose fame, I believe, has reached the extremities of the earth. I have chosen my counsellors from men of prudence, wisdom, and veracity, and I have always been happy to receive their advice.

" With the aid of God, nine monasteries and one nunnery, founded by my ancestors in Normandy, have received additions from me, and been gorgeously embellished by my presents. Since I have governed the duchy, seventeen monasteries and six nunneries have been built; divine service has been daily celebrated in them, and abundant alms has been distributed for the love of the Supreme Being. Thus Normandy is filled with spiritual fortresses, in which mortals learn to combat the demons and the lusts of the flesh. By the inspiration of God I have been the founder of these houses,—their protector and their friend. I have cheerfully confirmed, both in Normandy and in England, all grants of lands and revenues that my nobility have made to God and the saints, for the salvation of their souls; and I have protected, by my superior authority, all charters of donations against the attacks of envy, fraud, and rapine.

" Such have been my cares from my youth upwards,— such are the obligations that I impose on my successors. Do you, my sons, constantly imitate me in

this point, that you may be honoured before God and
man.  You who are of my blood, I enjoin you to attach yourselves to men of worth and wisdom, and to
follow their advice, that you may possess a durable
glory.  This is the doctrine of pious philosophers—to
discern good from evil, to follow justice in all things,
and spare no effort to avoid wickedness ; to assist the
poor, infirm, and honest ;  to curb and punish the
proud and selfish ; to prevent them injuring their
neighbours; devoutly to attend holy church, to prefer the worship of God to worldly wealth, and, nightly
and daily, in prosperity and adversity, to observe
rigorously the divine law.  Before I fought Harold at
Hastings, I had given Normandy to my eldest son Robert ;  as he has already received the homage of nearly
all the barons of the country, no one can deprive him
of what I have bestowed.  Nevertheless, I know that
the country subjected to his power will be truly miserable.  In fact, he is proud, reckless, extravagant, and
intemperate in his passions :  he will have long to endure the most cruel misfortunes.  I appoint no one my
successor to the throne of England ; I dare not give
that kingdom, which I have acquired with so many
crimes, to any unless to God.  It is not by hereditary
right that I possess so great an honour ; I seized the
sceptre from the perjured Harold, after a cruel battle
and a fearful effusion of blood ; and I only subjected
it to my dominion, after having killed or banished the
partisans of that prince.  I hated, more than I ought
to have done, the natives of that country.  I persecuted
the nobles and the people ; I unjustly disinherited
several ; I caused many to perish from hunger, more
from the sword, particularly in Yorkshire.  The men

of Durham and Northumberland supported the Danish
army of Sweyn against me; they not only killed Robert Comyn and a thousand of my soldiers in the walls
of Durham, but many of my bravest and most devoted knights in other places.    These hostilities inflamed me with the most violent resentment: I rushed
like a furious lion against the people of the north; I
ordered the houses of the rebels to be burnt, with their
crops, their implements of husbandry, and domestic
furniture, and their cattle of every kind to be slaughtered.    Thus did I punish a multitude of both sexes
with famine.    For these reasons I dare not bestow,
unless on God alone, the sceptre of that kingdom which
I have obtained by so many sins, for fear that, after
my death, great calamities may happen.    I desire that
my son William, who, from infancy, has always been
dutiful to me, and who has obeyed me in all things to
the best of his power, may keep himself in the ways of
God, and if it be the divine will and pleasure, I hope
he may happily enjoy the royal throne." [1]

This long and affecting address the dying monarch
frequently interrupted with his tears, and when he had
terminated the narrative of his life and partial confession of his sins, his youngest son, Henry, finding
that he was excluded from the parental succession,
approached his father, and said, "What, then, do you
give to me?"    William answered, "I give you five
thousand pounds weight of silver out of my treasure."
Henry rejoined, "What shall I do with that gift, if I
have no land to dwell in?"    His father replied, "My
son, be satisfied with your lot, and trust in the Lord;
suffer your brothers peaceably to precede you.    Robert

1 Ord. Vit. liv. vii. vol. iii. p. 197, et seq.

will have Normandy, and William, England. As to
you, when your time comes, you will possess all that I
have acquired, and surpass your brothers in power and
riches," a prediction that was afterwards realized.

The king retained to the last all the prudent cir-
cumspection that had formed a distinguishing feature
in his character.  He wrote to Archbishop Lanfranc,
to express his wish that William should obtain the
crown of England, and ordered him to prepare the nobility to receive him as his successor; he then desired
his son to cross over at once to England.   William had
no sooner reached Wuissant, on the coast of Boulogne,
(the Portus Iccius from which Julius Cæsar embarked
when he invaded Britain,) than he heard of the death
of his father, and he hastened forward without delay.
Henry, on his part, was equally active to secure the
money bequeathed to him, to verify the exact weight,
to surround himself with proved friends, and to provide a place of safety in which to deposit his treasure.

The apartment of the dying monarch was still
crowded with physicians, ministers of state, and the chief
nobility; and he was now importuned, as a matter of
grace and favour, to liberate the prisoners of rank
whom he had incarcerated.   To these solicitations the
king thus answered : " For a long time I have held in
strict custody Morcar, a noble English count, and
most unjustly; but I did so, fearing that he would
create trouble in England if I gave him his liberty.  I
have retained in irons Roger de Breteuil, because he
displayed the most furious hatred to my person, and
provoked his brother-in-law, Raoul de Guader, to revolt, as well as many others ; and I swore that he should

never leave his prison while I lived. I arrested several persons to punish them for their perversity, and others because I suspected them of rebellious designs. In fact, the maintenance of public order required this severity, and the divine law, announced by Moses, enjoins sovereigns to restrain the guilty, lest the innocent should suffer. Now feeling the immediate approach of death, as I desire to be saved and absolved of my sins by the mercy of God, I order that all the prisons be opened, and that all the prisoners, except the Bishop of Bayeux, my brother, be liberated for the love of God, that he may show me mercy. However, I make it a condition that the prisoners, before they receive this free pardon, take an oath to my ministers not to disturb the tranquillity of the state, but to maintain peace in Normandy and England, and resist to the utmost of their power all who foment rebellion."

When Robert, Earl of Mortain, heard this sentence, which condemned his brother to perpetual imprisonment, he was deeply affected. Herlouin de Conteville had married Arlette, after the death of Duke Robert, father of the Conqueror, by whom he had two sons, Odo and Robert. William had loaded his father-in-law with wealth and honours, both in Normandy and England, and even extended his favours to Raoul, a son that Herlouin had by a second wife, for he always behaved most generously to his maternal relatives. He had created Odo, Bishop of Bayeux and Earl of Kent, and raised Robert to the dignity of Earl of Mortain; but the ingratitude and treachery of Odo, already noticed, compelled William to constitute him a prisoner. He had now languished four years in the tower of Rouen, and so convinced was the Conqueror

of his dangerous character, that he deemed it essential
to the public safety to make him an exception to the
royal clemency. But the Earl of Mortain refused to
quit the presence of the dying monarch, till he had
obtained the pardon of his brother, and he was seconded
in his entreaties by several of the most influential
barons. Worn out at length by this continued im-
portunity, the resolution of William failed him, and he
thus addressed the audience:—

"I am astonished that your foresight has not penetrated the real character of the criminal whose liberation you so urgently request. Is not the man for whom
you intercede an enemy to true religion and the perfidious author of the most dangerous seditions? Did
not the bishop, whom I appointed to act as a just
viceroy over the English, become the most cruel oppressor of the people, and the despoiler of the monasteries? In demanding the liberty of this traitor you
plead for an unworthy object, and are preparing for
yourselves the most grievous misfortunes. It is evident that my brother Odo is flighty and ambitious,
cruel and fond of worldly possessions, and too much
attached to vain pomp and pleasure. This I have often
and clearly experienced, wherefore I put in irons, not
the prelate, but the tyrant. Without doubt, should he
recover his liberty, he will again disturb the peace and
cause the death of thousands. I do not thus speak
from hatred of an enemy, but as the father of my
country, and watchful over the welfare of a Christian
people. In fact, were he to conduct himself with that
chastity and modesty which becomes a minister of God,
I should feel in my heart a greater joy than I can
express."

The Earl of Mortain and his friends, gaining courage from this last expression, pledged themselves that Odo would correct his mode of conduct, and out of gratitude lead a tranquil and loyal life. The king then said, "Whether I will it or not, your demand shall be granted, for a great revolution will follow my death. It is in spite of myself that I deliver my brother out of prison. Be assured, however, that he will cause the death of many, and occasion great calamities. I will also do another act of clemency; I took from Baudri, the son of Nicolas, all his lands, because, without my permission, he quitted my service, and passed over into Spain. I now restore them to him for the love of God: I do not believe there is a better knight under arms than he, but he is changeable and prodigal, and fond of roving into foreign countries."

On the morning of the 9th of September, 1087, the last hour of the Conqueror approached. He was roused from a restless sleep by the sound of the cathedral bells. Raising his eyes to heaven, and with an air of fervent devotion, he exclaimed, "I commend myself to the holy Mary, mother of God, my sovereign, that by her prayers I may be reconciled with her dearly beloved Son, our Saviour, Jesus Christ." As soon as he uttered these words he expired. No sooner had the king breathed his last than his palace was deserted; the nobles retired to their castles to put their property in safety; the guards abandoned their post, and the domestics plundered with impunity the vases, weapons, linen, and, in short, every article that was moveable. The body was left alone without a single attendant, while the gates of the palace were accessible to every intruder.

The news of the king's death soon spread through
Rouen, when the monks and priests assembled and
ordered a procession.  The archbishop, after this ceremony was terminated, directed that the corpse should
be transported to Caen, and buried in the church of
St. Stephen's.  The brothers and cousins of the king
had already retired, and those who had lived on his
bounty had shamefully abandoned their post.  Herlouin
de Conteville, his step-father, alone remained faithful : he arranged matters for the funeral and conveyed
the body to Caen.

Gislebert, bishop of Evreux, read the burial-service,
and pronounced a panegyric on the deceased; but in
the middle of the ceremony an alarming fire broke out
which consumed a large part of the town, and all the
priests and monks hurried away to stifle the flames.
The body was removed to an adjoining convent.
Shortly afterwards, all the bishops and abbots of Normandy assembled at Caen, and the obsequies of the
monarch were performed with great solemnity.

On this occasion an extraordinary event occurred,
worthy of being recorded, as showing the powerful influence of the laws of Rollo, the founder of the duchy.
When William built the great abbey of St. Stephen's
at Caen, he pulled down several houses to obtain a
spacious area, and he did not compensate all the owners for their loss.  When the body of the Conqueror
was about to be deposited in the vault, Ascelin, the son
of Arthur, stepped forward, and thus addressed Prince
Henry and the bishops :—

" He who oppressed kingdoms by his arms, has
been my oppressor also, and has kept me under a
continual fear of death.  Since I have outlived him

who injured me, I mean not to acquit him now that he is dead. The ground wherein you are going to lay this man, is mine; and I affirm that none may, in justice, bury their dead in property that belongs to another. If, after he has departed this life, force and violence are still used to withhold my right from me, I appeal to Rollo, the father and founder of our nation, who, though dead, *lives in his laws!* I take refuge in those laws, owning no authority above them."

This demand was investigated on the spot, and the claim of Ascelin was confirmed by the testimony of his neighbours. None offered him violence for having interrupted the ceremony; on the contrary, all respected the Haro, or appeal to Rollo; the complainant received sixty sous, with a promise that the full amount of his loss should be paid at an early day.

The character of William has been variously estimated by the Norman and English chroniclers, the former loading him with every praise, the latter reproaching him with every crime. Both of these portraits have been overcharged; his virtues have been as extravagantly lauded as his vices have been ungenerously magnified. None can dispute his courage, his prudence, his indefatigable industry, and the vigilance of his administration. Undoubtedly he was a great sovereign and the hero of his age. He conquered difficulties under which an ordinary mind would have succumbed. With the exception of the invasion of England, he cannot fairly be reproached with a love of war, for his continental battles were defensive. He was liberal and generous, and though covetous, and fond of amassing wealth, he rewarded his friends with princely munificence. When he had subdued his

enemies he was usually lenient; and if he was cruel
to the people of Alençon, who had grossly insulted his
mother, it must be allowed that he had ample provocation for his severity. The excesses he committed at
York and Mantes are not to be excused, but in his dying speech he confessed his guilt, and evinced his
repentance. The foulest stain on his honour was the
murder of the English count, Waltheof, who had re-
vealed a conspiracy against his person in which he had
himself been concerned; but William became reconciled
to him, treated him as a friend, and then treacherously
caused him to be put to death. His forcible seizure of
the English crown was an act of unjustifiable ambition,
and the artifice he adopted to fix perjury on Harold
was mean and despicable. He deprived the Anglo-
Saxons of their constitutional monarch, freely elected
by their own choice, irrespective of the will of Edward
the Confessor, and ruled his new subjects with a rod of
iron. Never were a people more degraded under the
yoke of bondage; under his tyrannic sway, lands,
honours, and power, civil, military, and ecclesiastical,
were exclusively bestowed on the Normans. He himself admitted the injustice of his conduct, and the sins
he had committed weighed so heavily on his soul, that
he dreaded appointing a successor to the throne he
had usurped; a confession of itself sufficient to prove
the extent and heinousness of his crimes. That William was truly pious, according to the spirit of his age,
must be admitted; but his conduct shows how loosely
religion exerts its influence on men devoured by ambition. He founded abbeys and burnt cities; he patron-
ized the monks and slaughtered the laity; he loaded
the monasteries with wealth and spread famine in

England; he knelt himself before a bishop or an abbot, and smote the widow and the fatherless with the sharp edge of the sword. As a successful warrior he will be admired by the soldier; as a wise administrator he will be esteemed by the politician; as a zealous supporter of the church he will be venerated by the clergy; but the impartial historian, while giving every merit to William that he justly deserved, will denounce his ambition, his thirst for gold, and his cruelties. The Conqueror was the glory and the buckler of Normandy, but the curse and scourge of England.

# ROBERT THE SECOND,

## EIGHTH DUKE OF NORMANDY,

### Surnamed Courte-Heuse.

———

ROBERT was at Abbeville when his father died, and
as soon as he received intelligence of that event he repaired to Rouen, where he received the ducal crown
and mantle from the archbishop, in presence of several
of the barons, who took the oaths of homage and fealty.

This prince possessed all the courage and boldness of
his ancestors; but he was prodigal, inconsiderate, a
slave to sensual passions, irresolute and vacillating.
He enriched his personal friends, but impoverished his
people; he rashly gave up some of the strongest castles to his barons, and thus diminished his own power.
The reins of government floated loosely in his incapable hands; his finances soon fell into a dilapidated
state; justice was openly violated, and rapine and
disorder convulsed the duchy.

Requiring money to satisfy his wants, he applied to
his brother Henry for a loan, which was refused, unless
a sufficient security were given for repayment; on
which Robert proposed to sell the Cotentin, containing
one third of Normandy, for three thousand pounds
weight of silver, and these terms Henry accepted.
The pound weight of silver was worth two marks; the

H

mark, from Charlemagne to Louis the Sixth, that is to say from 763 to 1113, was worth fifteen sous; under Louis the Fifteenth and Sixteenth it increased to forty-nine francs sixteen sous; the three thousand pounds' weight of silver, with which Henry purchased the Cotentin, were equal in our money to two hundred and ninety-eight thousand eight hundred francs.

The next imprudent step adopted by Robert was to appoint his uncle, the Bishop of Bayeux, prime-minister: he restored him to all his honours, confided the sole government of the duchy to his charge, unmindful of the dying speech of his father, in which the depraved and intriguing character of Odo is so well described.

William Rufus had been crowned King of England on the 29th of September, 1087, and Odo determined to wrest the sceptre from his hand. In this design he was supported by Eustace, Count of Boulogne, Robert de Bellesme, and other powerful barons, who were induced to pursue this policy in consequence of the separation of England from Normandy. " If," said they, " we serve Robert faithfully, we shall offend his brother William, who will despoil us of the lands and dignities we hold in England; if, on the other hand, we are obedient to William, Duke Robert will deprive us of the patrimonies we enjoy in Normandy. It is our interest, therefore, to dethrone William, who is young and arrogant, and to whom we owe nothing. Let us then place Robert on the thrones of England and Neustria, to maintain the unity of the two states: he is the eldest, we served him when his father lived, and we took the oaths of fidelity to him for both countries."

This resolution was communicated to Robert by

Odo, and the rash and thoughtless prince was charmed
with the project, promising every assistance to his adherents, provided they would commence the enterprize.
The conspirators, thus emboldened, sailed for England
about Christmas, 1087, fortified their castles, seduced
many restless spirits to join their party, and succeeded
in fomenting a civil war.

William soon received intelligence of the meditated
insurrection, and prepared to repel force by force.
He besieged Odo in the city of Rochester, in Kent,
where the prelate was expecting the arrival of Robert
with the Norman reinforcements, but he was too indo-
lent to cross the sea. Disease broke out among the
garrison, and the chiefs of the insurgents sent deputies
to the royal camp, offering to surrender the place on condition of their retaining their lands and fiefs, and swearing to recognize William as their lawful sovereign.
When the king heard these proposals he was greatly incensed ; he dismissed the deputies in fierce anger, swearing that he would hang the principal rebels on gibbets,
and put the remainder to death by various modes of
torture. In the royal army were many barons and
knights who had friends and relatives in the besieged
city, and who endeavoured to appease the wrath of
William, putting forth their own faithful services as
the grounds on which they requested him to show
mercy to the garrison. To their entreaties the king
answered : " I acknowledge my obligations to you, but
you ought not to ask me to sheathe the sword of justice.
Whoever spares brigands and traitors, who have committed perjury, deprives the innocent and loyal of the
peace and security to which they are entitled. What
have I done to justify this revolt? Have I ever injured

these rebels? Why should they seek to despoil me of my inheritance, bestowed on me by my father, or seek my life? I have not seized their property, nor molested their persons; they have attacked me without any provocation, and a severe punishment will operate as an example, and prevent future rebellions."

The barons renewed their entreaties, and appealed to his royal clemency. "The Bishop of Bayeux," they said, " is your uncle; he greatly aided your father in the conquest of England, and in many affairs of difficulty: you will not lay violent hands on a minister of God, or shed his blood. The Count of Boulogne was always faithful to your father, and assisted him valiantly in his most arduous undertakings. Robert de Bellesme was his personal friend, and through his bounty received most extensive estates in Normandy. Forget, then, the injuries they have meditated against you, and pardon them for the services they rendered to your father: you have vanquished them, and can be generous without hazarding your dignity."[1]

William at length yielded to these pressing solicitations: he abandoned his threats of death and mutilation, and allowed the garrison to march out with their horses and arms; but he deprived the rebels of all their English estates, vowing that they should never recover them during his life. It was the custom in those times, whenever a fortress or city was carried by force, for the victorious party to announce their triumph by a flourish of trumpets, and Odo desired that this ceremony should not be performed; but William sternly refused to spare him that humiliation. The Bishop of Bayeux was formally and ignominiously expelled from England,

[1] Ord. Vital. liv. viii. vol. iii. p. 237.

to which country he never again returned, and retired
to his diocese covered with shame and confusion. The
siege of Rochester terminated in the summer of 1088.

Immediately after these events, Prince Henry, bearing the Norman title of Earl of the Cotentin, visited
England, to demand of his brother William the inheritance of their mother, Matilda, which the Conqueror
had bestowed on him. He was accompanied by Robert de Bellesme. The English monarch acceded to
the request of his brother, and put him into possession
of the maternal estates, but he afterwards took them
from Henry, and conferred them on Robert Fitz-Aimon, a transfer which subsequently led to a rupture
between the two brothers.

The restless and intriguing spirit of the Bishop of
Bayeux now found another pretext to disturb the
peace of the duchy. He persuaded Robert that
Prince Henry and Robert de Bellesme had been to
England to mature a plot against his life, and demanded permission to arrest them on their return. This was granted, and the former was incarcerated at Neuilly, and the latter at Bayeux. When
Roger, Earl of Shrewsbury, father of Robert de Bellesme, received intelligence of the imprisonment of his
son, he obtained permission from the king to pass over
into Normandy, and fortify his castles, justly apprehending that the duke intended to seize on his estates.
The Bishop of Bayeux now resolved on the destruction of this powerful family, intending to enrich himself by the confiscation of their domains; and he accordingly summoned a council at Rouen, with a view
to carry his criminal projects into effect. He thus addressed the duke and the audience:—

" Whoever holds the reins of government should
show himself mild or severe, as reason admonishes him;
gentle as a lamb towards the good, the humble, and
the submissive; severe as a lion towards the wicked,
the rebellious, and the insolent.    You see, Duke
of Normandy, lawless men committing all sorts
of excesses, rivalling even the pagans in their
crimes.    The monks and widows raise their cries
to you, but you sleep.    You are aware of these enormities, but they seem to give you no concern.    This is
not the way in which holy David acted, nor Alexander the Great, nor Julius Cæsar, nor Annibal the
Carthaginian, nor Scipio Africanus, nor the Persian
Cyrus, nor the Roman Marius.    But why do I cite
the barbarians whose names are unknown to you?  Let
me speak of princes with whom you are acquainted,
and who are of our blood.    Call to mind your fathers
and ancestors whose magnanimity and valour was so
much admired and dreaded by the French, valiant as
they are.    I speak of Rollo, William Longsword, the
three Richards, your grandfather, Robert, and your father, William, the most illustrious of your predecessors.
Imitate their firmness and vigour, which obtained them
dominion, curbed tyrants, and subjected cruel nations.
Rouse from your slumbers, assemble the invincible
army of Normandy, and march on the town of Mans.
There your garrisons occupy the castle built by your
father ; all the people of the town obey you, especially
Hoel, its venerable bishop.    Summon the nobles of
Maine ; treat them graciously, and give them the praises
they merit.    Attack with vigour those who despise your
authority.    Besiege them in their strong holds, if they
do not at once submit.    After having subjugated the

Manceaux, attack Earl Roger and expel him and
his family from the Norman soil. You already hold in
irons Robert, eldest son of Roger. If you act with
the energy which becomes a valiant prince, you may
chase away for ever the seditious family of Talvas.
Their race is accursed; their vices and crimes are hereditary; this is certain from the horrible deaths they have
died, quite dissimilar from the rest of mortals. If you do
not extirpate the whole of them, they will become too
powerful for the throne. They now hold the strongest
castles at Bellesme, Urson, Essai, Alençon, Domfront,
St. Ceneri, Motte d'Igé, and many other places, which
by fraud or violence they have ravished from the legitimate owners. Your father held all these castles;
but Robert, whom you hold prisoner, as soon as he
heard of his death, drove out your garrisons, and
placed in them creatures of his own, to rob you of your
inheritance. Weigh, then, maturely what I have said,
and act with vigour in defence of the church and the
poor, both being oppressed by these civil feuds." [1]

This speech elicited great applause, as each of the
audience hoped to gain some share of the spoils of the
family of Bellesme. The duke marched to Mans,
where he was well received by the inhabitants, and
where he was joined by Geoffery of Mayenne, Robert
of Burgundy, and other powerful barons, eager to
serve him. The castle of Balon, belonging to the Earl
of Shrewsbury, was the first conquest of Robert, who
then besieged Saint Ceneri, which was gallantly defended by Robert Quarrel, a brave knight and remarkable for his personal strength. After a protracted defence he was obliged to surrender for want of pro-

[1] Ord. Vital. liv. viii. vol. iii. p. 253.

visions, when the duke had the barbarity to put out his eyes, and many of his officers were mutilated by a sentence of the ducal court. This severity alarmed the followers of the Bellesme family, and several had resolved to submit, but Robert was incapable of continued action, and wishing to return to his pleasures he disbanded his army. The Earl of Shrewsbury sent deputies to the duke, and succeeded in obtaining the liberty of his son, and on the general demand of the nobles and people Prince Henry was also released.

William Rufus had been deeply incensed against Robert for having fomented the disturbances in England which terminated in the capture of Rochester and the expulsion of Odo. Had he not been restrained by Archbishop Lanfranc, the faithful friend of the Conqueror and his family, he would have taken an immediate revenge, but that prelate interposed, and prevented any retaliation on Normandy. But his death, which occurred in 1890, was the signal for hostilities between the two brothers, and William commenced his plans by sending emissaries across the water, and corrupting several of the ducal vassals. In this extremity Robert applied for aid to Philip, King of France, who promised succour: William forwarded money to Paris; the bribe was accepted, but not a single soldier crossed the frontier. Deserted by his suzerain, who was bound to have sent armed assistance, Robert was still more embarrassed by the revolt of the Manceaux, who profited by his difficulties to declare their independence. He applied to the Count of Anjou to quell these disturbances, who consented, on condition that he received the daughter of the Count de Montfort in marriage: to this her father demurred, unless Robert restored to him the estates of his uncle, Raoul Tête d'Ane, which the Conqueror had confiscated. The duke was obliged to comply, and purchased temporary tranquillity in Maine, by weakening his personal power in Normandy.

The intrigues of Rufus, and the bad administration of Robert, had reduced the duchy into a state of lawless insubordination. The Cotentin alone was free from rapine, under the prudent government of Henry, who, however, only wanted an opportunity to attack both of his brothers. He was incensed against William for having given his maternal inheritance to Fitz-Aimon, and he had to avenge himself on Robert for having imprisoned him. In the present posture of affairs he resolved to assist Robert, in order to thwart the views of William, and marched to Rouen on the 3rd of November, 1090, where he was joined by the Counts of Evreux, Bellesme, Breteuil, and the Baron de l'Aigle.

Rufus had succeeded in forming a powerful party in the metropolis of Normandy, at the head of which was Conan, a man of immense wealth and unbounded influence. He had agreed to give up the town to the king, and when he had matured his conspiracy, he fixed a day for the royal troops, stationed at Gournay, to advance on Rouen. When the insurrection broke out, the duke deserted his capital, embarked on the Seine, and secreted himself in the church of Sainte Marie du Pré, at Emendreville,—an act of cowardice which covered him with eternal disgrace. A fierce battle ensued, in which a great number of the citizens were slain, but victory remained with the duke's party, and Conan, the instigator of these troubles, was taken prisoner. He was brought before Prince Henry, on the platform of the great tower of Rouen, who thus addressed him : " Look, Conan, from this eminence, at the beautiful country you attempted to subjugate. On the south is a magnificent park ; to the east are fertile meadows; here is the Seine, which waters these walls, and daily brings to the city vessels loaded with various merchandize. Observe the strength of the fortifications, the number of churches and houses, and reflect on the courage and intelligence of the population. Rouen has from the most ancient times justly commanded all Normandy." Conan, alarmed at the ironical taunts of Henry, fell on his knees, and invoked his clemency. " I am," said he, " conscious of my guilt, and condemned by my own crime, but I crave your pardon. I will give you all my treasures, and those of my family to ransom my life, and swear fidelity for the future." Henry replied, " By the soul of my mother, I will show no favour to a traitor: prepare for the death you merit." Then Conan, groaning bitterly, cried with a loud voice, " For the love of God, give me time to confess myself to a priest;" but Henry, furious with rage, and deaf to his entreaties, seized the traitor with both his arms, and hurled him through a window of the tower. The body was tied to the tail of a horse, and dragged ignominiously through the streets of Rouen. [1]

When Duke Robert returned to his capital he was touched with pity at the massacre of his subjects, and still more affected at the treatment of the prisoners. Robert de Bellesme and William de Breteuil insisted on receiving ransoms from their captives, in default of

Ord. Vital. liv. viii. vol. v. p. 312.

which they immured them in their castles. The duke
dared not interfere, or resist those barons who had
perilled their lives in defence of his crown.

The plans of Rufus were thus disconcerted; but
though Normandy was free, during a few months, from
foreign enemies, it continued to be the scene of domestic troubles. Robert de Bellesme employed the
plunder he had gathered at Rouen in building two
strong castles, one at La Fourche and the other at La
Courbe, with the intention of attacking his neighbours,
Hugh de Grentemesnil and Richard de Courcy. In
self-defence they raised troops, and many conflicts and
skirmishes ensued, but Robert, at the request of De
Bellesme, marched to his aid, thus espousing the quarrel of one vassal against others, who were, in fact,
more worthy of his protection. The duke laid siege to
the castle of Courcy, but was soon obliged to raise it,
as an English army had landed at Eu, and again threatened to dispossess him of his duchy. This invasion
Robert had neither the power nor the firmness to repel,
but obtained peace on the most disadvantageous terms,
giving up to Rufus, Cherbourg, Mont St. Michel, Aumale, St. Valery, Eu, and Fécamp, the keys of Normandy, and many strong fortresses. William, on his
part, stipulated to restore their English estates to all
the barons who had been faithful to Robert; but this
concession only strengthened the subject, without
adding to the power of the dukedom; the two brothers
also reciprocally covenanted that, in case either of them
should die without issue, the survivor should inherit
either England or the duchy, as the case might be.
These articles were signed by twelve English and
twelve Norman barons.

This treaty reconciled the king and the duke, but it necessarily raised a quarrel between them and their younger brother, Henry; for Cherbourg and Mont St. Michel formed part of the Cotentin, which he had purchased of Robert. Henry knew perfectly well that neither of his kinsmen would pay the slightest attention to the claims of justice, and that force alone could secure the alienated part of his dominions: he accordingly threw a strong garrison into Mont St. Michel, and fortified his other castles. William and Robert combined their armies, and marched against Henry, who, being much feebler than his competitors, was soon abandoned by many officers, whom bribes and menaces induced to surrender up the forts entrusted to their charge, and the deserted prince was compelled to seek shelter in Mont St. Michel. Henry defended himself with courage, made frequent sallies, and killed great numbers of his opponents; but after a resistance of fifteen days, want of water compelled him to surrender. He passed into Brittany, and then into the French Vexin, where he remained during two years in poverty and exile.

Two interesting anecdotes are connected with this siege of Mont St. Michel, which took place in the middle of Lent, 1091, and they merit record. In one of the sallies made by the besieged, the King of England, hurried away by his impetuosity, advanced singly in front of his line of battle, and defied the boldest knight to combat. The challenge was soon accepted, and a powerful thrust of a lance threw his majesty to the ground; his assailant, quickly dismounting, drew his sword, and was on the point of cutting off his head, when William exclaimed, "Stay

your hand, sir knight, I am the king!" The knight
lowered the point of his sword, returned it into its
scabbard, approached the prostrate monarch with
marked respect, and raised him up in his arms.  This
extraordinary encounter and its consequences had the
effect of causing a temporary suspension of hostilities;
besiegers and besieged crowded round William, who
was mounted on a fresh charger.  He was struck by
the chivalrous generosity of the knight, and asked
aloud that he would come forward.  "Sire," replied
the knight, "I stand in your presence: if I have
failed in respect to your majesty, I crave your pardon.  I thought my opponent was a simple knight, as I
am, and not a powerful monarch."  "I do not only
pardon you," rejoined William, "but I wish to number you among my personal friends: you shall be my
knight of honour, and I swear by Saint Luke to place
you on my register, and give you the highest posts, in
token of my esteem and good-will." [1]

This trait of generosity does honour to the character
of William, but the other anecdote which we are now
about to relate exhibits him under a very different light.
Robert, knowing that his brother Henry was sorely
distressed for water, sent him a large quantity, and
some wine; at this William was highly incensed, insisting that he ought to be reduced by famine; but Ro-

[1] "Solus in multos irruit...moxque occiso sub fœminibus deturbatus equo...etiam
diû per pedem tractus est; sed fides loricæ obstitit ne læderetur.  Jamque miles qui
dejecerat manum ad capulum optabat ut feriret, cum ille periculo extremo territus
exclamaret: Tolle nebulo; rex Angliæ sum ego.  Tremuit notâ voce jacentis vul-
gus militum, statimque reverenter de terrâ levato alterum equum adducunt.  Ille
non expectato ascensori sonipedem insiliens; Quis, inquit, me dejecit?  Musitan-
tibus cunctis, miles audacis facti conscius, non defuit patrocinio suo dicens: Ego,
qui non te putarem esse regem, sed militem.  Tum verò rex placidus, vultuque
serenus, per vultum, ait, de Lucca (sicenim jurabat) meus eris, et meo albo insertus
laudabilis militiæ præmia reportabis." *Willelm. Malmsbury,* L iv. p. 68.

bert replied, " Shall we allow our brother to die of
thirst? When he is no more, how shall we replace
him?" [1]

The King of England having possessed himself of
Mont St. Michel quitted Normandy for his transmarine
dominions, and rendered himself unpopular with the
clergy, by attempting to extort money from Anselm,
Archbishop of Canterbury, to defray the expense of
the late war. This prelate, formerly Abbot of Bec, in
Normandy, had succeeded Lanfranc, and he offered
William five hundred pounds weight of silver, but
twice that amount was demanded: it was refused, and
Anselm retained his money and retired from the court.
Nor was this the only difference between them. Anselm demanded permission to travel to Rome to receive the *pallium* from the pope; the king observed
that he would never place the archbishopric under the
controul of the Roman pontiff; that such an act would
compromise the rights of the crown; that all the
cathedrals and churches were under his royal protection; and that he would hold any prelate guilty of
high-treason who accepted his installation from his
holiness. A contest between the spiritual and temporal jurisdictions now seemed inevitable, but the im-
pending storm was happily averted by the arrival of a
papal legate, who delivered the *pallium* to the king, by
whom it was conferred upon the archbishop.

In 1092, Prince Henry, then in exile, was invited
by the inhabitants of Domfront, who had long groaned

[1] " Quod cum relatum regi esset, ut semper calori pronus erat, comiti dixit : Bene
acis actitare guerram, qui hostibus præbes aquæ copiam; et quomodo eos domabimus,
si eis in pastu et in potu induserimus? At ille renidens illud, comé et merito famo-
sum verbum emisit. Papæ! dimitterem fratrem nostrum mori siti? et quem
alium habebimus, si eum amiserimus." *Willelm. Malmsbury*, l. iv. p. 71.

under the scourge of Robert de Bellesme, to take possession of their city and the territory attached to it. They annexed two conditions to this arrangement, first, that he would in no respect change their laws and customs, and, secondly, that he would never surrender his rights on Domfront, or transfer them to any other person. These terms were accepted, and Henry, though attacked by Robert, successfully maintained his position, and even conquered large tracts of the surrounding country, living in comple independence of his brother. [1]

We have now arrived at the period of the first crusade, under the celebrated Peter the Hermit, which threw almost the whole adult population of Europe into Palestine. Among the princes who joined this memorable expedition was Robert Courte-Heuse, who quitted Normandy in September, 1096, accompanied by many of the barons and knights of the duchy ; among these, Ordericus Vitalis mentions Odo, Bishop of Bayeux ; Rotrou, son of Geoffrey, Count of Mortain ; Walter of St. Valery-sur-Somme, and his son Bernard ; William de Ferrieres ; Gerard de Gournay ; the two sons of Hugh de Grentemesnil, and several distinguished knights.

To appear with splendour and distinction among the crusaders, the Duke of Normandy required money, and as his own treasury was exhausted, he mortgaged his duchy to king William for five years, receiving ten thousand marks of silver. When this disgraceful bargain was concluded, Robert set out on his journey to the Holy Land, where he rivalled the bravest in feats of arms, So great indeed was his reputation that the crusaders hesitated whether they should elect

Ord. Vital. liv. viii. vol. iii. p. 339.

him King of Jerusalem or Godfrey of Bouillon, and
some historians declare that Robert voluntarily declined the honour which was offered to him.  At the
battle of Ascalon, he seized with his own hands the
principal standard of the infidels, and this highly
valued trophy was deposited in the temple of the Holy
Sepulchre. [1]

After the departure of his brother, William Rufus
made frequent visits to Normandy, under the pretext
of maintaining tranquillity, but his real motive was to
corrupt the fidelity of the barons and knights who had
remained at home, so that, at the expiration of the five
years stipulated in the mortgage, he might make himself absolute master of the duchy.  He carried his
arms into Brittany, and in the spring of 1097, appeared before Nantes with a powerful army, and as
the inhabitants were unable to make any effectual resistance, they delivered up the keys of the town, and
recognized him as their sovereign.

In the summer of the same year, Rufus demanded
from Philip, King of France, the province of Vexin,
and the fortresses of Pontoise, Chaumont, and Mantes,
which were refused.  Philip was too old to take the field
in person, and his son Louis was too young: not having one of their princes at their head, the French
fought with little resolution ; many of the barons were

---

[1] According to Wace, v. 14820. p. 323, of the Roman de Rou, Robert deposited the
standard in the church his mother, Matilda, had founded at Caen.  But this is expressly denied by Albert of Aix, who admits that the duke seized the standard,
but declares that it was left in the Holy Sepulchre: " Longissima hasta, argento oper-
ta per totum, quod vocatur *standart* et quæ Regis Babyloniæ exercitui signum præ-
ferebatur, et circâ quam præcipua virtus densabatur, ad quam victi et dissipati
revertebantur, capta est à Roberto Nortmannorum principe, et in templum
Dominici Sepulchri transmissa, et usque in hodiernum diem ob memoriam vic-
toriæ Christianorum attitulata est."  *Hist. Hieros.* lib. vi. c. 49.

bribed, and surrendered for money strong castles on
the frontier; and though William did not succeed in
obtaining the territory he claimed, he was enabled to
build the strong castle of Gisors, one of the most formidable ramparts of Normandy.

The disturbances which had agitated the duchy since
the accession of Robert, had prevented him keeping
the Manceaux in subjection, and Maine had recovered
its independence for six years before the duke departed for Palestine. The reigning sovereign of that
province was Hélier de la Fleche, who enjoyed the
castle of that name as his patrimonial inheritance: by
his marriage he became possessed of four other strong
fortresses. Château-du-Loir, Mayet, Lucé, and Ostilli.
Hélier was desirous of joining the crusaders, and had
indeed made a vow to repair to the Holy Land, but
fearing lest, in his absence, Rufus should attack his
territories, he went to Rouen and demanded an audience of the king. Having stated his intentions,
Hélier said, " I now demand your friendship, as my
suzerain, as I desire to undertake my pilgrimage in
peace with you." Rufus answered, "Go whither you
please, but put into my hands the town of Mans and
all Maine, for I will have what my father held."
Hélier rejoined, " I hold my possessions of my ancestors by hereditary right, and, with the blessing of God,
I will leave them free to my posterity. If you deny
my right I will leave the point to be adjudged by kings,
earls, or bishops." William haughtily rejoined, " I
will know no other umpires, but swords, lances, and
flights of arrows." Hélier, indignant at this treatment,
warned the king that he was a soldier of Christ; that
to attack his territories when he was absent, combating

the infidels, would be an act of impiety; and finally
challenged him to put his menace into execution.[1]

The Earl of La Fleche then quitted Rouen, returned to Maine, put his castles into a state of defence,
and built the fort of Dangeul, to arrest the incursions
of Robert de Bellesme. This ambitious and powerful
baron, being thus checked in his schemes of plunder,
urged Rufus to lose no time in leading his troops
against Danguel, and the Norman army was soon in
motion. Hélier received early intelligence of this invasion, and being fully prepared to meet the enemy,
no decided battle was fought, but the territory of
Maine was cruelly devastated by fire and sword.
Three hundred prisoners, who fell into the power of
Robert de Bellesme, were starved to death in his dungeons, although considerable ransoms were offered for
their liberation, and refused.

In 1098, Hélier was surprised by Robert de Bellesme, when only attended by seven knights. The
Norman baron had planned an ambuscade near to
Dangeul, and succeeded in capturing his formidable
enemy, whom he led prisoner to Rouen, and delivered up to the king, by whose orders he was incarcerated at Bayeux. This fortunate circumstance induced
Rufus again to attempt the conquest of Maine; but he
was vigorously opposed by the Earl of Anjou, who
espoused the cause of the captive Hélier. Hains of
Montdoubleau, an ancient friend of the Normans, put
the king into possession of the strong castle of Ballon,
which was immediately garrisoned by the indefatigable Robert de Bellesme, and Rufus advanced against
Mans: but the desolated condition of the country

[1] Ord. Vital. liv. x. vol. iv. p. 29.

preserved the city; for provisions failing in the royal camp, the besiegers were compelled to retire, though not before they had destroyed all the vineyards in the neighbourhood.

The Earl of Anjou then marched out of Mans, and laid siege to Ballon, but without success, and as the king, after having recruited his troops, returned to the scene of action, the earl quickly regained his former quarters. A council was held in the beleagured city, and the inhabitants being satisfied that they were too feeble to resist the united forces of England and Normandy, consented to surrender the place and abandon all the territory which William the Conqueror had subjugated, on condition that Hélier should be set at liberty and the prisoners on both sides be exchanged. The terms were mutually agreed to, and peace was restored.

When Hélier was released from his prison at Bayeux, he went to Rouen, and had an interview with the king. " Powerful monarch," said he, " deign to befriend me with your bounty. For a long time I have enjoyed the rank and title of an Earl, for I possessed a noble earldom by hereditary right; but fortune has changed, and I am now deprived both of my dignity and my estates. Consequently, I pray to be admitted to a command in your armies, with permission to retain my ancient name and title, and I will repay you by faithful services. I abandon all claim to the city of Mans, and the other strong places I have lost, unless you should be pleased, out of your royal munificence, to restore them to me. · I now aspire to no other rank than to be enrolled among your followers, and to enjoy your friendship and esteem."

Rufus, touched with compassion, and flattered by
this unreserved proffer of service, wished to accede to
this demand, but he was dissuaded by Robert, Count
of Meulan. This crafty baron was all-powerful with
the king, presiding at his councils and at his ducal
court of justice, and he feared to introduce within the
palace a man who was his equal, if not his superior, lest
he might meet his rival. He said to William, "All
the people of Maine are wily, deceitful, and unworthy
of confidence; they contrive to obtain by stratagem
what they cannot accomplish by force. What is the
true object of Hélier, your enemy, whom you have
vanquished, and who now insidiously courts your
friendship? It is to pry into your secrets, by being
near your person, that he may know the best opportunity of betraying you."

William was swayed by this advice, and at once
changed his opinion, and though Hélier still pressed
his request, all solicitation was fruitless. Incensed at this
conduct, he thus addressed the king: " I would have
served you honourably as a loyal knight, had you accepted the tender of my services. Henceforward be not
offended or surprised, if I carry what talents I have
elsewhere. I cannot tamely endure the loss of my
inheritance. You refuse me a bare act of justice. Be
not then astonished if I strain every nerve to recover
the dominions of my father." The king, in anger,
replied, " Go, and do the worst you can against
me." [1]

Hélier returned to La Fleche and fortified his five
castles. His virtues and his misfortunes soon drew
around him many devoted friends; and as the people

[1] Ord. Vital. liv. x. vol. iv. p. 41.

of Mans detested the Norman yoke, he was soon in a
condition to renew hostilities.   He assaulted the
Planches Godefroi, a strong fortification in the vicinity
of that city; but the garrison being well provisioned,
offered a stern resistance, and compelled the besiegers
to retire.   In the mean time, the vigilant Robert de
Bellesme had secured the important castle of Ballon,
and he instantly dispatched a messenger to William,
then in England, announcing the revolt of Hélier,
with a strong request that he would immediately embark for his continental dominions.

William was hunting in the New Forest when he
received this intelligence: he instantly rode down to
Southampton, and though the wind was adverse, he
embarked on the first vessel he saw, and, without any
retinue, hurried over to Normandy, which he reached
in safety.   He pressed rapidly forward to encounter
his enemy, passed though Bonneville, refused to
rest a single night on the road, and took no repose ere
he had arrived before Mayet, to which he laid siege.
But his activity was of no avail, the walls were strong
and the garrison resolute, while Hélier, at the head
of a considerable force, was encamped at Château-au-
Loir, prepared to take advantage of any favourable
contingency.   His most experienced officers advised
the king to abandon this hopeless enterprize, and he at
length consented, and disbanded his army.   These
events occurred in July, 1099.

From this time hostilities were suspended till the
summer of 1100, when Rufus prepared for another continental campaign, which was interrupted by his
death.   Ordericus Vitalis relates many marvels and
prodigies which prognosticated the decease of the

king, stating that several monks in different monasteries, in dreams and visions, had received omens of his untimely end. Serlon, Abbot of Gloucester, had written to William, announcing his fears that some evil attended him, but the monarch laughed at the friendly caution of the priest. On the morning of the 2nd of August, 1100, he prepared to hunt in the New Forest, as was his custom after dinner. A smith brought him six new arrows, with which he was highly pleased: he kept four himself, and gave two to his friend Walter Tyrrel, saying, " It is just that an archer whose aim is unerring should have the sharpest-pointed arrows." Tyrrel was a knight of great distinction in France, possessing the lordships of Poix and Pontoise, rich, warlike, and of an illustrious family. He was a great favourite with William, and lived with him on terms of intimate familiarity. Just before they started for the chase, a monk presented himself, and delivered a second letter from the Abbot of Gloucester. William read it, with loud laughter, and showing it to Tyrrel said, " Be sure to do justice to the arrows I have given you." His companion answered, " I will do my best." The king then said aloud to the monk, " I am astonished that Serlon should send me such idle letters, for I thought he was a man of more sense and discretion. In the excess of his simplicity, he narrates the dreams of his monks, as if they were oracles of truth. Does he think that I shall imitate the English, who put off journeys of pleasure or business, because some old woman has had the night-mare ?"

Then dismissing the messenger, he mounted his horse and galloped to the New Forest. His brother,

Prince Henry, the Earl of Breteuil, and other persons of distinction were of the party: they separated on reaching the woods. The king and Walter de Poix remained together: a buck darted from the thicket, when Walter drew his cross-bow; the arrow grazed the back of the animal, glanced off, and stretched the king dead on the ground. Tyrrel immediately rode to the coast, embarked on board a vessel, and sought refuge on his estates in France.

Whether the death of Rufus was accidental or premeditated has been doubted. Ordericus Vitalis, from whom we have borrowed the preceding details relative to Abbot Serlon, and the conversation that passed between the king and Tyrrel before they set out from the palace at Winchester, relates the fact as a pure matter of chance; but Wace, in the Roman de Rou, Eadmer, and John of Salisbury more than hint that Walter committed a deliberate murder. Suger, in his Life of Louis Le Gros, declares positively, that he himself had heard Walter Tyrrel, long after the event, when he had nothing to hope or fear, declare that he did not kill the king, that he was not hunting in the same part of the forest, and that he had not seen him at all after their first entrance into the wood. If this be true, it is difficult to understand why Tyrrel should have absconded; but as he received no reward from Henry, and had no apparent motive to slay William, who was his personal friend, it is most probable that Tyrrel was the cause, though the innocent one, of his death.

The fall of the king was soon spread through the New Forest, and Prince Henry galloped to Winchester, where the royal treasure was deposited, but William de Breteuil reached the palace as soon as he, and refused to surrender the keys. " We should loyally," said De Breteuil, " keep the faith we have pledged to your brother Robert. He is the eldest son of your father; you and I have both done him homage. We ought to be faithful to him in all things, absent as well as present. For many years he has been fighting as a soldier of Christ, who now gives him, without striking a blow, with the crown his father conquered, the duchy which he quitted as a pilgrim for the love of heaven."

This resistance irritated Henry: he drew his sword, and insisted on having the keys of the treasury, avowing his resolution to claim the paternal sceptre. He was warmly supported by his personal friends; and many fearing that a refusal would lead to a civil war, persuaded De Breteuil to submit, when the castle was surrendered to the prince. Thus was Robert a second time deprived of the crown of England by a younger brother. His first exclusion was founded on the will of his father, but the second was in no respect authorised; on the contrary, Henry was expressly deprived of the right of succession by the treaty between Robert and Rufus, concluded in 1090, by which it was stipulated that, in the event of the death of either without issue, the survivor should inherit the crown, or the duchy, as the case might be. To justify the usurpation of Henry it was urged that he was born after the coronation of the Conqueror, and therefore that he was the eldest son of the king, while Robert was only the eldest son of the duke; but this sophism would have had no weight had Henry been absent and Robert present when Rufus was slain.

Not one of the courtiers of William manifested the

least respect to his memory; they left the removal and
interment of his body to servants and the peasantry of
the forest, solely anxious to ingratiate themselves with
his successor.   Ordericus Vitalis says that his mortal
remains were covered with mere rags, and conveyed to
Winchester, as a wild boar killed by the hunter.   According to Mathew Paris, he was placed in a coal-cart.
Some monks and foresters followed this humble funeral, and the corpse was deposited without any ceremony in the old monastery of St. Peter's at Winchester.   As he had made himself obnoxious to the clergy,
by plundering the churches, few bells were tolled at
his burial; and, having died a violent death without receiving absolution, he was considered justly punished
for his crimes.

Three days after the death of Rufus, on the 5th of
August, 1100, Henry was crowned at London by Mau-
rice, Bishop of London, for Anselm, Archbishop of Canterbury, was in exile.   Henry was thirty years of
age, and he commenced his reign with prudence, endeavouring to conciliate all ranks by acts of clemency
and munificence.   He recalled Anselm, and reinstated him in the archiepiscopal throne, and filled up
all the vacant benefices with men of piety and learning.   Having thus secured the powerful support of the
church, he next ingratiated himself with the people,
by marrying Matilda, daughter of Malcolm the Third,
King of Scotland, and Mary of England, sister of
Edgar Atheling, an act of great popularity, as the
English were warmly attached to the Anglo-Saxon
line of princes.   He acted with equal discretion in attaching the most powerful barons in England and
Normandy to his interests, by confirming them in all

their rights and titles, and guaranteeing to the Normans
all their estates in England, while he received among
his counsellors Robert de Meulan, the prime-minister of
Rufus, Richard de Reviers, Roger Bigod, and Hugh
de Chester.

In September, 1100, Duke Robert returned from the
Holy Land, and landed at Mont St. Michel. He
was accompanied by his wife, Sybilla of Conversano,
daughter of Robert, Duke de la Pouille. Free from
his obligation to pay the ten thousand marks of silver
he had borrowed from Rufus, and indignant at the
usurpation of Henry, he meditated his dethronement.
But his attention was first called to the affairs of
Maine.

When Hélier de la Fleche was assured of the death
of William, he entered Mans with his troops, where,
being favourably received by the inhabitants, and
supported by the Earl of Anjou, he laid siege to
the citadel. It was commanded by Haimeri de Mo-
rie and Walter of Rouen, at the head of a strong
garrison. They were well supplied with provisions
and implements of war. The attack and defence
were carried on in a spirit of courteous chivalry peculiar to that age. Hélier was permitted to visit
the castle whenever he pleased, on condition that he
wore a white tunic, as a symbol of peace. One
day they fought, on the next besiegers and besieged
joined in friendly banquets. At the end of some
weeks, the Norman commanders thus addressed Hélier: " We guard the citadel, confided to us by
our prince, which is strong and well victualled: we
neither fear you nor your war-engines, and we shall
resist as long as we please. We can assail you with

stones and arrows, because from these heights we command the town; but through the fear of God, and the
esteem we have for you personally, we spare you:
moreover, we know not for whom we keep the fortress;
wherefore we deem it just and mutually advantageous to conclude a truce, during which we will send
a messenger to our princes, who are masters of England and Normandy. When he has returned, we shall
act according to our instructions." Hélier was delighted with this proposal, and communicated it to the
Earl of Anjou, who having approved of it, a truce
was granted.

The messenger first waited on Duke Robert, and expressed himself in these terms : " Walter and Haimeri, your faithful vassals, guard the citadel of Mans,
in obedience to the orders of the late King William;
they are besieged by the Manceaux and the Angevins,
and demand your succour. They also desire to know
your wishes. If you intend to keep possession of that
strong fortress, advance with a powerful army to repel
the besiegers; if not, advise your officers how they
may escape death." Robert answered, " I am fatigued with my pilgrimage and the hardships I have
undergone ; the duchy of Normandy suffices for me.
Moreover, the English barons invite me to cross the
sea, and they promise to receive me as their sovereign."

When the messenger received this reply, he departed, and crossing the Channel had an interview
with Henry, to whom he made the same representation as he had done to Robert. The King of England
praised the loyalty of the commanders of the citadel,
but declined to interfere, saying, that the reduction of

Mans was the duty of his brother, and that he was sufficiently occupied with his own affairs. He then dismissed the envoy with valuable presents.

When the messenger reported to Walter and Haimeri the answers of the two princes, they invited Hélier to array himself in his white tunic, and enter the castle. " You may now," they said, " rejoice with good reason, for at length we are in the position we have so long desired. If you have a good round sum of money in your treasury, you may make a good bargain with us." Hélier having asked what he was to understand by this language, they replied, " The powerful William, Conqueror of England, built this fortress, which his son confided to us ; but, alas ! he is dead. Consequently we cede it to you, and henceforward you will be Count of the Manceaux. If we wished to resist you longer, we should not be alarmed by your valour, nor deprived of courage. We have arms and provisions, but we have no lawful sovereign, to whom we can consecrate our lives. Therefore, brave warrior, knowing your merit, we elect you, and after having surrendered the place, we will declare you Earl of Maine." This extraordinary contract was faithfully executed, the garrison marched out with all the honours of war, and Hélier was put into possession of this fine province by the two commanders, and enjoyed his acquisition in peace for ten years.[1]

At this time the barons of England and Normandy were equally discontented ; the former urged Henry to seize on the duchy, the latter instigated Robert to demand the crown. Robert collected his fleet and army,

[1] Ord. Vital. li . x. vol. iv. p. 81.

and crossed the Channel: he landed safely at Portsmouth at the close of the autumn of 1101. He was there joined by several barons, among others by Robert de Bellesme and William de Warenne, Earl of Surrey, and marched boldly forward to encounter his brother, whose forces were already in the field. Henry sent an ambassador to demand of Robert why he had the audacity to enter England in hostile array. The duke replied, " I have come to claim what is due to me by the right of primogeniture."

In a few days the two armies were in sight of each other : there were relatives and friends in the opposing camps, while the war itself was of a fratricidal character. A moral feeling made the combatants anxious to avoid an encounter, and after some negociation it was arranged that Robert and Henry should meet together in the open plain, and endeavour to arrange their differences amicably. The brothers approached each other, embraced, and were reconciled ; and it was agreed between them, first, that Robert should renounce in favour of Henry all pretensions to the crown of England ; secondly, that Henry, on account of his royal dignity, should be released from his oath of homage to Robert ; thirdly, that Henry should pay to his brother an annual sum of three thousand pounds sterling, and abandon the Cotentin, and all his possessions in Normandy, except Domfront, which town he was bound by his oath never to alienate out of his own hand. They concluded a treaty of alliance, offensive and defensive, and bound themselves to punish any of their respective barons who disputed either the royal or ducal authority.

Robert remained two months in England, after

which he returned to Normandy. The king, now
strengthened on his throne, wreaked his vengeance
on those barons who had encouraged the pretensions of
his brother; some he fined in heavy sums, others he
banished, after having deprived them of their estates.
Among the latter was William de Warenne, Earl of
Surrey, whose annual revenue from that county Ordericus Vitalis fixes at one thousand pounds weight in
silver. This nobleman crossed the Channel and laid
his griefs before Robert, who warmly espoused his
cause, and passed over into England to intercede with
his brother for the restoration of De Warenne's estates.
Henry was indignant at this interference, and would
have arrested his brother, had he not been dissuaded
by Robert de Meulan, who painted in lively colours the
infamy and disloyalty of such a violent proceeding.
The king, thus constrained to dissemble his real feelings, affected to receive his brother with friendship,
and so craftily did he work on his facile and generous
disposition, that Robert released him from the annual
tribute of three thousand pounds sterling, transferring
it as a gift to Queen Matilda. This was the price of
their reconciliation, and of the pardon of William de
Warenne, who was restored to his earldom, and reinstated in the county of Surrey.

On his return to Normandy, Robert became an object of contempt to his subjects, who despised him for
his weak concessions to Henry; and the barons, disdaining his authority, not only warred against each
other, but ravaged with impunity the ducal domains.
Anarchy and confusion prevailed, the laws were a dead
letter, agriculture was neglected, commerce abandoned,
and the whole country subjected to the sword. Nor

was England tranquillized, for Robert de Bellesme raised his standard against the king, and when cited to appear before the royal court to answer forty-five charges of sedition and treason, he only answered by a bold and uncompromising defiance. This powerful and skilful baron, one of the most remarkable military characters of that warlike age, was only reduced into submission after four years' resistance, when all his English estates were confiscated, and sentence of perpetual banishment was pronounced against him. He repaired to Normandy breathing vengeance against the king.

While Henry was engaged in quelling the insurrections raised by Robert de Bellesme in England, he had frequently insisted that Robert should seize the Norman estates held by that refractory baron, in compliance with the offensive and defensive treaty signed by the two brothers. The duke, however, would never comply with this demand, and Henry resolved, after the expulsion of De Bellesme, to cross the Channel and strip him of his lands by force. The king still had a footing in Normandy by the retention of Domfront, and his first measure was to erect a strong castle at Tinchebrai, in which he could deposit his military stores, for though his ostensible pretext for invading Normandy was to punish Robert de Bellesme, his real motive was to dispossess Robert of the duchy.

Henry had many partizans in the province, and was powerfully supported by the clergy, whose wealth was daily plundered by the lawless barons, whom the feebleness of Robert could not coerce. Serlon, Bishop of Seez, who had been driven out of his diocese by De Bellesme, distinguished himself by the violence with which he preached a sort of crusade, not only against that earl, but against the duke himself. This prelate preached a sermon at Carentan, before Henry, on the Saturday before Easter, 1105, and as the church was full of various property deposited therein by the peasants for safe custody, the bishop drew all the materials of his discourse from that fact, showing that the duchy was one universal scene of rapine, and praying that God would send a protector for the clergy, the widow, and the poor.

The finances of the duke were reduced to the lowest ebb; he had not the means of paying his troops, and to supply his deficiencies excessive taxes were raised, in the towns, on the trading classes. This exaction increased his unpopularity, while it strengthened the party of his brother, for any change was deemed preferable to the existing state of things. The politic Henry, having observed the tone of public opinion, saw that the moment had arrived when he could successfully strike a decisive blow, and accomplish the ends both of his vengeance and ambition. He returned to England to make preparations for conducting the war on an extended scale, and in the autumn of 1106, landed in Normandy at the head of a powerful army.

William, Count of Mortain, nephew to Robert de Bellesme, was then besieging Tinchebrai, and the latter, unequal to cope with the royal forces single-handed, demanded the aid of Duke Robert, as his sovereign to whom he owed homage, and who was therefore bound to protect his vassal. Robert marched to his assistance, and sent a messenger to Henry, desiring him to quit Normandy, or that he would expel him by force. The king defied his brother to battle. He was supported by Hélier, Earl of Maine, William,

Count of Evreux, Robert, Count of Meulan, William
de Warenne, and many other barons of inferior note.
The principal followers of the duke were the Count of
Mortain, Robert de Bellesme, Robert d'Estouteville,
and William de Ferriéres.   The royal army was superior in cavalry ; but the Normans were more numerous
in infantry.   When the hostile forces were in sight of
each other, Henry sent the following message to his
brother :  " I have not come hither from any desire of
worldly wealth, nor have I resolved on despoiling you
of your duchy ; but, invoked by the tears and the
complaints of the poor, I desire to succour the church
of God, which, like a vessel without a pilot, runs great
danger in the midst of a stormy sea.   As to you, you
stand on this earth as a barren tree, nor do you offer
to your Creator any equitable sacrifice.   You have, it
is true, the name of duke, but you are an object of
public ridicule to your subjects, nor dare you resent
the indignities put upon you.   Thus the cruel children of iniquity, under colour of your name, oppress a
Christian nation ; many parishes in Normandy have
been wholly depopulated.   When I contemplate these
calamities, I feel myself glowing with a zeal for God,
and I cheerfully hazard my life for the safety of my
brethren, for a people whom I love, for my native land.
Take these things into your consideration, and I beseech you to profit by my advice, and you will see
that I am not influenced by ambition, but by good
motives.   Give up to me all your strong places, all
civil and criminal jurisdiction throughout Normandy,
and half of the duchy ; and content yourself with the
remainder, free from the cares and duties of government ; I will pay you the value of your share every

I 5

year in advance. Then you may securely indulge in
banquets and gaming. For my part, to preserve
peace and order, I will take on my own shoulders all
the fearful weight of administration, and I will faithfully discharge my engagements to you, while you
take your pleasure; besides, with the aid of God, I
will curb the rebellious, and protèct the subjects against
oppression." [1]

The duke convened his counsellors, and read them
the royal message: all loudly expressed their indignation at this mixture of craft and hyprocrisy, and determined to try the fate of arms, rather than to submit
to such humiliating terms. Henry divided his forces
into three divisions; the first was commanded by
Ranulf of Bayeux; the second, by Robert, Count of
Meulan, and the third by William de Warenne.
These consisted of cavalry. The king placed himself
at the head of the English and Norman infantry;
while Hélier, Earl of Maine, with the Manceaux and
Breton auxiliaries, formed a corps of reserve.

In the ducal army the Count of Mortain commanded
the first division, and Robert de Bellesme, the second.
The king's troops charged with an impetuosity that
deranged their ranks, which the duke observing, he
fell upon them with fury, and drove them back in all
directions. Robert made himself sure of victory, but
Henry advanced with his infantry, and thus gave time
to his soldiers to re-form and rally. Prodigies of valour were performed on both sides, and Robert displayed all the talents of a general,—all the courage of a
warrior, nor was Henry less active or intrepid. For
some hours success was doubtful, when the fate of the

1 Ord. Vital. vol. iv. p. 198.

day was decided by Hélier, Count of Maine, who advanced with his troopers at a sharp trot, charged the Normans on the flank, and put the division under the Earl of Mortain, where the duke fought in person, to complete route. At this critical juncture Robert de Bellesme belied his martial reputation; he was seized with a panic and fled. The duke, the Earl of Mortain, Robert D'Estouteville, William de Ferriéres, and four hundred gentlemen of distinction were made prisoners. The battle of Tinchebrai was fought on the eve of Michaelmas day, 1106, and the victory obtained by Henry put him in full possession of Normandy, thus realizing the prophecy of the Conqueror, on his death-bed.

# HENRY THE FIRST,

### KING OF ENGLAND, AND NINTH DUKE OF NORMANDY.

———

THE battle of Tinchebrai was followed by the submission of all the adherents of Robert; and the towns and castles, which had resisted Henry, now opened their gates to his lieutenants. Through the intervention of Hélier, Earl of Maine, Robert de Bellesme obtained his pardon: he was compelled to surrender the bishopric of Seez and the city of Argentan, but confirmed in the title of Viscount of Falaise, and all the Norman dignities enjoyed by his father, Roger de Montgommeri. The Earl of Mortain, though cousin-german of the king and the duke, was not only stripped of all his estates, which were given to Stephen of Blois, but he was subjected to a close and cruel captivity, and deprived of his eye-sight, a fact not known till after the death of Henry.[1]

But the foulest stain on the memory of the English monarch was his atrocious treatment of his unfortunate brother. All the claims of fraternal affection were violated; the common rights of humanity were foully outraged, nor did a sense of gratitude for past

[1] Hist. de Geoffroi de Plantagenet, par Jean de Marmoutier, l. i. p. 81.

favours soothe the ferocity of this merciless tyrant.
Henry forgot the generous conduct of Robert at the
siege of Mont St. Michel, when Rufus would have
starved him and his garrison; nor did he choose to
remember the liberal transfer to his queen of the annual tribute, he had engaged to pay to the Duke of
Normandy. Robert was confined in the castle of Car-
diff, in Wales. He at first enjoyed some degree of
liberty, being allowed to walk in the neighbouring
forest with guards; but having one day seized a horse,
and attempted to escape, he was conducted back to his
dungeon, and by the order of the brutal Henry, his
eyes were extinguished. He endured this miserable
captivity for a period of twenty-seven years, with a
dignity and fortitude worthy of a better fate. One
day some new clothes were brought to him, which, by
touch, he discovered were torn: he was told that
Henry had tried to wear them, but, being too small, a
rent had been made in drawing them on. He threw
them from him with anger, exclaiming, "Does my
brother, my traitor, the base clerk who has deprived
me of my inheritance and my sight, think me so humble and degraded,—me, who have acquired so much
honour and renown in Palestine,—as to accept his
cast-off garments as an alms, as though I were his
lacquey "[1]

Robert had been affianced, in the life of his father,
to Margaret, daughter of the Earl of Maine, but she
died before attaining to nubile age. He had three
illegitimate children by the daughter of a priest in the
French Vexin. The eldest was killed at the chase, the

[1] "En frater, meus, immo proditor meus, et supplantator, et ignavus clericus,
qui me incarceravit, et incarceratum excœcavit."—*Math. Paris*, p. 50.

second died in the Holy Land, and the third was married to Hélier of Saint-Saëns. By his wife Sybilla he had one son, who neither inherited the dignity nor the misfortune of his father, but whose career was marked by alternate hope and disappointment.

There is an anecdote related of the death of Sybilla which has a touching interest, though it is not mentioned by any cotemporary historian. Robert had been struck by a poisoned arrow, and the physicians declared his death inevitable, unless the venom was sucked out of the wound. "Let me die, then," said the duke: "I will never be so cruelly unjust as to owe my existence to the loss of another's life." Sybilla, when her husband was asleep, sucked the wound, and fell a victim to her conjugal tenderness.[1]

Henry was now undisputed master of England and Normandy, nor had he any rival to contest his pretensions, for William Cliton, son of the unfortunate Robert, was yet a child; but his uncle, looking forward to future events, feared that when the boy became a man he might claim his paternal inheritance, and avenge the indignities of his father. It became, therefore, the royal policy to secure the person of the young prince, who had been confided to the custody of Hélier of Saint Saëns, the husband of his illegitimate sister. Robert de Beauchamp, Viscount of Arques, was accordingly empowered to demand the child from his guardian, and he presented himself before the castle of Saint Saëns with an armed force: his appearance alarmed the inhabitants, who were the more embarrassed on account of the temporary absence of Hélier. However, the design was suspected, and the boy

[1] Essais sur Paris, par Sainte Foix, tome iii. p. 19.

removed in the night to a place of safety. The viscount, enraged at the escape of his prize, seized the castle in the name of the king, which was afterwards conferred on William de Warrenne, Earl of Surrey, and this dispossession of Hélier is sufficient presumptive proof that the king would not have treated his nephew more humanely than his brother.

William Cliton was conducted to Hélier, by whom he was diligently and faithfully protected, and trained in every accomplishment suited to his birth. Hélier easily won over Robert de Bellesme to his party, and they both intended, when the boy was old enough, to take the field, and make a vigorous effort to raise him to the dukedom. His active and devoted guardian introduced him at the court of France; he then, in succession, took him to Brittany, Burgundy, and Poitou, everywhere proclaiming the tyranny of Henry, the wrongs of Robert, and the legitimate claims of his pupil. He so powerfully interested the Count of Anjou in favour of his youthful charge, that that sovereign promised him his daughter in marriage, with the province of Maine for her dowry.

The King of England soon received intelligence of these meditated arrangements, and the approaching elevation of his nephew; he strained every nerve to prevent the completion of this alliance. He first menaced the Count of Anjou with hostilities; but this threat was disregarded, as the count knew that he would be supported by all the neighbouring princes, who were jealous of the vast power that Henry had concentrated in his own hands. Thus baffled, he had recourse to bribes, by which he succeeded; but the count, not daring thus disloyally to break his word without some

ostensible pretext, urged the ties of relationship as a
bar to the marriage. This plea was not without foundation. Richard, son of Gonnor, was father of Duke
Robert the First, who was father of the Conqueror, and his son Robert was father of William Cliton. On the other side, Robert, Archbishop
of Rouen, and brother of Duke Richard, had a son
Richard, who was Count of Evreux ; this Richard was
father of Agnes, wife of Simon de Montfort, and
mother of Bertrade, who was the mother of Fulk,
Count of Anjou.[1] This degree of propinquity put an
end to the whole negociation, and William Cliton,
after vainly demanding aid in various quarters, repaired to Flanders, where the count, called Baldwin of
the Axe, received him with kindness and promised
him protection.

Having succeeded in dissolving this proposed alliance, Henry was gratified by an embassy from the
Emperor of Germany, demanding his daughter Matilda in marriage, though then only six years of age.
To this union the king gave his consent, and the
young princess was confided to Burchard, Archbishop
of Cambray, under whose care she was to receive her
education, till the marriage was solemnized.

Normandy now enjoyed an interval of repose for
three years, but at the commencement of 1112 peace
was again disturbed by Fulk, Count of Anjou. He
had married the daughter of Hélier, Count of Maine,
and on the death of his father-in-law, claimed the
province in right of his wife, refusing any fealty or
homage to the Duke of Normandy. This was the
signal of another war, in which Fulk was encouraged by

[1] Orderic. Vital. t. iv. p. 257.

his uncle, Amauri de Montfort and Robert de Bellesme, both of whom detested Henry. But these hostilities were unattended by any decisive results; Henry strengthened his frontiers by building new fortresses, and the Angevins made no impression on his duchy. The king, however, cited Robert de Bellesme to appear before him at Bonneville-sur-Touques, and this audacious rebel, though a vassal of Normandy, had the effrontery to present himself in the character of ambassador from the King of France: when called upon to account for his numerous delinquencies, he declined the jurisdiction of his sovereign, and pleaded his privilege as the envoy of a foreign prince. He was condemned for contumacy, on the 4th of November, 1112, and imprisoned at Cherbourg, where he died.

This great fomenter of conspiracy and revolt being now secured, Fulk and his friends were disposed to make peace with Henry, and negociators soon brought both parties to an amicable understanding. The king and the Count of Anjou had an interview at the Pierre Percée, probably the Pont Percé, a league distant from Alençon, when it was agreed that Fulk should do homage to Henry for Maine, and that his daughter should marry William Adelin, son of the King of England.[1]

Philip the First, King of France, died on the 29th of July, 1108. He was a mere tool in the hands of his second wife Bertrade de Montfort, who meditated the death of Louis, son by his former marriage with Bertha. This young prince visited England in 1103, and Bertrade, knowing how Henry had treated his brother Robert, proposed to him the assassination of Louis, in

[1] Orderic. Vital. t. iv. p. 266.

order that the sons she had had by Philip might succeed to the throne. But the King of England had no
motive to violate the laws of hospitality, or disgrace
his memory by an act from which he could not derive
any personal advantage. The prince was treated by
him with kindness and honour. On his return to
France, however, the queen resolved to accomplish
herself what she had vainly asked of Henry: Louis
was poisoned, and though the effects were not fatal,
the extreme paleness of his countenance left visible
proof of the injury he had sustained. The physicians
of the court pronounced his disease incurable, but he
was saved by a foreign charlatan. At the earnest
prayer of his father he pardoned Bertrade, and succeeded to the crown of France in 1108.

The residence of Louis at the court of England, and
the gratitude he expressed to Henry for not having
conspired against his life, made both the Normans and
English anticipate long years of harmony and friendship between the two sovereigns. But these hopes
were disappointed. Louis, in spite of his extreme
bulk of body, on account of which he was named Le
Gros, had all the fire and activity of a warlike prince;
while the ambition of Henry could not brook a superior. The former considered the latter as his vassal,
because he owed him homage for Normandy; while
the King of England spurned at the dependence and
inferiority which such a claim entailed. What more
was wanting to embroil them in hostilities?

The first rupture between the two monarchs took
place in 1110, Louis having preferred claims to Maine
and Brittany. He offered to decide his quarrel by a
duel of three, or of two, on each side, but Henry had

the good sense to reject these offers, being then secure
in the castle of Gisors, a position which enabled him at
one and the same time to protect Normandy and invade France. This campaign was protracted for two
years, during which no decisive battle was fought, and
Louis at length obtained peace by abandoning all his
pretensions to Maine and Brittany.

In 1118 Henry had again to take the field against a
formidable confederacy. On the 18th of April of that
year, William, Count of Evreux died, and his nephew,
Amauri de Montfort, claimed the succession. By the
advice of Audin, Bishop of Evreux, the king refused
this demand, on which Amauri rose up in arms, being
supported by Hugh de Gournay, Eustace de Breteuil,
Richard de L'Aigle, and other barons, who resolved
to reinstate William Cliton in his paternal rights. They
were joined by Baldwin, the young Earl of Flanders, who
brought forward all his troops against Henry. The
king was advised of this plot in time to seize Hugh de
Gournay and the Count of Eu at Rouen, both of whom
he put into irons. Baldwin, at the head of his Flemings, penetrated as far as Arques, and burnt the small
town of Falou in sight of his majesty, who, however,
contented himself with fortifying Bures, which he
garrisoned with English and Bretons, distrusting the
Norman soldiery, who had shown strong symptoms of
their attachment to the cause of William Cliton.
Baldwin soon presented himself before Bures, and
defied the garrison to battle. They sallied out, and a
valiant knight, named Hugh de Boterel, severely
wounded the Count of Flanders, who was compelled to
suspend hostilities and retire to Aumale ; his wound was
badly dressed, and after languishing from September to

June he died. He was succeeded by his cousin, Charles D'Ancre, who made peace with the King of England.

The Norman barons, however, refused to lay down their arms, and Amauri de Montfort even refused to accept Evreux, when offered to him by the king as the price of his submission. They persuaded Louis le Gros to aid them with his troops, and the hostile armies came in sight of each other at Brenneville, a vast plain situate between Andely St. Clair, and the castle of Noyon. In this battle Henry nearly lost his life, having been fiercely attacked by William Crespin, who had fought against him at Tinchebrai, and who, being a personal friend of Duke Robert, burned with a desire to avenge himself on his persecutor. He pierced the line of troops, and struck the king so violent a blow with his sabre on the head, that nothing but the firm temper of his helmet could have saved him from instant death. This valiant knight, being alone in the midst of his enemies, was compelled to surrender himself prisoner, and Henry, roused to fury by this encounter, charged his enemies so impetuously that they were completely routed.

The King of France, though defeated, displayed all the courage of a soldier and all the skill of an able general. When retiring from the field, his bridle-rein was seized by an English knight, who, exulting in his prize, exclaimed, "The king is taken!" Louis raised his sword and laid his assailant dead at his feet, saying, "Know you not the king is never taken, not even at the game of chess." Having thus escaped, he sought shelter in the woods of Andely; but as the paths were unknown to him, he roamed about for many hours, fearful of being surprised by the enemy: he was at

length met by a forester, who conducted him in safety
to the castle of Andely.  Henry did not push the advantage he might have derived from the battle of
Brenneville, but returned to England ; and though the
war was suspended on both sides by mutual consent,
yet petty skirmishes were still continued, each baron
pillaging his neighbour when opportunity offered.

In 1119, the marriage of William Adelin, son of the
King of England, with Sybilla, daughter of Fulk,
Count of Anjou, was solemnized at Lisieux in Normandy, on which occasion, at the earnest request of
Fulk, William Talvas, son of Robert de Bellesme, was
taken into the royal favour, and he received all the
estates that his father had held in Normandy.  Robert
de Saint Ceneri was also pardoned, and put into possession of Montreuil and Echafour.  This marriage
secured the king against any attacks from Maine and
Anjou, and the politic clemency he manifested to the
heir of the powerful family of De Bellesme, who were
beloved by the soldiery, though detested by the monks
and the peasants, shielded him against internal rebellion.

Shortly after this event, Pope Calixtus the Second
arrived at Rouen, and Louis and Henry both appeared
before him to state their respective grievances, and submit their pretensions and claims to his arbitrament.
The meeting was held in the metropolitan church of
the Norman capital on the 19th of October, 1119, in
the presence of numerous bishops of France and Normandy, and the chief nobility of each country.  Ordericus Vitalis has narrated all these proceedings with
exact minuteness of detail, nor does it seem possible to
convey a better idea of the spirit of these times, or to

give a clearer view of the sentiments of Louis and
Henry, than by translating the speeches attributed by
that old and most accurate historian to the rival princes.
The king of France first addressed the assembly.

"I come," said he, "holy father, to this solemn and
sacred meeting, with my barons, humbly to crave your
advice : deign to listen to me.   The King of England,
who for a long period was my ally, has caused me and
my subjects very many vexations, and inflicted on us
severe injuries.   He has violently invaded Normandy,
which is a fief of my crown ; and against all right and
justice he has treated with detestable barbarity Robert,
Duke of the Normans.   That prince, who is not only
my vassal, but who is also brother to Henry, and his
lawful sovereign, has endured a variety of tortures :  he
is a prisoner;  his eyes have been blinded, and to this
hour he is in a dungeon.   Henry has also robbed of his
inheritance the son of Robert, William Cliton, who
now presents himself with me before your holiness.
Through bishops, earls, and other persons of rank and
note I have demanded the release of the prisoner; but
I have never been able to obtain any satisfaction from
Henry on that head.   In his own court he arrested
Robert de Bellesme, my ambassador, loaded him with
chains, and confined him in prison.   Theobald, Count
of Blois, also my vassal, has been instigated by his
uncle Henry to revolt against me.   Proud of his
wealth and power, he has taken up arms against me,
and faithless to his obligations, waged an atrocious
war, and disturbed my dominions.   He now holds in
his dungeons the good and loyal William, Count of
Nevers, whom your holiness knows perfectly well,
having captured him when returning from an expedi-

tion against an excommunicated thief, who occupied
a castle and cavern full of brigands, a residence fitted
for the devil. Pious prelates had justly denounced
the enormities of Thomas de Marle, who spread sedition throughout the province; wherefore they besought me to besiege this public enemy of travellers
and of all honest people: the loyal barons of France
flocked to my standard to punish these crimes. It was
on his peaceable return from this expedition, and
under my protection, that the knight of whom I speak
was made prisoner, and he is still confined by Count
Theobald, though his liberation has been demanded
even with prayers, and all the lands of Theobald have
been cursed with anathema by the bishops for his refusal."

The King of England being called on to reply to
these charges, thus made answer to the King of France:
"Reverend father, I have promised to obey you in all
things reasonable, and I repeat that promise. Deign
to listen to my defence, and examine how I have com-
ported myself. I did not despoil my brother of the
duchy of Normandy; I claimed, with arms in my
hand, the inheritance of my father, which neither my
brother nor my nephew possessed in fact, for the
duchy was devastated by brigandage and sacrilege.
No respect was paid to the priests or other servants of
God; the manners of the Gentiles prevailed almost
throughout the whole of Normandy. The monasteries,
founded by our ancestors for the salvation of souls,
were destroyed, and the monks dispersed to perish for
want of food. The churches were plundered, many
were burned, and those who sought refuge in them
were dragged from the sanctuary with profane vio-

lence. The inhabitants murdered each other, and the
whole country was a scene of outrage. These misfortunes pressed on Normandy for seven years, and there
was no liberty, no security. The repeated prayers of
the ministers of God reached me, they implored my
assistance for the love of heaven, and prayed that I
would no longer permit a host of brigands to oppress
the innocent. Thus urgently invited, I crossed over
to Normandy; I was well received by the illustrious
Counts, William of Evreux and Robert de Meulan, as
well as other loyal barons and knights; I was sorely
distressed at seeing the desolation of the lands of my
ancestors, but I could only assist the unfortunate by
force of arms. My brother openly protected the
authors and fomenters of the public disturbances, and
even followed the counsels of the very men who rendered him odious to, and despised by, his subjects.
Thus Gunhier d'Aunai, Roger de Laci, Robert de
Bellesme, and other brigands, became the scourges of
Normandy, and, acting in the name of a mere phan-
tom of a prince, ruled imperiously over the prelates,
the clergy, and the people. Even those whom I had
banished from England, on account of their criminal
excesses, my brother selected as his intimate friends
and confidential advisers, and entrusted to them all the
important offices of state. In all directions there were
committed murders, fires, and other atrocities of a
nature and to an extent incredible to all who had not
witnessed them. I frequently requested my brother
to follow my advice, and promised to support him with
all my power; but he despised me, and aided my
enemies against me. Under such circumstances, I
could not refuse to protect the church, our holy mother,

and I diligently endeavoured to discharge the duty
which God had so evidently confided to my hands.
Thus, valiantly fighting with fire and sword, I captured Bayeux from Gunhier, and Caen from Enguerrand.   In fighting against these tyrants, I conquered
several other places which formed part of the dominions of my father.   My brother had bestowed them
on perjured parasites, and while they were rich, he
was so impoverished that he could not pay the wages
of his domestic servants.   Ultimately I was compelled
to besiege Tinchebrai, a real den of demons, where
William, Count of Mortain, led my brother against
me with a strong army: in the name of the LORD and
in defence of my native land I gave him battle.   There,
with the aid of God, who knows the purity of my
motives, I vanquished my enemies;   I made prisoners
two counts, my brother, and my cousin, and many
nobles who had betrayed me;  and, up to this hour, I
have vigilantly guarded them in prison, lest they
should excite fresh disturbances against me or the
state.   Thus I recovered the inheritance of my father,
and I devoted myself to maintain the laws in obedience
to the will of God, and for the repose of my people.   I
did not load my brother with chains as a captive
enemy ;  I placed him in a royal castle, as a noble pilgrim, fatigued and worn out by long misfortunes, and
supplied him abundantly with every delicacy, every
amusement, and all that could make life agreeable.   I
entrusted his son, then five years of age, to Hélier,
son-in-law to my brother, desiring to treat him as a
child of my own, that he might be trained in wisdom,
courage, and prudence.   But Hélier, at the instigation of his accomplices, absconded with my nephew,

K

abandoning the castle of Saint Saëns, which he possessed, and fled to strange countries; after which he
did all in his power to annoy me by numerous attacks
and conspiracies. Nevertheless, being opposed by
God, he never succeeded in his projects. He armed
against me the Burgundians, the French, and other
people; but, unless I am deceived, he did more mis-
chief to them than to me. I have often demanded that
my nephew should be restored to my protection; I
have begged him in a spirit of friendship, through
several envoys, to come to my court, and share the
royal riches with my son. I offered him three counties in England, as an independent principality; I
beseeched him to approach me that he might have his
education perfected by my counsellors, that he might
learn how to comport himself with prudence and
sagacity before rich and poor, and how to exercise
sovereign justice and maintain military discipline.
All these offers he has rejected, preferring the exile of
a beggar among brigands to the enjoyments of my
palaces. As witnesses of the numerous calamities I
have stated, I appeal to the uncultivated fields, houses
burned, villages devastated, churches demolished, and
to a whole people groaning under the butchery of their
friends and the pillage of their property. I now pray
your Holiness to examine and weigh these things
calmly, and give a sentence just and equitable both to
those who command and to those who obey."

When the king ceased to speak, the pope lavished
the highest praise on his conduct, and then addressed
him in the following terms. " You have given me
a sufficient explanation of all that concerns Duke Robert and his son; let me therefore speak to you on
other subjects. The king of the French complains

that you have unjustly broken the treaties you concluded with him, and that you have done him, and
his people, much injury.  Henry answered : " Louis
himself first violated our treaty and our friendship.
He has on repeated occasions aided my enemies; he
has induced my vassals to revolt.  Nevertheless, if he
will compensate me for the evils I have suffered at his
hands, and pledge himself to keep good faith with me
for the future, I am ready to obey in all particulars
whatever you may please to direct."

The pope highly pleased at this dutiful submission to
him, as umpire of these disputes, then observed :
" King Louis complains of the injury he has received
from Count Theobald, your nephew, who made the
Count of Nevers prisoner on his return from the siege
which the king himself, with the French prelates, undertook against Thomas de Marle, to prevent that
lawless man from continuing to oppress the innocent."
Henry replied : " I will not neglect any opportunity
of following your paternal advice, in order to secure
peace and tranquillity, and, for the public good, I
will make my nephew, Theobald, submit to your
orders, and you will find him to be a strict observer of
justice.  I also now advise my other nephew, William
Cliton, to take advantage of this peace; and I again
offer him, through the mediation of your holiness, the
same favours as I have heretofore proffered, because I
desire that you may be satisfied in all respects, and
because I am anxious to procure a general and lasting
state of tranquillity for my people, and I am as much
interested in the welfare of my nephew, as in that of
my son." [1]

[1] Ord. Vital. vol iv. liv. xii. p. 322, et seq.

The result of these explanations was peace between
France and England, and the following terms were
mutually accepted :—First, that all the strong places
on either side, captured during the war, should be
surrendered. Secondly, that all prisoners should be
liberated without ransom. Thirdly, that all things
should remain as they were before the breaking out of
hostilities. Fourthly, that the King of France should
abandon the son of Duke Robert. Fifthly, that Normandy should remain in the possession of Henry.
Sixthly, that the two kings, as neighbours and allies,
should live in friendship and harmony.

It is impossible to peruse the speech addressed by
Henry to the pope, without being shocked at the moral baseness of his character. Mendacity and hypocrisy breathe in every line. Though he had reduced
his brother to the most deplorable condition, having
deprived him of his personal liberty and his eye-sight,
he audaciously affirmed that he had treated him with
affection and honour. The hollow and insidious offers
of friendship to his nephew were the mere flimsy cover
of the blackest intentions ; for who can suppose that
he would have shown less mercy to the son than to the
father ? His charge against Hélier of Saint Saëns was
without a shadow of foundation ; that faithful and devoted guardian of the young prince having abandoned
his property, rather than compromise the safety of
William Cliton. The only truth that Henry uttered
was the bad administration of Duke Robert, but that
neither justified his usurpation of the duchy, the tortures inflicted on his brother, or the expulsion of his
nephew from his paternal inheritance. How sincere
his compassion was for the wrongs done to the church,
may be judged by his putting out the eyes of Robert

and the Earl of Mortain, acts of barbarity which nullify all his hypocritical appeals to Heaven.

When the treaty of peace was signed, Henry invested his son William with the duchy of Normandy; the latter did homage for the province to the king of France, and the Norman barons took the oaths of fealty to the young prince, who was then eighteen years of age.

Henry now thought himself at the pinnacle of human grandeur and human prosperity, and made preparations for his return to England, with his two sons, William and Richard, and his principal barons. All repaired to Barfleur, the port from which they were to sail, but the house of rejoicing was soon to be converted into a house of mourning. The injuries of Duke Robert were about to be severely and sternly avenged.

On the morning of the 25th of December, 1120, a pilot named Thomas Airard demanded an interview of the king, and offering for his acceptance a mark of gold, thus addressed him :—" Stephen, son of Airard, was my father, and during his life he served your father on the sea. It was he who carried Duke William over to England, when he went to fight Harold. To his death his services were accepted, and the Conqueror so enriched him with presents, that he lived honourably among his countrymen. I request the same favours of your majesty : I have ready for the royal service a vessel perfectly equipped; it is called the "Blanche Nef."[1] The king made him this answer, " I grant your request; but having selected a vessel in which I shall cross the channel, I shall not change

[1] Candida Navis, the white ship. Ord. Vital. iv. tom. p. 353.

it; but I will entrust to you my sons, William and Richard, whom I love as myself, and with them you will take over the chief nobles of my realms."

The pilot was delighted with this honourable appointment, and having reported his good fortune to his crew, they all waited on the royal princes, and demanded wine that they might make merry. They received three measures of sixty gallons each, and became intoxicated. About three hundred persons embarked on the Blanche-Nef. There were fifty rowers. Some of the passengers, apprehending danger from the drunken state of the sailors, returned on shore, among whom Ordericus Vitalis mentions two monks of Tyron, Stephen, count of Mortain, William de Roumare, the chamberlain Rabel, and Edward of Salisbury. The royal treasures were placed on board this vessel. At the given signal, the rowers vigorously pulled their oars, anxious to overtake the ship in which the king had sailed, but Thomas Airard, stupified with liquor, ran the Blanche Nef on a tide rock, which was always covered with the flood and left dry with the ebb. Two planks started from the violence of the shock, and the vessel instantly sunk in deep water. Two men only clung to the main-boom, on which they floated during the night, expecting aid when the morning dawned. One of them was a butcher of Rouen, named Berold, the other a young nobleman, named Goisfred, son of Gislebert de L'Aigle.

When this catastrophe happened, the moon shone brightly, and the sea was smooth. The pilot Airard soon recovered his senses, and swimming towards the two survivors, called out, " What has become of the

king's son." They answered, that he had perished
with all his companions. Airard then said, " I will live
no longer," and plunged into the deep.  The night
was severely cold; the young Goisfred, who was
thinly clad, felt his limbs benumbed ; he could no longer hold on the floating spar, and recommending his
companion to God, he sunk to rise no more.  Berold
owed his life to his poverty, being clothed in a coarse
dress of sheep's-skin, which shielded him from the in-
clemency of the weather; on the following morning
he was picked up by three fishermen.  From his narrative, these details of the wreck were made known,
and preserved by Ordericus Vitalis, who says that Berold survived this fatal event twenty years.

Other historians relate that when the Blanche-Nef
was sinking, the king's son, William Adelin, got into
the boat, and reached the shore in safety.  As soon as
he landed, he enquired after his brother and sisters,
as well as his personal friends.  From the margin
of the sea he saw his natural sister, the Countess of
Perche, buffeting with the waves, and heard her
shrieks for assistance.  William tenderly loved this
young princess, and hesitated not an instant to launch
the boat, and row to her aid.  The countess was safely
placed in this frail embarkation, but so many others
crowded into it, that it sunk under the excess of
weight.  This addition to the account of Ordericus has a touching interest, but it cannot be
depended on as an historical fact, since none of the
parties alluded to escaped, and the only survivor is
not only silent on these details, but states expressly
that he saw the prince perish when the vessel sunk.

It has been erroneously stated, by some authors,

that the Blanche-Nef was wrecked on the Casket
Rocks, off the island of Alderney. This is wholly an
error. The cries of the drowning were heard at Barfleur, and on board of the king's ship, which facts
completely disprove the assumed locality. Moreover,
Ordericus Vitalis states that the wreck was brought on
shore on the day following the catastrophe, and all
the royal treasure saved. Several bodies were washed on
the beach, among others that of Richard, Earl of
Chester. None of these circumstances could have
happened, had the vessel foundered on the Caskets. It is
indeed beyond doubt that the Blanche-Nef struck on
a rock called the *Ras-de-Catte*, now known as the
Ras de Cattevile, off Barfleur.[1]

When Henry received intelligence of this sad event,
which deprived him of his sons, his friends, and the
flower of the nobility, his grief was poignant and unbounded. He never smiled again. The old Norman
chroniclers are peculiarly eloquent on his excess of
sorrow, comparing him to Jacob when he lost Joseph,
and to David when he mourned for Absalom. The
English historians, however, viewed the matter in a
different light, considering the death of William Adelin a just visitation of Providence, for the crimes of
his father and his own personal vices. The prince
had openly manifested his dislike to the English, and
used to say that if ever he became king he would make
the miserable Saxons draw ploughs as oxen.[2] Gervase
of Canterbury and Brompton dwell on the calmness of
the sea when the vessel foundered, as a proof of special

[1] " In quodam loco maris periculossimo qui ab incolis Cata Ras dicitur." *Guill.
Gemet. Hist. Norman.* p. 257.
[2] " Palam comminatus fuerat Anglis quod si quando acciperet dominatum super
eos, eos, quasi boves ad aratrum, trahere faceret." *Jo. Brompton.* p. 1013.

divine interposition, keeping out of view the intoxi-
cation of the pilot,[1]  Henry of Huntingdon speaks of
his death with a taunting sneer.  " He thought,"
says that historian, " of his future reign; but God
said, ' It shall not be, impious man, it shall not be.'  It
happened to him that instead of having his head enriched with a crown of gold, it was beaten to pieces
against rocks." [2]

Henry, being thus deprived of heirs male to his
large possessions, determined on a second marriage,
and on the 3rd of January, 1121, he espoused Adeline,
daughter of the Duke of Louvain, by whom, however,
he had no children.  Matilda, wife of William Adelin,
quitted England, and retired to her native country,
where, by the advice of Goisfred, Bishop of Chartres,
she took the veil.  Henry bestowed all his affection
on his natural son Robert, called Robert of Caen,
whom he created Earl of Gloucester, in England, and
Lord of Thorigny, in Normandy.  It is this prince who
took so prominent a part in opposing King Stephen in
the subsequent interregnum.

Of the blood royal of England, there now only remained Matilda, married to the Emperor of Germany,
and she was childless.   In these circumstances, the
Norman barons again came forward to support the
claims of William Cliton, whom they resolved at least
to place on the ducal throne, and at the head of this
confederacy was Amauri, Earl of Evreux.  This powerful noble went to Fulk, Earl of Anjou, who was his

---

[1] " Manifestum Dei judicium...mare tranquillo perierunt." *Gervace Cantuariens,*
p. 1339.  " Enormiter in mari tranquillissimo." *Jo. Brompton.* p. 240.

[2] " Ille de regno futuro cogitabat; Deus autem dicebat: Non sic, impie, non
sic.   Contigit autem ei quod pro coronâ auri, rupibus marinis scinderetur"
*Henry Huntingdon. Epist. De Contemptu Mundi, Anglia Sacra.* vol. ii. p.
696.

nephew, and persuaded him to promise his daughter
Sybilla in marriage to William Cliton: Fulk did
more, for he gave the young prince the province of
Maine for his subsistence, till he could obtain possession of the duchy.   When Amauri made this alliance
known, his partizans daily increased, including the
highest ranks of the nobility, among whom were Galeran, Count of Meulan, William de Roumare, Hugh
de Montfort, Hugh de Neuf-Chatel, and Paien de
Gisors.   Civil war raged till 1124, when the good
fortune of Henry again triumphed over his enemies,
but he stained his victory by mutilating his prisoners,
and particularly in the cases of Goisfred de Tourvill
and Odard Du Pin, both of whom had their eyes
put out.   The same punishment was awarded to Luc
de la Barre, who had not taken up arms, but who had
written some songs offensive to the king.

The hopes of William Cliton were again disappointed, for Fulk now retracted the promise he had
made, and the marriage of his daughter was broken
off.   The unfortunate prince was again a wanderer on
the earth, but still faithfully followed in his misfortunes by Hélier of Saint Saëns and Tyrrel de ·Main-
ieres.   In this unfriended condition he remained during three years, when he again obtained the protection
of Louis Le Gros.

In 1127, the King of France convened his barons,
and having with great eloquence and feeling described the unmerited misfortunes of the son of Duke
Robert, besought their aid to put him into possession
of his paternal inheritance. This appeal was responded
to both by the French and Norman nobility, and
preparations on an extended scale were quickly

adopted to seize the duchy by force of arms. William
Cliton was now twenty-six years of age, and Louis, to
add weight to his pretensions, gave him in marriage
the uterine sister of the Queen of France. The king
also conferred on the young prince the districts of
Pontoise, Chaumont, Nantes, and all the French
Vexin. William then proceeded to Gisors and formally claimed the duchy, and the great mass of the
Normans respected his demand, as they recognized in
him their legitimate prince.

Under these favourable circumstances his prospects
of success were more than usually flattering, and his
hopes were still further buoyed up by a tragical event
in Flanders, with which indeed he had no concern, but
from which he casually derived a great advantage.
On the 1st of March, 1228, Charles, Duke of Flanders, was murdered in the cathedral of Bruges, by
Baldwin of Lille. The assassin and his confederates
were attacked by Louis Le Gros and William Cliton,
and being taken prisoners, were hurled from the walls
of the castle of Bruges and put to death. The King
of France seized the duchy, and transferred it to the
Norman prince, taking back the French territories assigned to him on his marriage. William conferred
the castle of Montreuil on his faithful friend Hélier of
St. Saëns, and severely punished all who were implicated in the murder of Duke Charles.

But he was not allowed to hold his new dominions
in peace. The friends of Baldwin of Lille sought for
vengeance, and persuaded Thierri, Count of Alsace,
to claim Flanders. He readily acceded to their
wishes and levying troops, fortified himself at Alost,
against which town William marched. At this siege,

he displayed all the martial virtues of his ancestors, but, unfortunately wounded himself in the arm with a lance, which he had taken from one of his own soldiers. The injury sustained was fatal; mortification ensued, and in five days he expired, on the 28th of July, 1128.

The death of William Cliton removed out of the path of Henry every competitor to his paternal dominions. His daughter, Matilda, widow of the Emperor of Germany, and yet young, was the only surviving member of his family in a direct line from the Conqueror, and on her his hopes were now fixed to perpetuate his race. He declared her his successor, and she was recognized in that character by the prelates and barons of the realm. The next object of the king was to ally her to one of the continental princes, and he selected Geoffrey Plantagenet,[1] son of Fulk, Count of Anjou, by whom his proposals were readily accepted, and the marriage was solemnized in 1129. After the ceremony was performed, Fulk repaired to the Holy-Land, and married the daughter of Baldwin, second King of Jerusalem, and on the death of his father-in-law, which followed in the ensuing year, 1130, he took possession of the throne, which he occupied for six years.

In 1132, Matilda gave birth to a son, who afterwards became Henry the Second, the most powerful prince of his family by the extent of his dominions. The king was so delighted at this auspicious event that he again convoked the prelates and barons at Oxford, and

[1] The derivation of Plantagenet, is from " plante" and " genest." The former may be rendered " plant," and the latter " broom." Geoffrey used always to put a piece of " broom" in his cap, from which circumstance he received the distinctive epithet of Plantagenet.

confirmed the succession to his daughter and his grandson; and so great was his satisfaction that he promised the immediate investiture of Normandy to Geoffrey Plantagenet. But still the monarch was unhappy: age had calmed his passions; memory recalled the incidents of his past life, and his reflections alarmed and agonized his soul. He now felt that he had been the slave of unbridled ambition, that he had been an usurper and a tyrant; his criminal treatment of his brother Robert wreathed scorpions round his heart; that brother had saved his life, yet he had imprisoned him, and put out his eyes. His sleep was disturbed by frightful dreams, and the appearance of a comet, an eclipse, a violent storm, destroyed his peace of mind. When he reflected on the shipwreck of his children, he saw the retributive vengeance of heaven, and his tortured conscience made life unsupportable, while the prospect of death almost maddened his brain.

Hoping that change of scene might bring tranquillity, he quitted England, 1123, never to return, and landed in Normandy. He there found Matilda and her husband; and a second son, Geoffrey, increased the happiness of the parents. But the king was still melancholy: even the sight of his grandchildren soured his temper; he envied his son-in-law, the grandeur of whose posterity he saw in perspective, and he compared his prospects with what his own might have been, had his sons survived. This bitterness of spirit was increased, by the demand of Geoffrey to receive the investiture of the duchy, which Henry had promised him on the birth of his first child, but of that promise he had evaded the performance. He feared

lest this concession should make his son-in-law aspire
to the crown of England, and was apprehensive that
he might share a fate similar to that which he had
awarded to his own brother.

Geoffrey indignant at this violation of good faith,
determined to seize the duchy by force of arms. He
besieged and burned the town of Beaumont, in the
bailwick of Evreux. This open act of hostility determined the king to break off all intercourse with his
son-in-law, and to return to England with his
daughter; but she espoused the cause of her husband,
and refused to leave him. Thus abandoned by his only
surviving child, and bearded by Geoffrey, the king
became still more miserable, and the anguish of his
mind seriously impaired his health. It is indeed affirmed, that he disinherited Matilda and her children,
but whether that be true or false, it was the pretext
by which Stephen of Blois usurped the throne of England at his death.

The strength of Henry now daily declined, and he
was advised by his physicians to take active exercise
to dispel the chagrin and melancholy which preyed
upon his constitution. He accordingly repaired to
Lions-la-Foret, seven leagues from Rouen, where he
had a hunting establishment. There he died on the
1st of December, 1135.[1] The proximate cause of his
death has been ascribed to eating immoderately of
lampreys, but the fever which gnawed his vitals, and
which had never left him for twelve months, sufficiently accounts for his decease. He lingered in this
last illness from Tuesday to Sunday, in which time
he sent for the Archbishop of Rouen to whom he con-

[1] Ordericus Vitalis. t. iv. p. 460.

fessed, and from whom he received the last holy
offices of the church.   By the advice of that prelate,
he pardoned all criminals, recalled all whom he had
banished, and returned their patrimony to those whose
estates he had confiscated.   He directed his natural
son, Robert de Caen, Earl of Gloucester, to take
sixty thousand pounds out of his treasury, at Falaise,
and distribute it among his domestic servants and the
soldiers of his body-guard.   He was attended in his
last moments by Robert de Caen, William de Warenne, Rotrou de Mortagne, Galeran de Meulan, and
Robert de Leicester.

On the day after his decease his body was conveyed
to Rouen, attended by twenty thousand men.   His
corpse was embalmed ; his intestines were placed in a
vase, and deposited in the church of Sainte-Marie-du-
Pré, which his mother had commenced, and which
he had finished.   The body was then taken to Caen to
be embarked for England, where contrary winds detained the procession during four weeks.   It was ultimately placed in the church of Reading, in presence of
Stephen, who had usurped the throne of England, and
many prelates and barons, who paid this last mark of
respect to the departed monarch.

# INTERREGNUM.

THE death of Henry was followed by the usurpation of
the throne of England. Stephen, Count of Bologne,
second son of Stephen, Count of Blois, who had married Adéle, daughter of the Conqueror, resolved to
seize the dominions of his deceased uncle. This young
prince had been educated at the court of Henry,
who had taken the greatest care in the cultivation of
his talents, from the warm attachment he felt to his
mother. Stephen was at Rouen when the king died,
and, ambition conquering every feeling of gratitude, he
stopped not to pay the last token of respect to his relative, but, rapidly crossing the Channel, arrived in
London, where, being well received by the spiritual
and temporal peers, he was crowned by the Archbishop
of Canterbury, on the 15th of December, only a fort-
night after the death of his predecessor.

When this intelligence reached Normandy, the
barons of the duchy, assembled at Neubourg, were
discontented, it being their wish to elect Theobald, elder
brother of Stephen; but reflecting that the English
had already declared their choice, and taking into

consideration that they held lands in both countries, they were induced by motives of personal policy to abandon their opposition lest they might place their own possessions in jeopardy.

Geoffrey, Count of Anjou, husband of Matilda of England, was not of a character tamely to submit to this usurpation, and his first measure was to march into Normandy, and there strengthen his party. He found both friends and enemies, and the province became a scene of anarchy, some adhering to Stephen, others to Matilda, but neither was legally recognized as duke or duchess. The English partizans of Geoffrey reminded the barons of that country that they had sworn to accept Matilda and her son, as joint heirs of the deceased king, and accused them of disloyalty and perfidy in supporting an usurper; but Hugh Bigod, Senechal of England, declared on oath, that Henry had disinherited his daughter on account of the revolt of her husband, and therefore maintained that they were all released from their oaths. This impudent assertion satisfied the doubts of the wavering, though it is certain that Hugh Bigod was not present when the king died; moreover, those who attended him in his last moments attested that the dying monarch most distinctly declared Matilda, Countess of Anjou, to be his only legitimate heir, as Queen of England and Duchess of Normandy.

The strongest argument in favour of Stephen was the unsettled law of succession that prevailed at this period, for hereditary title was not yet so firmly established as to supersede election. Precedents were brought forward against the claims of Matilda, sanctioned by the conduct of her own family; thus the Con-

queror was preferred to Edgar Atheling, under colour
of the will of the Confessor; Rufus set aside primogeniture in seizing the crown to the prejudice of his elder
brother Robert, and his example was imitated by
Henry the First.

A threatened invasion of the Northern counties of
England by David, King of Scotland, prevented Ste-
phen from crossing over to Normandy, but to strengthen
his party in that province, he betrothed his daugh-
ter, only two years of age, to Galeran, Count of
Meulan, and appointed him his lieutenant.  The
Count of Anjou applied for assistance to the crown of
France, and Louis the Seventh, otherwise known in
history, as Louis le Jeune, declared in his favour.
The French generals invaded the Boulonnais, and
Louis and Geoffrey together entered Normandy, which
they subdued, when the Count ceded Gisors and the
French Vexin to his ally, as a compensation for his
services.

This union was of short duration.  When Stephen had arranged his English affairs, he attacked
Normandy with a body of chosen troops, and regained
it as easily as it had been subdued.  The rapidity of
the conquest alarmed Louis, who, fearful of losing Gisors and the Vexin, concluded a treaty of peace with
the king of England, by which he abandoned Geoffrey
and Matilda.  A league, offensive and defensive, was
concluded between them, and, to give it a character of
permanency, it was stipulated that Constance, daughter of Louis le Gros and sister of Louis le Jeune, should
be affianced to Eustace, son of Stephen of Blois.

Though thus abandoned by the king of France, the
Count of Anjou persisted in his claims; and, as he had

numerous partizans in the duchy, and drew powerful
aid from his hereditary dominions, civil war continued
to rage with fury and alternate success.   It would be
uninteresting to dwell minutely on the skirmishes and
sieges between the barons of either party, which are
related in detail by the old chroniclers; suffice it to
say, that anarchy and confusion reigned till 1441,
when the battle of Lincoln brought some temporary
repose.

   During five years after the death of Henry, Robert
Earl of Gloucester, his natural son, seems to have been
an inactive spectator of the struggle between Stephen
and Matilda.   In June 1140, Ordericus Vitalis states,
that Geoffrey, by prayers and promises, prevailed on
him to join the party of his sister, and that he consented
to attach Caen and Bayeux, of which he was the
governor, to her cause.[1]   The Earl had great power in
England.   He commanded Gloucester and Canterbury, Bristol, Lynn and Dover.   In the wars on the
Continent he had acquired a great military reputation
for personal courage, and he possessed much of the
prudence and sagacity of his father.   When it was
known in England that Robert had openly espoused
the defence of Matilda, many of the prelates and
barons who had submitted to Stephen, rather from
necessity than choice, determined to transfer their allegiance to the Countess of Anjou, and when she was
assured of meeting a favourable reception, she crossed
the channel with the Earl of Gloucester and a feeble
retinue of only twelve knights and some domestic servants.   Matilda took up her quarters in the castle of

[1] T. iv. p 510.

Arundel, where she was received by William D'Aubigny, whom she had created Earl of Arundel.

The Earl of Gloucester soon collected a powerful
army, and marched against Stephen, who was besieging
Lincoln. The king arranged his forces in three divisions; the enemy made a similar disposition. In front
of the royal line were stationed the Flemings and the
Bretons, commanded by William D'Ypres and Olain
of Dinan; these were furiously attacked by the Welsh
auxiliaries of Matilda. The king and his principal
barons dismounted from their chargers, and fought on
foot. Ranulf, Earl of Chester, father-in-law of Robert
of Gloucester, imitated this gallant example. The
charge was desperate, the resistance firm; each party
feeling that a crown was at stake. Stephen had the
advantage in cavalry, his opponent in infantry. The
fortune of the day was decided by the cowardice or
treachery of the Flemings and Bretons, who precipitately fled from the field after the first encounter. The
king discharged all the duties of a general, and displayed all the courage of his heroic race, but skill and
bravery were vain; he was defeated, taken prisoner,
and confined in the castle of Bristol.[1]

This victory restored Matilda to the throne of England, but her excessive pride, and the indignities she
exercised on the Londoners, soon precipitated her from
her elevation. The Bishop of Winchester, brother to
Stephen, who at first had deserted his cause and supported that of his rival, was incensed at the ill-treatment he experienced as the reward of his services, and
taking advantage of the unpopularity of the queen, he
soon stirred up a civil war. Eustace, son of Stephen,

[1] Ord. Vital. t. iv. p. 528.

crossed over from the Continent with chosen troops, and was favourably received in the capital. Hostilities were renewed; the Earl of Gloucester was captured, and as without him the party of Matilda was powerless, he was exchanged for Stephen, who thus recovered his liberty and his crown.

While these events were passing in England, the State of Normandy was equally distracted by the claims of the competitors. Geoffrey held the strongest castles in the duchy, but Eustace, supported by Louis the Seventh, occupied the open country with superior forces. These circumstances prevented the Earl of Anjou from assisting the Earl of Gloucester in England, for had he quitted Normandy, it would have been overrun by the son of Stephen; on the other hand, Eustace could not subdue Geoffrey, as the King of France could only spare him detachments of his army, being himself at war with the Count of Champagne.

In 1144, Geoffrey presented himself before the gates of Rouen, where William de Warenne, Earl of Surrey, commanded for Stephen. Eustace had been compelled to retire to the Boulonnais to raise fresh levies, but De Warenne, firm in his loyalty, refused to surrender the capital of Normandy. After sustaining a blockade for some months, he capitulated, and the duchy submitted to Matilda, after a resistance of nine years. Geoffrey immediately convened the States at Rouen, and caused his son Henry to be acknowledged duke by the prelates and barons, who swore allegiance and fidelity to the young prince; but the Earl of Anjou reserved to himself the functions of regent during the minority.

Many of the French and Norman historians have
classed Eustace of Boulogne and Geoffrey of Anjou
among the dukes of Normandy, but in this they have
erred ; neither of them held dominion over the province in that character ; their right was simply that
conferred by the chances of war, and it was maintained
by the edge of the sword, not by the sanction of law ;
neither received homage from the people, nor were the
brows of either girded by the ducal tiara.   It is true
that Eustace had the investiture conferred upon him
by Louis the Seventh of France, but that conveyed no
valid title, the act being unsanctioned by the States
of the duchy ; when Eustace was subdued, Geoffrey
never pretended to be more than temporary viceroy, a
dignity to which he was entitled, as the natural guardian of his own son.

The success of Stephen in England compelled Matilda and the Earl of Gloucester to return to Normandy,
but far from being disposed to submit to the usurper,
the Earl recruited fresh levies, and as his friends in
England were numerous, powerful, and faithful, he
soon crossed the Channel, taking with him his nephew,
the youthful Henry, then ten years of age.   Robert of
Gloucester was an accomplished prince, and he devoted
himself with untiring zeal to advance the education of
his young charge, and train him in English habits and
English feelings, that he might better ingratiate himself with the people.   While the earl remained at
Wareham in Dorsetshire, he sent Henry into Somersetshire, where he was cordially received by the friends
of Matilda.   Civil war was carried on with doubtful
success and alternate triumphs and defeats for three
years; but in 1147 the Earl of Gloucester died, when the

queen and her son, deprived of his protection, returned to Normandy.

In 1149, Prince Henry journeyed to Carlisle, accompanied by the Earls of Chester and Hereford, where he was received by his grand-uncle, David, King of Scotland, who conferred on him the order of knighthood. At the close of the year, Henry returned to Normandy, followed by Eustace of Boulogne, who laid siege to the castle of Arques, near to Dieppe; but though he was aided by the troops of Louis the Seventh, he feared to attack Geoffrey, and signed a truce. The English crossed the sea, and the King of France, fearing to lose the Vexin, acknowledged the pretensions of Henry, who did him homage for the duchy.

In September 1151, Geoffrey, Earl of Anjou, died. This prince was brave, generous, and just, a good husband, a good father, and a good monarch. He was respected by his contemporaries for his courage in battle, and his moderation in treaties.[1] Satisfied with the patrimony of his ancestors, he was engaged in long wars, not from personal ambition, but to maintain the rights of his wife and son. He expired at the Chateau-du-Loir, in Maine, and was buried in the cathedral of Mans. His monument was preserved up to 1793, on which the following epitaph was engraved:—

Ense tuo, princeps, prædonum turba fugatur;
Ecclesiisque quies, pace vigente, datur.

[1] Le Comte de Segur, in the fourth volume of his History of France, page 307, speaking of the Earl of Anjou, applies to him the epithets of "bigot, deloyal, et ambitieux." This censure is without the least foundation, and we are astonished to see such a passage in the work of so distinguished an author.

# HENRY THE SECOND,

## TENTH DUKE OF NORMANDY.

On the death of his father, Henry, then nineteen years of age, received the ducal sword, mantle and tiara, in presence of the barons of Normandy. This ceremony being completed, he visited Maine, and Anjou, where he was recognized as successor to his paternal dominions, with the customary formalities of homage and fealty.

At this epoch died the celebrated Suger, minister of Louis the Seventh King of France, whose prudent counsels had restrained that monarch from taking the rash step he had for a long time meditated, and which he now determined to carry into execution. Louis had married the beautiful Eleonora, Duchess of Guienne and Countess of Poitou; the charge of conjugal infidelity has been thrown upon her moral character, but, in the absence of any positive proof, it is more charitable to limit her guilt to giddiness and indiscretion, increased by her aversion to a husband whose jealous temper interfered with her gaiety and love of pleasure. Her conduct, however, became the subject of solemn investigation before the Archbishop of Rheims,

and several of the principal barons, and prelates, who
assembled at Baugency, and the result of the inquiry
was a sentence of divorce.  When the royal pair separated, Louis restored to Eleonora the dower she had
brought, and removed the French troops out of Guienne and Poitou, thus leaving her absolute mistress
of her hereditary dominions, without annexing any
condition to the surrender — an act of disinterested
generosity which we must admire, but an error in
policy which must be condemned.

Duke Henry had seen Eleonora at the court of
France, and if he was smitten by her charms, it is certain that the queen regarded him with no common interest.  She was now at liberty to dispose of her hand,
and her rich possessions attracted numerous suitors.
Theobald, Count of Champagne, attempted to seize
her by force, but she was apprized of his intentions, and
secured herself at Tours.  There she narrowly escaped
from another ravisher, Geoffrey, brother of the Duke
of Normandy.  Within six weeks after her departure
from Paris, she arrived at Bourdeaux, whence she
wrote to Henry and made him the offer of her hand.
The young prince eagerly accepted the brilliant proposal, and their nuptials were celebrated with extraordinary pomp and magnificence.  Thus, at twenty
years of age, Henry was master of Normandy, Maine,
Anjou, Poitou, and Guienne, a territory extending
from the Seine to the Garonne, and comprising a
fifth part of the French monarchy.

Louis detested the wife whom he had repudiated,
but he saw with regret the annexation of these extensive provinces to the dominions of a vassal already too
powerful.  He accordingly formed a league with Ste-

phen, and entering Normandy with a strong army,
laid siege to the castle of Neuf-Marchais, near to
Gournay. Henry arrived too late for its defence; it
had already surrendered. But Eleonora had made
him acquainted with the real character of Louis, and
the duke successfully worked on the vanity of the
French king, so as to obtain a truce, the grand object
of his policy being the dethronement of Stephen,
which he could not have attempted with any hope of
success, had his continental possessions been endan-
gered by hostilities with Louis.

Stephen was fully aware of the designs of Henry,
and dreaded his recent augmentation of power. To
strengthen his authority, he convened the prelates and
barons at London, desiring them to declare the throne
hereditary in his family, and nominate his son
Eustace his successor. The Archbishop of Canterbury, though indebted to the king for his episcopal
dignity, strongly opposed this demand, and he was
supported in his opposition by the whole assembly.
He was banished, and sought refuge in Normandy.

While Henry was making preparations to invade
England, disturbances broke out in the duchy, which,
however, were soon quelled by his firmness and activity. The fomenter of this revolt was Geoffrey, brother to the duke, who, dissatisfied with his father's will,
which only gave him the castles of Chinon, Loudun,
and Mirebeau, with their dependencies, attempted by
force of arms to obtain a larger share of the patrimonial inheritance. He was supported by William de
Montfort, but the duke having made this baron prisoner, Geoffrey was intimidated and made peace
with his brother.

Internal tranquillity being thus restored, Henry placed garrisons in all the strong castles of Normandy, and set sail for England, with fifty knights and three thousand infantry. He took possession of Malmsbury in Wiltshire. When Stephen heard of this invasion, he marched against his competitor with very superior forces, and offered battle: Henry eagerly desired to accept the challenge, but Robert de Beaumont, Earl of Leicester, dissuaded him from the unequal contest; and the Normans entrenched themselves so securely, that the royal army did not dare to attack their position. The Earl of Leicester had been the friend of Stephen, and his appearance in the camp at Malmsbury operated strongly in favour of Henry, who soon was in possession of thirty castles.

There were friends and relatives in either army, and the barons, fearful of having their estates confiscated by the victor, were anxious to settle the dispute by a compromise. As these feelings influenced all parties, an interview between the rival princes was appointed to take place, and they met on opposite banks of the Thames. The result of the conference was a suspension of hostilities, and the basis of a permanent peace was considered to be safely established.

Eustace saw these friendly proceedings with extreme jealousy, fearing that his personal interests would be perilled. Determined to resist any accommodation which might interfere with his right to the succession, he levied troops, and ravaged the county of Cambridge. Henry made immediate preparations to repel force by force, but the sudden death of Eustace rendered it unnecessary for him to take the field,

That prince died at Bury St. Edmunds, in Suffolk, in consequence of indigestion, after dining with the monks of that monastery.

The last acts of hostility between Stephen and Henry were the capture of Ipswich by the former, and of Nottingham by the latter. The friends of peace now pointed out to the king, that the death of his son had removed every obstacle to an amicable arrangement: they proposed that he should retain the crown for life, and that Henry should be declared his successor, to the exclusion of his illegitimate children. The prelates and barons convened at Westminster solemnly adopted this settlement.

This important act has been variously represented by the historians of the time. According to some, Stephen adopted Henry as his son, and by virtue of this preliminary act, the prelates and barons acknowledged him as lawful inheritor of the throne; [1] others state that the king first recognized the personal and hereditary right of the son of Matilda, and that the latter of his own free will permitted him to reign during the term of his natural life. [2] Thus contemporaries, equally worthy of belief, establish, on principles diametrically opposed, the legitimacy conferred on the grandson of Henry the First. Which, then, are we to believe? Neither. The truth is that the same barons who elected Stephen, in violation of the oath they had pledged to Matilda,—who subsequently elected Matilda in vio-

---

[1] " Et rex quidem ducem adoptans in filium, eum solemniter successorem proprium declaravit." *William of Newbridge ap. Script. re. Francia.* t. xiii. p. 100.

[2] " Rex recognovit hæreditarium jus quod dux Henricus habebat in regno, et dux benignè concessit ut rex, tôtâ vitâ suâ, si vellet, regnum teneret." *Chronic. Norman.* p. 989.

lation of the oath they had pledged to Stephen,—
again, by a fresh act of their own volition, designated the son of Matilda successor to Stephen, thus
formally excluding Matilda.   Their will alone determined this settlement; a clear proof that in the earlier
ages of the monarchy the crown was not hereditary,
but elective.

In the following year Stephen died, on the 25th of
October, 1154.   Henry embarked at Barfleur, and arrived in London on the 7th of December.   He was
received with every demonstration of joy, and on the
15th was crowned by the Archbishop of Canterbury.
Among the Norman prelates who attended the ceremony were Hugh, Archbishop of Rouen, Philip, Bishop
of Evreux, Arnulphus, of Lisieux, and Herbert of Avranches.   Both nations were flattered by the vast
empire centered in their sovereign, for while the territory of the King of France was limited by the Loire,
the Sâone, and the Meuse, that of Henry included
the whole of the western part of Gaul, between the
Somme and the Pyrenees, with the single exception of
Brittany.

At the commencement of his reign Henry displayed
sagacity and firmness: he selected able counsellors,
and enforced the law.   The castles built by the barons
during the civil war were dismantled, and thus all the
usual retreats of rebellious subjects were destroyed.
It is said by the early historians that twelve thousand
fortresses were razed to the ground.   Having made
these and other judicious provisions for the public
tranquillity of England, the king repaired to Normandy in 1156.

Louis summoned Henry on his arrival to do him

homage for his continental dominions, and Henry, satisfied with possessing that real superiority which
power confers, had the prudence to comply ; while the
King of France, gratified by the barren acknowledgment of nominal sovereignty, confirmed the title of his
rival to Normandy, Guienne, Poitou, Touraine, Anjou, and Maine.  Shortly afterwards Louis married
Constance, daughter of Alphonso the Seventh, King
of Leon and Castile, and gave his sister, also named
Constance, in marriage to Raymond, Count of Toulouse.  In the same year the French and English monarchs signed a treaty of alliance and friendship, in
terms the most formal ; and as they were subsequently
engaged in almost unceasing hostilities, it is well to
exhibit the document as a proof how fatally ambition
triumphs over good faith.

" We wish all the world to know that such is, and
such ever will be, our friendship, that each of us will
defend the life of the other, his members, dignity, and
possessions.  I, Henry, will aid with all my forces
Louis, King of France, my suzerain ; I, Louis, will
aid with all my power Henry, King of England, my
man, and my vassal ; excepting only the obligations
we reciprocally owe to our respective vassals, so long
as they are faithful." [1]

Having concluded these arrangements, Henry met
his family who were assembled to give effect to the
last will and testament of his father, the Earl of
Anjou.  It was stipulated in that instrument that
Geoffrey should only enjoy Chinon, Loudun, and Mirebeau with their dependencies, as it has already been
remarked ; but it also directed that, in the event of

[1] Segur. Hist. de France, t. iv. p. 313.

Henry obtaining the English throne, Geoffrey was to
receive Anjou, Maine, and Touraine, and William,
the youngest brother, was to be put into possession
of Mortain. The Earl of Anjou, aware of the avarice
and ambition of his eldest son, had given instructions
that his body should not be buried till Henry had
sworn faithfully to observe this testament; and that
oath he took, fearing to be branded with infamy, or to
be excommunicated by the church, if his refusal deprived his father of the rites of sepulture. Now possessed of the crown of England, he refused to surrender to his brothers their share of the patrimonial inheritance, and obtained absolution from Pope Adrian, an
Englishman by birth, from the oath he had taken on
his father's death.

Geoffrey appealed to arms: he was supported by
the Count of Champagne and Louis the Seventh, not
from any sense of justice, nor from motives of sympathy or friendship, but because it was their obvious
policy to weaken Henry, by dismembering his vast,
and to them formidable possessions. The army of the
confederates soon spread over the Norman Vexin;
that of Henry was encamped between the Andelle,
and the Epte; but neither party acted on the offensive.
The King of France and the Count of Champagne retired on Gisors; Geoffrey marched into Anjou; Henry
pursued him; Chinon, Loudun, and Mirebeau quickly
fell into his hands; Geoffrey was compelled to submit
and purchase peace by abandoning all his right to
those castles, receiving as an indemnity, an annuity of
one thousand pounds sterling.

At this period, Hoël, Count of Brittany, was expelled from Nantes, and the people of that city and

the territory depending on it, offered their small principality to Geoffrey. This he accepted, and was installed in his new dignity, but he lived only a short time to enjoy the acquisition, dying in 1568. Henry declared himself heir to his deceased brother, and in that character pretended to claim, as a matter of right, a government which had been conferred on Geoffrey by election; and as the king enforced his title by the sword, the people of Nantes were compelled to submit to his usurpation.

Eleonora, Queen of England, had legal pretensions to Toulouse, which her first husband, Louis the Seventh, had vainly attempted to enforce, and Henry now resolved to attempt the conquest of that city. He laid siege to the place with a powerful army, and would, undoubtedly, have succeeded, had not Louis marched to the aid of Count Raymond, his brother-in-law. The advantages of this campaign were balanced on either side, and peace was again concluded on terms that promised to give some permanency to the arrangment. It was stipulated that Margaret, daughter of Louis, should marry Henry, eldest son of the King of England, and that Alice, sister of Margaret, should espouse Richard, his second son. Both the princesses were entrusted to Henry, that they might be brought up in the observances of the English court. Gisors, and other castles of the French Vexin, were to form the dowry of Margaret, and Richard was to receive the investiture of Poitiers and Guienne.

Henry now flattered himself with the prospect of a tranquil reign, but his hopes were miserably disappointed. Peace was indeed maintained for four years; but from the time that the king raised Thomas Becket

to the primacy to the hour of his death, his life was
one continued scene of vexation and disappointment.
The history of Becket more strictly belongs to England than Normandy; but as his disputes with Henry
broke the alliance with Louis, and caused continual
wars, it is necessary to sketch the outline of his character and conduct.

It had been the invariable policy of the Norman
conquerors to exclude from every office of trust and
dignity the descendants of the Anglo-Saxons, and
Becket was the first of that oppressed race who was
elevated to power.    In early life he was sent to
France, to study the continental languages, and he
thus entirely lost the English accent, a certain badge
of slavery in those days, and which alone would have
barred his admission into the upper classes of Norman
society.   Becket was of a gay and lively temperament,
skilled in hunting and hawking, with a pleasing address, and insinuating manners: these qualities introduced him to a rich baron in the neighbourhood of
London, who presented his young friend to Theobald,
Archbishop of Canterbury.    Thomas soon became
Archdeacon of that see, and was entrusted with the
delicate task of persuading the pope formally to forbid the coronation of Eustace, son of Stephen. When
Henry obtained the throne, Theobald presented Becket
to his majesty, warmly praising his important services
during the usurpation; and from that hour he became
the personal and intimate friend of the monarch, who
raised his favourite to the high office of chancellor.
Becket followed Henry to the wars, and though in
deacon's orders, he was the first to scale the walls of

fortresses in the campaign against the Count of Toulouse.

The chancellor vigorously maintained the royal prerogative, and though menaced with excommunication
by his early patron, Theobald, he insisted on subjecting
the mitre to the crown.  When Henry made preparations to besiege Toulouse, a tax was levied on every
landed proprietor whose estate was sufficiently large to
maintain a man-at-arms; it was called *escuage*, or
shield-money.  The rich prelates and abbots, all of
Norman extraction, had paid this tax, while danger
was to be apprehended from the revolts of the Anglo-
Saxons, but being now secure against any spolia-
tion of their lands by that completely subdued people, they refused any further contribution.  " We
are bound," said they, " not to shed blood, and
therefore we should violate our holy office were we to
pay money for the encouragement of war."  Becket
would not listen to this evasion, but compelled the
clergy to advance their proportions, for which conduct
he was branded with ecclesiastical censures, but rose
higher in favour with the king.

In 1162, Henry and the chancellor were in Normandy, when intelligence arrived of the death of Theobald, Archbishop of Canterbury.  The king immediately summoned Becket into his presence, and told
him that he would shortly have to return to England
on an important mission.  " I am ready to obey," said
Thomas, " as soon as I have received my instructions."
" What !" replied the monarch, with great emphasis
and an expressive gesture, " do you not guess at my
meaning?  Are you not aware of my firm resolution
to give you the primacy ?"  Becket smiled, and raising

up the skirt of his richly embroidered robe, " Behold,"
said he, "the holy man, to whom you propose to confide
the religion of the country.  Besides, your majesty has
views on the church which I can never sanction; and
if you make me archbishop, I fear that our friendship
will cease."[1]  The king treated this answer as a mere
effusion of sportive raillery, little anticipating the
truth of his favourite's prediction.

Becket was ordained a priest on the Saturday before
Whitsuntide, in the year 1162, and consecrated on the
following day by the Bishop of Winchester.  He at
once assumed a character which excited universal astonishment.   His sumptuous furniture was removed
from his palace; the plainest fare succeeded the most
luxurious diet; the society of his noble friends was
abandoned, and the poor and the oppressed became his
sole and constant companions.  His marked partiality
for all of Saxon descent roused the suspicions of the
Norman nobility, who saw in Becket the rallying point
for revolt, while the native population looked up
to him as the patriot of his fallen country.

Shortly after his elevation to the primacy, Becket
returned the royal seal to the king, saying that he had
not time to attend fully to his ecclesiastical duties,
and consequently could not discharge those attached
to the secular office.  Henry received this message as
the signal of hostility, and his former attachment was
converted into the bitterest hatred.  From that date
commenced a series of royal vexations which only
ceased with the murder of the primate.

Before the conquest, there was no separation between

---

1 " Citissime à me auferes animum: et gratia, quæ nunc inter nos tanta est, in
atrocissimum odium converteretur." Script. re. Fran. t. xiv. p. 453.

the civil and ecclesiastical jurisdiction.  The bishop
took his seat in the hall of justice by the side of the
sheriff or alderman.  There was one law and one tribunal for laics and clergy.  This system was entirely
changed by the Conqueror; he exempted the clergy
from the controul of the secular authorities, and empowered every bishop to hold a court of justice in his
own house, or in any other place that he might select;
and causes were there tried, not according to the law
of the land, but according to the ecclesiastical canons
and episcopal decrees.  Such was the state of affairs
when Becket became primate.

The first blow which Henry struck at the archbishop
was the nomination of a priest, who had been un-
frocked in Normandy for his vices, to the abbey of
Saint Augustin, near to Canterbury.  Becket summoned him to take the oath of canonical obedience, by
virtue of an order established by Lanfranc; but the
priest, whose name was Clerambault, refused to appear
to the citation, and at the instigation of the king, referred his cause to the pope.  He pleaded that in ancient times, that is to say, before the conquest, his
abbey was free; Becket replied that the laws of the
Conqueror had destroyed the original immunities;
but his holiness decided in favour of Clerambault, thus
violating the decrees of Pope Gregory the Seventh,
for the sole purpose of supporting the illegal pretensions of a Norman abbot against an archbishop of
English extraction.

The pride of Becket was mortified by this reversal
of his sentence, but he found ample revenge in gene-
ralizing on the new principle of church-government
thus established.  As he was commanded to submit to
rules in force before the conquest, he now insisted on

all the ecclesiastical privileges enjoyed by the church
under the Anglo-Saxon dynasty.  To bring this point
to issue, he summoned Gilbert de Clare to restore the
estate of Tunbridge to the see of Canterbury, which
had been conferred on his family by the Conqueror;
and he thus placed in jeopardy the titles of all who held
property which had anciently belonged to the church.
Gilbert de Clare pleaded prescription in bar to the
summons, but Thomas answered that there was no
prescription to robbery and injustice.

This vigorous blow was followed by another equally
formidable.  The tenants in chief of the crown appointed priests to all the churches on their estates, and
this right of presentation Becket resolved to attack.
He nominated an incumbent to the vacant church of
Alresford, which stood on the lands of a Norman baron.
The Norman expelled the priest by force, on which Becket
excommunicated him for laying violent hands on a clerk.
The king now interposed, and declared the sentence
of the church null and void, as directed against one
of his tenants in chief, who was bound to attend the
royal council, and there give his advice on matters of
state.  The archbishop was compelled to submit, but
he yielded reluctantly and with a bad grace : on this
occasion Henry said openly, " All is now ended between this man and me."

Shortly after these transactions the king's justici-
aries summoned a priest, accused of rape and murder,
before the secular tribunal: Becket pronounced the citation illegal, as it contravened the express ordinance of the
Conqueror.  The culprit however was arraigned before
the ecclesiastical court, found guilty, deprived of his
preferment, publicly flogged, and suspended from his

clerical functions.   In this affair the primate was
supported by the Norman prelates, and opposed by the
Norman barons.   Henry summoned a council, and
proposed to revive a pretended law of his grandfather's
for the punishment of priests: it was put to the vote,
and accepted by the Norman barons; but the clergy,
with Becket at their head, added this proviso, " Save
and except the honour of God and of holy church."
" There is venom in the words," said the king, and
abruptly broke up the meeting.

The struggle between the secular and ecclesiastical
jurisdiction now approached to a crisis, and it was
evident that either the crown or the mitre would gain
a complete ascendency, as all compromise would have
been equally rejected by both parties.   Henry bribed the
pope, and his holiness commanded all the clérgy to
adopt such laws as the king might promulgate.   Then
were enacted the famous Constitutions of Clarendon, so
called from a small village, three miles distant from
Salisbury, where the assembly was held which carried
them into execution.   Becket alone hesitated to give
his assent: he asked time to consider the various
clauses of the new document, but he was ultimately
foiled in his opposition, and the sixteen articles were
declared to be part of the law of the land.

These Constitutions were not limited to England, for
the king commanded their observance throughout his
continental dominions.   But the clergy of Normandy,
Anjou, Maine, Poitou, and Guienne, who took no
personal interest in the quarrel between Henry and
Becket, and were jealous of their ecclesiastical privileges, murmured at the new edict, and Rotrou, Primate of Rouen, visted Rome, hoping to persuade the

pope to interfere, and at least obtain some modification
of the Constitutions of Clarendon.    His holiness thus
appealed to by a Norman, entered into the details of
the subject, which he had neglected to do at the request of an Anglo-Saxon, and though he did not
venture formally to negative the wishes of Henry, he
postponed his pontifical sanction, that he might be free
to act according to circumstances.

The king now thought himself strong enough to
strike a decisive blow at Becket, and deprive him of
the primacy.    For this purpose he sent an embassy to
the pope, requesting him to appoint the Archbishop of
York his apostolic legate; but his holiness refused:
however, he vested Henry himself with that authority,
with a strict injunction that the powers thus granted
should not be used to depose Thomas.    This reserva-
tion defeated the whole scheme, and Henry now resolved to adopt other means to destroy his formidable
rival.

Becket was summoned to appear before a council
held at Northampton, and account for monies he had
received when he exercised the office of chancellor.
He was accused of having embezzled forty-four thousand marks.    "The king knows," said Thomas, "as
well as myself, that on the day when I was consecrated
archbishop, the Barons of the Exchequer and Richard
de Lucy, Justiciary of England, passed my accounts,
and exonerated me from all future liabilities."    Had
this prosecution been opened to obtain justice, the
receipt of these high functionaries would alone have
proved an acquittal, but vengeance was the sole aim
of Henry.    Becket proudly and indignantly repelled
the charge of malversation; on which the king turned

round to the barons, saying, " By the fealty you owe
me, inflict justice on this my liege subject, who, duly
summoned, refuses to answer in my court." Sentence
of imprisonment was pronounced on the primate, but
when Robert, Earl of Leicester, approached to seize
him, Becket exclaimed, " Earl, I command you, in
the name of the Most High, not to lay hands on me,
who am your spiritual father. I appeal to the sovereign pontiff, and cite you to appear before his tribunal."

The archbishop then rose from his seat and walked
towards the door. A burst of anger now shook the
hall. " Is the perjured traitor about to escape ? Does
he dare to evade the punishment due to his crimes ?"
Becket scornfully answered, " It is well for those who
insult me that I am a priest : time was when I would
have resented such insolence with sword and lance."
He mounted his horse, and reached Sandwich, under
the feigned name of Dearman, whence he embarked
for France, and landing at Gravelines, walked to the
monastery of Saint Bertin, in the town of Saint Omer.

When the flight of the primate was ascertained,
Henry sent letters under the great seal of England to
the King of France and the Earl of Flanders, requesting them to expel the fugitive from their territories ;
but Louis refused to persecute the unfortunate exile,
and, after some delays, the pope allowed him to retire
to the abbey of Pontigny, on the confines of Burgundy
and Champagne, where he assumed the dress of the
monks of Citeaux, and cheerfully underwent all the
privations and discipline of a monastic life.

The resentment of Henry was not yet appeased.
All the relations of Becket in the ascending and

descending line, including old men, pregnant women,
and infants, were condemned to banishment.   All the
revenues of the archbishop and of his adherents, real
or suspected, were sequestrated, and John, Bishop of
Poitiers, accused of favouring Becket, narrowly escaped assassination.

Thomas remained on the Continent eight years,
sometimes protected, sometimes abandoned by the
King of France, as it suited his policy.   During his
exile, Becket, when at Sens, had to subsist on casual
alms, but his firm and undaunted spirit never quailed.
He had several interviews with Henry, which were
unsatisfactory ; and the king had widened the breach
between them, by causing his eldest son to be crowned
by the Archbishop of York.   On the 22nd of July,
1170, they met on a vast plain between Freteval and
La Ferté Bernard, the King of France being present.
Becket first demanded permission to punish the Archbishop of York, for having usurped his prerogative.
" The coronation of your son," said he,  " by any prelate but myself, was a violent invasion of the ancient
prerogatives of the primacy."   " But who," answered
Henry, "crowned my grandfather, William, the Conqueror of England ?—was it not the Archbishop of
York ?"   Thomas replied, that on that occasion the
see of Canterbury had no legitimate pastor, as Stigand,
the nominal primate, was then under the censure of
the pope.   The king seemed content with this explanation, and promised Becket full satisfaction on that
point.

Thomas next demanded the kiss of peace, a formality
in those days indispensable among parties who had
been enemies, as the open and solemn proof of the

sincerity of their reconciliation. "The kiss of any other but the king," said he, "of his son for example, would be insufficient; for the people might suppose that the archbishop had been received into favour with the son rather than with the father." Henry evaded compliance with this request, saying, with an air of politeness, "We shall see each other again in England, and then we will embrace."

They parted with mutual demonstrations of respect: Becket inclined his knee to his majesty, and Henry held the stirrup of the archbishop's saddle, when he mounted his horse. The king wrote thus to his son Henry: "Know that Thomas of Canterbury has made his peace with me, to my entire satisfaction. I therefore command you to restore his property, and that of his friends, now under sequestration." The order was never obeyed, but treated with ridicule. Thomas was advised from Rome to distrust the king, and warned against returning to England. He had a second interview with Henry, but it was cold and repulsive. They appointed to meet at Rouen; the king, however, absented himself, nor had he given instructions for Becket to receive a sum of money promised him to pay his debts and defray his travelling expenses.

Becket borrowed three hundred pounds in the capital of Normandy, and proceeded to the little port of Wissant, near to Calais. The Count of Boulogne sent a messenger to him, advising him not to cross the Channel, as armed men, stationed on the shore, had received orders to put him to death. But the archbishop was determined to proceed at all hazards, and disembarked at Sandwich. When Gervaise, Viscount

of Kent, knew that he had landed, he swore by a fearful
oath that he would cut off his head with his own
hand.   He summoned his troops to put his threat into
execution, but the people of Dover, of English extraction, marched towards Canterbury in his defence, and
the whole population rose in mass.   The Normans,
alarmed at the popular excitement, retired to their
castles, and Becket entered his cathedral, where he at
once preached a sermon from the text, "I come to you
to die among you."

It was the policy of the court of Rome, while yield-
ing to Henry, to uphold the primate, as the instrument
of the king's submission to pontifical supremacy.   The
pope, accordingly, had furnished Becket with full
power to punish the Archbishop of York, and the other
prelates who had crowned the king's eldest son.   It
was soon reported that he was armed with this irresistible authority, and his enemies well knew that the
thunders of the Vatican would soon be launched from
his vigorous arm.   The Archbishop of York hurried
over to Normandy, and, presenting himself to the king,
said, "I implore your royal aid for the repose of the
clergy and the tranquillity of the realm.   Becket is
putting England in flames; he moves about with
horse and foot before him and behind him, hovering
about the royal castles, and seeking to corrupt the
governors."   On hearing this exaggerated statement,
Henry was seized with one of those ungovernable
transports of rage which had become habitual to him.
"What!" he furiously exclaimed, "is a wretch who
has lived upon my bounty, a beggar who came to my
court on a lame horse, carrying all his wealth behind
him on a crupper, to insult his king, the royal family,

and the nation? and have none of those spiritless
knights who feed at my table courage enough to deliver
me from a priest who dares to pluck me by the beard?"[1]
The language of the king was not to be mistaken.
Richard the Breton, Hugh de Morville, William de
Traci, and Regnault, son of Ours, swore to put
Becket to death, and, suddenly departing, crossed the
Channel.

Five days after the festival of Christmas they
entered Canterbury, and went to the palace of the
archbishop. He received them courteously, demanding the object of their visit. "We come," said Regnault, "on the part of the king, with his commands
that all the persons who have been excommunicated
may be absolved, and that you account for your own
conduct." "It is not I," replied Becket, "but the
sovereign pontiff, who has excommunicated the Archbishop of York, and consequently his Holiness can
alone absolve him. As to the bishops who assisted him
in invading my prerogative, I will restore them to
their functions when they have paid me a proper submission." "From whom, then," rejoined Regnault,
"do you hold your archbishopric, from the king or the
pope?" "I hold my spiritual rights from God and
the pope, and my temporal rights from the king."
"What!" exclaimed the Normans, "has not the king
given you all that you possess?" "By no means,"
said Thomas. The knights were indignant at this distinction, which they roundly termed mere casuistry,

1 "Unus homo qui manducavit panem meum, unus homo qui in manicato ju-
mento claudo prorupit in curiam, dehonestat totum genus regium, totum sine
vindice conculcat regnum . . . . se ignavos et ignobiles homines nutrivisse . . . .
qui ipsum de sacerdote uno non vindicarent." *Vita Thomæ, quadripart.* liv. iii.
cap. 11.

and manifested signs of impatience and anger. "You seem to menace me," said the primate, "but your threats are vain: were all the swords of England at my throat, my resolution would not be shaken." "Then," retorted Regnault, "we must cease merely to threaten, and begin to act."

They quitted the apartment, and put on their armour in the court-yard. The servants of Becket closed and secured the door of the room. Regnault soon returned, and being refused admittance, took an axe from a carpenter who chanced to be present, and attempted to break open the door. The domestics, dreading the violence of the Normans, besought the primate to take shelter in the church through a private gallery that communicated with his palace, which he refused; but when told that the hour of vespers had struck, he observed, "It is then my duty to go to the cathedral." He stood at the altar, separated from the nave by an open grating of iron, when Regnault appeared at the other end of the building, cased in a coat of mail, with a drawn sword in his hand, crying aloud, "To me, to me, loyal servants of the king!" The other conspirators followed him, similarly accoutred. The friends of Becket wished to close the iron grating, but he forbade them, nor would he attempt to escape by a secret passage to the crypt, or subterranean chapel. The assassins now approached, shouting out, "Where is the traitor?" Becket answered not. "Where is the archbishop?" "Here," said Thomas, "is the archbishop, but no traitor! Why come ye into the house of God thus girded for war?" "To slay you," was the ferocious reply. "I am resigned," said the primate. "I fly not from your swords: but, in the name of the Most

High, touch not one of my companions, be he clerk or
layman, high or low."[1] At this moment he received
a blow on the back with the flat of a sword, and the
person who struck him said, " Fly, or you are a dead
man." But he remained immoveable. The murderers
attempted to drag their victim out of the cathedral, for
they had scruples to slay him on the steps of the altar;
the archbishop resisted, resolved not to quit the sanctuary. William de Traci raised his sword, cut off the
arm of a monk named Edward Gryn, and wounded
Becket. A second blow from another Norman stretched
the primate on the floor, a third fractured his skull,
and the sword, striking on the pavement, was broken
in twain. A man-at-arms, named William Mautruit,
who had accompanied the Norman knights, trampled
on the prostrate body, tauntingly exclaiming, " Thus
perishes the traitor who has disturbed the kingdom,
and roused the English to insurrection !"

This rapid sketch of the character and conduct of
Thomas Becket differs from most historical portraitures
of that celebrated man, which generally represent him
in the most odious colours. He rose from obscurity to
the most exalted station by personal merit, and while
he held the office of chancellor, he discharged his trust
with fidelity and zeal, vigorously supporting the prerogative against the open and covert attacks of the
spiritual and temporal barons. When he was invested
with the primacy, a new sphere of duty opened to his
view, and he fulfilled it conscientiously. Had he
abandoned the rights of the church, and become the
tyrant of the poor, he might have been the most

1 " Prohibeo ex parte omnipotentis Dei, ne alicui, sive clerico sive laico, sive
majori sive minori, in aliquo noceatis." *Vita Thomæ quadripart.* cap. 17.

powerful subject of the realm; and justice must compel the impartial reader to admit that, had Becket been swayed by ambition, he would have retained the chancellorship with the primacy, and adopted all the views and caprices of Henry. He defended the rights of the clergy, established by the Conqueror, and sanctioned by the decrees of Pope Gregory the Seventh, seeking not to violate, but to uphold, the law; and with a loftiness of spirit and firmness of purpose which commands unqualified approbation, he struggled against the despotism of the king, even when abandoned by the pope. If vituperated by the Norman nobility, whose cruelty and avarice he repressed, he was idolized by the Anglo-Saxons, as the unflinching and patriotic friend of his oppressed countrymen. He endured the privations and indignities of exile with a noble fortitude, and his dying scene displayed the courage of a hero and a martyr. "*Frangas, non flectes,*" should have been inscribed on his monument.

The hatred of the Norman prelates pursued Becket beyond the grave. Sermons were preached, ascribing his death to divine judgment. The Archbishop of York compared him to Pharaoh, who perished amid the vauntings of his pride. Some of the prelates forbade the interment of his body in consecrated ground, desiring that it might be thrown into a ditch or exposed on a gibbet.[1] Armed men attempted to carry away by force the mortal remains of the Anglo-Saxon champion from the monks of Canterbury, but they were safely deposited in the crypt of the cathedral.

---

[1] " Dicentium corpus proditoris inter sanctos pontifices non esse humandum sed projiciendum in paludem viliorem aut suspendendum esse patibulo." *Epist. S.*
*Sarisb. apud script. re. Franc.* t. xvi. p. 618.

Louis was then rendering to Becket. Eleonora surrounded her son with her own creatures, who re-echoed her sentiments with fatal success.

When the king returned from an excursion to Ireland, in 1173, the young prince demanded the coronation of his consort, to which Henry willingly consented, the impediment to its celebration being removed by the death of the primate. He also requested permission to visit the court of France, which was granted; and after a short absence he returned more determined than ever to assert what he called his "rights." He complained that he had neither lands nor treasure, nor even a residence that he could call his own, and then formally demanded either the exclusive sovereignty of England, or the full dominion of Normandy, Anjou, and Maine, free from any homage or fealty to his father. Henry answered him as the Conqueror answered Robert, "Wait till my death for your succession." From that day there was no sincere friendship between them.

The king now resolved not to lose sight of his son, convinced that his mind had been poisoned by Eleonora, Louis, and their adherents; and being about to proceed to Aquitaine, he insisted on the young prince accompanying him. Raymond, Count of Toulouse, had broken his alliance with the King of France, and acknowledged himself the vassal of Henry; and as the feudal obligation bound him to keep the secret of his superior, and divulge the secret of his enemies, Raymond warned the king to fortify his castles in Poitou and Aquitaine, and beware of his wife and son. The soundness of this advice was soon proved, for the

young prince escaped from his father in the night, and
hurried into France.

When Henry ascertained the retreat of the fugitive,
he sent an embassy to Louis, demanding his surrender.
"From whom do you bring this message?" asked the
King of France. "From the King of England," was
the answer. "That cannot be true," replied Louis;
"the King of England is here present. If you speak
of the *former* king, know that he abandoned the throne
when his eldest son was crowned."

This conduct of Louis is a remarkable instance of
human inconsistency and infatuation. His probity is
lauded by his contemporaries; yet the sovereign who
scrupulously observed the most minute ceremonials of
superstitious devotion, did not shrink from violating
the most sacred of moral duties. He who had com-
promised his fortune, his crown, and his people to
defend the Holy Sepulchre, fomented a revolt between
a father and his children; he who was wont to kneel
with every mark of outward piety at the altar of a
GOD of LOVE, kindled civil war in a neighbouring
state, and sowed discord in the bosom of a royal
family.

If the conduct of Louis deserves severe censure, that
of the young Henry rouses the liveliest indignation,
for he attempted to justify his unnatural rebellion by
the basest hypocrisy and the rankest falsehood. He
thus wrote to the pope:—"I pass over in silence the
personal injuries I have received, to notice a fact
which has caused me the most poignant affliction. The
sacrilegious murderers, who, even at the very altar,
murdered my beloved tutor, the glorious martyr of
Christ, Saint Thomas of Canterbury, remain unpu-

nished; they still walk the earth; no act of royal justice has followed their atrocious crime. I cannot patiently endure this shameful negligence, and this has been the principal cause of the existing discord. The blood of the martyr cries aloud to me, but I cannot avenge him, nor render the honours due to his memory, though I have manifested my respect by visiting his place of sepulture. On that account my father broke out in anger against me; but surely I ought not to fear paternal displeasure when incurred through my devotion to Christ, for whose sake it is our duty to abandon father and mother. Such is the origin of our dissentions; listen to me, most holy father, and judge my cause, which will most assuredly be founded in justice, if sanctioned by your apostolic authority."[1]

It will be remembered that when the king was reconciled to Becket, he wrote to his son to restore the property of the archbishop and his adherents, then under sequestration, and that so far from this order being obeyed, it was treated with ridicule. Moreover, Prince Henry, of his own free will, issued an edict by which Becket was excluded from entering any town in England, except Canterbury; and the same instrument denounced every man as a public enemy, who aided, or even welcomed the exile. Whether the prince ever visited the tomb of the martyr is a doubtful fact, and even if he did, he was certainly not influenced by any worthy feeling, but simply by the hope of rendering his father odious. He clearly attempted to fix on the king the stain of murder, and the whole of his letter to the pope indicates the lowest depths of moral turpitude.

[1] Script. re. fr. t. xvi. p. 643.

The revolt of Prince Henry against his father was rendered still more formidable from his quarrel being espoused by his two brothers, Richard of Poitiers, and Geoffrey of Bretagne. They had accompanied their mother Eleonora to Aquitaine, and from thence proceeded to France, which they reached in safety; but Eleonora, disguised in male attire, was recognized, seized, and lodged in prison by order of her husband. Louis received the young princes with every token of kindness, but made them swear, as he had already made the eldest brother swear, not to conclude either peace or truce with their father, without the express sanction of the French barons.

The position of the King of England now became desperate, and he sought the protection of the pope, on terms which the Conqueror had haughtily rejected. He besought his holiness to excommunicate his enemies, and acknowledged himself the vassal of Rome, as the surest mode of accomplishing his wishes. His letter to Pope Alexander the Third contains the following passage: "My kingdom is under your jurisdiction; I am your feudatory; make then my enemies feel the extent of pontifical power. If you cannot protect the patrimony of St. Peter by temporal arms, prove at least to Europe that you can defend it by spiritual weapons."[1] This confession of vassalage gained the support of the pope, and the thunders of the Vatican menaced all the enemies of the King of England.

---

1 "Vestræ jurisdictionis est regnum Angliæ, et quantum ad feudatarii juris obligationem, vobis dumtaxat obnoxius teneor et astringor. Experiatur Anglia quid possit Romanus pontifex; et quia materialibus armis non utitur, patrimonium beati Petri spirituali gladio tueatur." *Recueil des Historiens de France*, t. xvi. an. 1173.

Secure in the protection of the church, Henry enlisted under his banners all the military adventurers he could collect, and who were ready to sell their swords for pay or pillage. These mercenaries were known by the various titles of Brabançons, Cotereaux, and Routiers, a restless and predatory association, bandits in peace, soldiers in war, ever ready for action, and superior in discipline to the regular baronial militia. At the head of these troops Henry marched against the revolted Bretons, defeated them in a pitched battle, and captured Dol after a short siege.

This victory over an important member of the coalition, changed the policy of Louis the Seventh; he saw that Henry could not be subdued without a great sacrifice of men and treasure, and he was not prepared to involve his subjects in a protracted and doubtful struggle. He therefore told the sons of Henry, that unless they could resist their father with their own private resources, they had better come to some accommodation, as he could no longer render them assistance: thus deserted, the young princes listened to terms of reconciliation, and the hostile parties had an interview between Trie and Gisors, under the lofty elm, which from time immemorial had marked the place in which the dukes of Normandy and the kings of France were wont to conclude their treaties.

The anxiety of Henry to terminate this unnatural war induced him to tender most liberal concessions to his rebellious children. He offered to give his eldest son one half of the royal revenues of England, and four strong castles, provided he would reside in that country; or, if his son preferred it, three castles in Normandy, one in Anjou, one in Maine, with all the

revenues of his ancestors in Anjou, and one half of the
revenues of Normandy.  Richard was to receive two
cities in Poitou, and half the revenues of that province,
while Geoffrey was to have half the revenues of Brittany.  This excess of generosity defeated itself: had
the proposals been accepted, Louis feared that the
reconciliation would have been permanent, which was
contrary to his interests; he therefore persuaded the
young princes that the extremely favourable terms
offered were no proof of the king's sense of justice, but
argued his weakness, and that they would be wrong
to accept a part, when a little firmness would secure
the whole.  This insidious counsel produced its intended effect; the conference was rudely broken up,
and fresh hostilities were commenced.

Richard raised the standard of revolt in Poitou,
where he was attacked by his father at the head of his
Brabançons, and  being unable to keep the open
field, the rebel prince sheltered himself and his
followers in the fortresses he had seized, while the
king devastated the country, tearing up the vines and
fruit-trees by the roots.  But he was soon compelled
to shift the scene of action, as his eldest son and the
Count of Flanders had equipped a naval armament,
and threatened a descent on England.  This menaced
invasion compelled Henry to quit the Continent, and
cross the Channel, which he speedily did, taking with
him, as prisoners, his wife, Eleonora, and Margaret of
France, his daughter-in-law.

The king landed at Southampton, and hastened to
Canterbury.  When he came in sight of the city, he
dismounted from his horse, and walked barefooted to the

church which contained the mortal remains of Becket. Arrived at the sanctuary, he threw himself prostrate on the ground, with his face to the earth, pretending the most poignant affliction. While in this position, Gilbert Foliot, Bishop of London, one of the bitterest enemies of Thomas, when living, and who had proposed in a sermon to throw his body into a ditch, addressed the audience, styling Becket a sainted martyr, and announced that the king, though quite innocent of the murder, would nevertheless submit to be scourged, because the assassins had pleaded in their justification a few hasty words which his majesty had incautiously uttered. This penance Henry underwent, presenting his bare back first to the bishops and afterwards to the monks, each of whom inflicted three or four stripes on the royal penitent. Many of the monks were of Anglo-Saxon descent, and secretly rejoiced at having the power of scourging the grandson of the Conqueror, a privilege conferred on them by superstition.

This ostentatious display of humility, and the hypocritical semblance of sorrow assumed for the occasion, were dictated by a profound policy, which was crowned with complete success. It was of the first importance to Henry to secure the loyal services of the Anglo-Saxon population, for had his eldest son and the Count of Flanders landed in England, and been supported by them, the throne would have been placed in imminent peril. The common people had canonized Becket, without waiting instructions from Rome, and popular belief ascribed miracles to his agency. Pleased with the homage thus paid to a native Englishman by a Norman sovereign, they rallied round his standard, and repulsed the King of Scotland, who had penetrated into the northern provinces.

Henry, now confident in the attachment of the English, returned to the Continent, and there exerted all his energies to conquer his rebellious sons. Many battles were fought, but victory constantly attended the royal arms, when Louis again recommended the young princes to solicit peace. A negociation was accordingly commenced, to which Louis himself became a party, and a treaty was eventually signed at Amboise, on the 30th of September, 1174. It consisted of the following eight articles :—

1. That all prisoners on both sides should be released without ransom.

2. That all who had taken part in the war should be reinstated in their property, and that their heirs should never be made responsible for any damage caused or committed.

3. That all castles built during the war should be razed to the ground.

4. That the King of England should give to his son Henry an annuity of fifteen thousand livres, currency of Anjou,[1] to be charged on the revenues of Normandy, with two fortresses in that country, which his son might garrison as he pleased.

5. That Richard, the second son, should enjoy half the revenues of Poitou, and two cities in that province.

6. That Geoffrey should receive half the revenues of Brittany.

---

[1] The Angevin livre corresponded to eleven sous three deniers, and was worth fifty-three livres nine sous and two deniers, of modern money.

7. That Prince Henry should ratify all the donations made, and to be made, by his father, as well to the churches as to his followers, and also those made to his youngest son, John.

8. That in order to consolidate a permanent union between the King of France and the King of England, Prince Richard should marry Alice, daughter of the King of France, and that this princess, being yet in infancy, should be entrusted to the King of England till of nubile age.

In the spring of the following year, Henry returned to England with his eldest son, and celebrated his reconciliation with his family by public rejoicings at London, which were repeated when he was joined by Richard and Geoffrey. He now fondly hoped to pass the remainder of his days in peace and happiness, but that hope was speedily disappointed.

Among the most remarkable men of this age was Bertrand de Born, Lord of Hautefort, in the diocese of Perigueux, a native of Guienne, and a patriot of the most decided character. The great object of his life was the independence of his country, and this he believed could only be secured by involving France and England in perpetual war. Guienne was too feeble of itself to resist either of the kings of those countries, and Bertrand used to compare it to a hammer placed between two anvils. In addition to every warlike accomplishment, he possessed the talents of poetry in an eminent degree, and was equally celebrated as a troubadour and a soldier. His activity was indefatigable, and while he roused the passions of his countrymen by the pen, he boldly defended their rights by the sword. Bertrand saw with regret the reconciliation of Henry

with his sons, and determined to break the general
peace ratified by the treaty of Amboise.

Queen Eleonora, captive in England, was a native
of Guienne, and Bertrand made the indignities to which
she was subjected the theme of his muse.  He successfully appealed to the chivalrous spirit of the age, and
persuaded the Viscounts of Ventadour, Limoges, Turenne, the Count of Perigord, and other powerful
chieftains, to insist on the liberty of their princess; and
to give stronger effect to the demand, they at once
fortified their castles, and commenced hostilities
against the royal garrisons.  This revolt was secretly
encouraged by the King of France, who promised
Bertrand de Born supplies of money, and all his influence to embroil the King of England with the pope.

When Henry received intelligence of this rebellion,
he sent for his son Richard, and gave him orders, as
the acknowledged heir of the insurgent province, to repair to Guienne, and punish the factious barons who
had taken up arms.  The young prince joyfully accepted this commission, and his courage and conduct
soon quelled the revolt, but he sullied his triumph by
cruelty, the more hateful, as it was exercised against
a people who had assisted him in his quarrels with his
father.  No sooner, however, had he put down this insurrection, than his restless temper prompted him to
renew the scandalous scenes in which he had been a
principal actor before the treaty of Amboise ; but the
chancellor of Poitou, having penetrated his intrigues,
communicated them to his father.  Incensed at this
disclosure, Richard caused the chancellor to be publicly flogged in the streets of Poitiers.  So gross
an outrage on so high a functionary, for the honest

performance of his duty, created general indignation, and Richard daily lost popularity by his severe administration.

These disturbances induced Henry to cross over to the Continent. He convened the States of Normandy at Rouen, and was there met by the papal legate, who imperiously commanded him to undertake a pilgrimage to the Holy Land, as an expiation for the murder of Becket, threatening, in case of refusal, to put all his dominions under an interdict. He further insisted that the marriage between Richard and Alice should forthwith be solemnized,—a demand that convinced Henry of the secret influence of the King of France, who indeed had bribed the legate to embarrass his rival, that he might be unable personally to interpose in the affairs of Poitou. The position of the King of England thus became very delicate, for he did not dare openly to disobey the pope, while, on the other hand, his absence in Palestine would have placed his territories in the most imminent danger. He therefore feigned acquiescence, only requiring time to make the necessary arrangements for his departure.

It is probable that he would not have succeeded in this manœuvre, had not Louis been deterred from his main object by the dangerous illness of his son, afterwards known in history, as Philip Augustus. This young prince, then fourteen years of age, was hunting in the forest of Compiegne, and lost his way. When night came on, an apparently colossal figure crossed his path; it seemed to be a man of gigantic stature, covered with black garments, carrying an axe on his shoulder, and holding in his hand a brazier, which at intervals emitted a brilliant flame. The obscurity, the solitude of the place, and the popular superstition of the age, made the affrighted prince mistake a collier for a spectre. Seized with terror, the royal youth, who in mature life exhibited all the martial virtues of an intrepid hero, fainted. The collier, having vainly attempted to restore him to sensibility, carried him in his arms to the palace. The health of Philip was seriously affected by this adventure, and it was long doubtful, even if his life were preserved, whether he would not sink into complete idiotcy.

Louis the Seventh depended more on superstition than medicine for the recovery of his son. He firmly believed in the miracles attributed to the tomb of Thomas Becket; and as he had afforded protection to the martyr, when an exile in France, he resolved on a pilgrimage to Canterbury, to beseech him to cure his son. The credulous monarch seems to have imagined that prelates, translated to heaven, were as fond of wealth and luxury as they usually are on earth, for he offered at the shrine a gold cup of great value, and bound himself to pay a rent of one hundred measures of wine, each containing sixty gallons. He also deposited a costly diamond, which Henry the Eighth of England wore as a ring, after he had destroyed the tomb of the martyr.

The King of England, though astonished at these proceedings, received Louis at Dover, and accompanied him to Canterbury. He was entertained with royal magnificence. Henry displayed his treasures, requesting his guest to select what he pleased : Louis accepted a few jewels as the gage of friendship, and they took leave of each other with the usual formalities, apparently as sincere as they were really hollow.

On his return to Paris, Louis found his son perfectly restored to health, and his recovery, attributed to Becket, wonderfully increased the popularity of the martyr. Desirous of associating Philip with him in the royal dignity, Louis fixed the day of All-saints, 1179, for his coronation, but a sudden stroke of apoplexy carried off the old monarch, who expired on the 18th of September of the same year, aged sixty years. Philip, however, was crowned on the appointed day; and Prince Henry of England, as Duke of Normandy, and in that quality first peer of France, carried the crown in the procession.

Bertrand de Born, now deprived of the alliance of Louis, applied to Prince Henry of England, who promised to espouse his cause, but he retracted when the time of action arrived; on which the patriotic troubadour published some biting verses against him, and the fear of being still further lampooned drew him back into the party of the insurgents. Henry undertook to plead the cause of the people of Guienne and Poitou, against his brother Richard, before their father, whom he roundly accused of unjust, vexatious, and tyrannical conduct; he even reproached the king himself with culpable neglect, in not protecting his subjects, and then proceeded to renew his old demands for an independent sovereignty. Henry, however, steadily refused any such concession, but consented that Richard and Geoffrey should swear homage to him for Poitou and Brittany. Geoffrey took the required oath, but Richard peremptorily refused.

Prince Henry, bitterly incensed against Richard, determined to invade his territories, and summoned Geoffrey, as his vassal, to aid him. The insurgent barons

flocked to his standard, and the young King of France
declared in his favour. This family quarrel now
threatened to kindle a general war, and the King of
England commanded his sons to lay down their arms ;
but they denied his right of interference. Conscious
that Richard could not resist the powerful confedera-
tion opposed to him, single-handed, the old monarch
hastened to his assistance, and fought against two of
his sons, while he defended the third.

Within a month after the renewal of hostilities,
Prince Henry repented of his conduct, returned to his
father, and betrayed the confidence of the associates
he had abandoned. He even placed his hand on the
Gospels, and swore never again to aid or abet any of
the enemies of the King of England; but his example
was not imitated by Geoffrey, who refused to submit,
partly from obstinacy of character, partly from a feeling of honour, which induced him to adhere steadily to
his engagements. The king attempted to negociate
with him, but in vain. A Norman priest earnestly
besought him to remember his duty, and return to
filial obedience. "What," exclaimed the young prince,
"would you have me abandon my inheritance?"
"Heaven forbid," rejoined the priest; "I wish you
good, not evil." "You do not comprehend me," said
the Count of Brittany; "it is the destiny of our
family not to love each other ; that is our inheritance,
and not one of us will abandon it."[1]

Though Prince Henry had returned to the camp of
his father, he still corresponded with many of the barons
of Aquitaine and Guienne, and particularly with Ber-

[1] " Non ignoras hoc nobis naturaliter fore proprium et ab atavis insertum ut
nemo nostrûm alterum diligat." *J. Brompton. apud Script. re. fr.* t. xiii. p. 215.

trand de Born, who had been his intimate friend, and
was the life and soul of the confederacy. The prince
conceived the foolish hope of reconciling all existing
differences by an amicable negociation; but it was not
the policy of Bertrand de Born to conclude any peace.
Henry, however, made the experiment, and went to
Limoges, which his father and Richard were besieging:
he was admitted within the walls, and after an interview with the chiefs, the gates were thrown open to
the king, who met Geoffrey in the market-place.
While they were conversing together, a flight of arrows
was discharged from the battlement, one of which
pierced the doublet of the old monarch, and had not
his horse started forward, he would probably have been
slain. Tears trickled down his aged cheeks: he
picked up the arrow, and handing it to Geoffrey, said,
" What has your unhappy father done, that he should
be made a butt for your archers?" The reproach was
natural from a father to a son, but the Count of Brittany was not morally responsible for this outrage; the
soldiers of the garrison were not in his pay, nor subject
to his immediate command: they were his allies, who
had national antipathies to avenge and satiate, quite
independent of any attachment to Geoffrey; they only
knew him as an associate in a common quarrel, but
did not recognize him as their chief.

Prince Henry, thus disappointed in his attempt at
negociation, completely changed his policy, and with
an inconsistency and tergiversation which indeed swayed
all his actions, quitted his father, and joined the insurgents at Dorat, in the marches of Poitou: his stay
with them was very short; he returned to the king,
assuring him that Limoges would surrender, if he sent

ambassadors, to whom hostages would be delivered up,
as the gage of peace.  Ambassadors accordingly presented themselves at the quarters of Geoffrey, and were
fiercely attacked before his eyes: two were killed, one
was severely wounded, and a fourth thrown from a
bridge into the river.

Thus a second time baffled in his expectations, Prince
Henry retired to Chateau Martel, in the vicinity of
Limoges, where he fell dangerously ill, and requested
to see his father; but the old monarch, fearing that
some plot was meditated against his personal safety,
did not obey the summons.  A second messenger announced his death, which happened on the 11th of
June, 1183, in the twenty-seventh year of his age.  In
his dying moments he made an ostentatious display of
repentance, desiring to be dragged from his bed with
a rope, and placed on sacks filled with cinders.  This
sudden event reconciled Geoffrey with his father.  The
day after the funeral, the king attacked Limoges and
carried it by storm.

The anger of Henry was fiercely directed against
Bertrand de Born, and he determined not to lay down
his arms till he had secured the person of this restless
and formidable partizan.  He marched with over-
whelming forces against the castle of Hautefort, accompanied by his sons, who scrupled not to attack
their old friend and companion, when he most needed
their protection.  To have attempted resistance would
have been fruitless, and Bertrand surrendered at discretion.  When brought into the royal presence, Henry
said to him, in terms of derision, " Bertrand, you used
to boast that you only needed to use half your brains
at once; in your present position you seem to require

the whole of them." "Sire," replied the dauntless
troubadour, "it is true that I have often said so, and
I spoke the truth." "I should say," rejoined the
king, "that you had lost your senses." "In that you
are right," observed Bertrand in a solemn tone: "I
lost my senses on the day that I heard of the death of
your valiant son." At the name of his child, which he
did not expect to hear, the king burst into tears and
fainted. When he recovered himself he was quite pacified; his projects of revenge disappeared, and he only
saw in his prisoner the ancient friend of his beloved son.
Instead of reproaches, he now used the language of
kindness: "Sir Bertrand, Sir Bertrand," said he, "it
is not surprising that your reason should have fled at
the death of my son, for he loved you more than he did
any other man; and I, from the affection I bear to his
memory, pardon you, and restore your property and
your castle. I pledge you my friendship, and give you
five hundred marks of silver as an indemnity for the
losses you have sustained."[1]

The death of Prince Henry and the pacification of
Poitou were followed by a complete reconciliation of
all the members of the royal family; and Queen Eleonora, after a captivity of ten years, was released from
prison. John, the youngest son, was now old enough
to be admitted to the paternal councils, and the king
once more indulged in the vain hope of future harmony among his children. While the three eldest sons
had been secretly plotting, or openly fighting, against
their father, John had been his solace: he was now
decidedly the favourite, and Henry promised to crown
him King of Ireland. This preference roused the jea-

[1] Thierry, t. iii. p. 356.

lousy of his brothers, and soon led to another rupture.
Geoffrey demanded Anjou, that he might unite it to
Brittany, and on meeting with a refusal, he retired to
the court of France, determined to enforce his claim
by the sword.  His sudden death prevented hostilities : he was thrown from his horse in a tournament,
and being trampled on and severely bruised, expired
of his wounds in 1185, being in his twenty-sixth year.

But though a family war was thus averted, the sword
was drawn by Philip Augustus of France.  His sister
Margaret, widow of Prince Henry of England, espoused Bela the Third, King of Hungary, two years
after the decease of her first husband, and her brother
now demanded back the French Vexin, which constituted her dowry when married to Henry.  He did not
wait an answer from the King of England, but at once
published a declaration of war, and invaded Berri: he
besieged Issodun, which immediately surrendered,
and then marched against Châteauroux, where the
English princes, Richard and John, were quartered.
Their presence emboldened the garrison to a vigorous
resistance, and Henry hastened to succour his children.
Both armies were drawn up in battle-array, but the
interposition of a papal legate prevented a hostile encounter.  A suspension of arms being agreed upon, the
question of the dowry was submitted to the peers of
France, who decided that the King of England should
retain the Vexin, on paying an annuity of £1750 to
Margaret.[1]

While these negociations were pending, Richard
and Philip were inseparable companions, and their intimacy apparently ripened into the warmest friendship.

[1] Segur. Hist. de France, t. iv. p. 369.

" Each day," says an historian of the time, "they ate
at the same table and from the same plate, and at night
slept in the same bed."[1]    Richard accompanied Philip
to Paris, and lived with him as a brother.    The King
of England, alarmed at this familiarity, summoned
Richard to join him in London; but instead of com-
plying with this order, the prince plundered the royal
treasury of Chinon, and once more attempted to assert
his independence in Poitou.    The people, remember-
ing his former tyranny, opposed him with such vigour
that he was compelled to return to his father, implore
his pardon, and swear on the Gospels, in presence of
the barons and prelates, never again to disturb the
public tranquillity.

While these events were passing in France, the
Christians had suffered severe reverses in Palestine.
Salah-Eddin, commonly called Saladin, had made himself master of Jerusalem, and taken possession of the
wood of the true cross, the holiest relic known in
Christendom.    The loss of this precious memorial of
the faith inflamed the zeal of Europe, which had cooled
down during the preceding half century, and the eloquence of William, Archbishop of Tyre, one of the
most remarkable men of his age, roused the chivalry of
France and England to attempt the recovery of Jerusalem.    The prelate met the princes and barons of the
two countries between Trie and Gisors, and addressed
them in the following terms :—

"We have lost Jerusalem, the holy city, which
Christian heroes, whose chiefs were your countrymen
and your relatives, had liberated from the yoke of the

[1] "Singulis diebus in unâ mensâ ad unum catinum manducabant, et in noctibus
non separabat eos lectus." *Rog. de Hoved.* p. 635.

Saracens: it has again fallen into slavery. Saladin
has captured it, and that formidable conqueror threatens
to expel us from Tyre, Antioch, and Tripoli, the remnant of our conquests, which once stretched from the
Red Sea to the Euphrates. The torrent will overwhelm
us, unless it be at once stemmed. You alone, pious
and valiant princes, can curb the ambition of Saladin,
recover the principality of Edessa and the kingdom of
Jerusalem, and restore to the Holy City, not only its
freedom, but the splendour it enjoyed when the banners of Godfrey, Boehmond, and Tancred waved over
its sacred walls. It is to you, generous princes, that
their posterity appeals, many of whom now groan in
the chains of Saladin; the remainder still combat
bravely, though with unequal forces, in the hope of
being assisted by your valour. March, then, heroically
to the East, in which your predecessors reaped so rich
a harvest of glory, and disdain not to add to your other
titles that of Liberators of Jerusalem."

This appeal to his warlike audience met with complete success: from the sovereign to the serf, all classes
were animated with one common fury against Saladin,
whom they swore to expel from Palestine or perish in
the struggle. The kings of France and England then
took leave of each other, to make suitable preparations
for the crusade.

To defray the expense of the expedition, a tax was
levied both in England and the continental dominions
of Henry, called "Saladin's tithe;" it was the tenth
part of all the revenues of the nation, charged both on
the clergy and the laity. It was raised in each parish
by a committee, composed of the parish priest, a knight-
templar, a knight-hospitaller, a royal commissioner,

one of the king's chaplains, and an officer and a chaplain appointed by the lord of the fief in which the parish was situated.  If the committee assessed an estate at too high a rate, the owner was permitted to appeal to six of the principal parishioners, and there depose on oath to its real value, and their sentence was final. This measure afforded some security against extortion, but it only extended to the Normans; the Anglo-Saxons were excluded from the protection of appeal. Those who offered the least resistance to the committee were imprisoned, as rebels, and the unhappy Jews were plundered without remorse.

The royal treasury was thus recruited, but Henry, instead of devoting the money raised to the object for which it was levied, determined to employ it against the King of France, to whom he had so recently sworn amity in presence of the Archbishop of Tyre.  He encouraged Richard to invade the territory of the Count of Toulouse, a personal friend of Philip's, hoping, by this stroke of policy, to embroil his son with the King of France, whose recent intimacy he regarded with a jealous eye.  Philip marched to the aid of the count, and Henry then took the field in defence of Richard.  The French were compelled to retreat, and Philip only escaped at Mantes through the devotedness of William des Barres, who lost his liberty in saving his king.  The chivalrous Richard was so pleased with this trait of gallantry, that he released his prisoner without ransom, and loaded him with presents.[1]

---

[1] In this campaign Henry destroyed the town of Clair-sur-Epte, where the treaty between Charles the Simple and Rollo was concluded.  It is now a mean village, though the locality will be always interesting from its historical associations.

Philip, whose high sense of honour was as keen and delicate as that of his illustrious opponent, was touched by the generosity of Richard, and proposed a suspension of arms. A conference was held at the usual place of *rendezvous* between Trie and Gisors, which, however, terminated without any accommodation, and Philip was so incensed that he cut down the ancient elm under which so many meetings had been held between the princes of France and Normandy. An old poet, William of Brittany, composed some indifferent verses in honour of this tree, and thus notices its destruction :—

> " Nunc (pudor et luctus patriæ totius) ab ipso
> Funditus est evulsa solo, sed adhuc locus ipse
> Ostentat, qualis fuerit dum tota vigeret."

Hostilities were renewed with activity on both sides; but Richard soon made private overtures to Philip, offering to submit his differences with the Count of Toulouse to the arbitration of the peers of France. To this arrangement Henry refused his sanction, and demanded a personal interview with Philip, which took place at Bonmoulins in Normandy.

That the King of France had been secretly intriguing with Richard is evident from the demands with which he insisted that Henry should comply. It has been already stated that by one of the clauses of the treaty of Amboise, Richard was bound to marry Alice of France ; the wars had hitherto been assigned as the reason why this union had never been consummated, but Philip now insisted that no further delay should retard its celebration. It is certain that Henry had himself seduced this young princess, promising to divorce Eleonora, and disinherit her children; but all his efforts to obtain the concurrence of the pope had proved unavailing. After the death of the fair Rosamond, Alice became his mistress. Philip further stipulated, that on the marriage being solemnized Richard should be declared sole heir to all the dominions of his father in England, Ireland, and the Continent.

These conditions Henry refused to accept, for he had experienced the temper of Richard on too many occasions not to distrust him. The king, however, offered to marry Alice to his son John, and declare him his heir, to the exclusion of Richard. To this Philip demurred, when the papal legate, who desired that the new crusade should be commenced, commanded the King of France to yield to the wishes of Henry, menacing to put his kingdom under an interdict, if he refused. This imprudent threat roused the indignation of Philip who accused the legate of having been bribed, and openly defied him to hurl the thunders of Rome either against his person or his dominions.

The impetuous Richard, incensed at the preference shown by his father to his younger brother, thus addressed Henry: " Since you will not recognize me as your successor, and as you wish not only to deprive me of my birth-right, but also of a princess long since affianced to me, I throw myself into the arms of the King of France, of whom I demand justice, and to whom alone I will do homage for the countries which are fiefs of his crown." So saying, he rushed furiously from the audience, mounted his horse and galloped away, at the head of some troops whom Philip had ordered to be in readiness for his protection.

Thus terminated the conference, the fatal effects of

which Henry too plainly saw : never had his position
been so critical; he could only muster seven hundred
soldiers, the remainder having deserted to his son, and
this force being much too feeble to meet the combined armies of Philip and Richard in the open plain,
the old monarch retreated to Mans, the place of his
birth and the depository of the ashes of his father.
These associations he hoped would ensure the fidelity
of the Manceaux.

In the meantime his enemies seized on his towns
and castles, and advanced into Touraine; but suddenly
retracing their steps, they presented themselves before
the gates of Mans.  Henry gave orders to break down
the bridge over the Sarthe, that he might place the
river between the town and the French camp; but
while the work of demolition was proceeding, Philip
attacked the labourers, and penetrated within the
walls.  The king had barely time to escape ; he tra-
versed Anjou, crossed the Loire, and fortified himself
at Chinon.  But all hopes of resistance were vain ;
Philip advanced against him from the north, the Bretons, from the west, the Poitevins, from the south ;
thus encompassed, without any authority or means of
defence, Henry was compelled to solicit peace on any
terms that the victor might dictate.

The two monarchs met on a plain between Tours
and Azay-sur-Cher, but Richard was not present.  The
conditions insisted on by Philip were harsh and humiliating: he demanded that Henry should acknowledge himself his vassal, and throw himself completely
on his mercy ; that Alice should be confided to five
trusty persons, till the crusade was finished ; that all
the cities and towns of Berry should be ceded to

France; that, as a ransom for his other continental dominions, Henry should pay Philip twenty thousand
marks of silver; and finally, that he should give
Richard the kiss of peace.

These terms were dictated in the open air, the two
sovereigns being on horseback. An old chronicler relates that the sky was serene and cloudless, when a
thunderbolt fell between them. Both were alarmed,
and suddenly retreated from each other: the panic
subsiding, they again approached, when the same
phenomenon was repeated, with a still louder explo-
sion. The King of England dropped the reins, and
would have fallen from his horse, had he not been supported by the attendants, who removed him in a faint-
ing state to his quarters.

Broken in spirit, dejected in mind, enfeebled in
health, the old king was placed in bed, and there received the French commissioners, who read the conditions of peace to him, article by article, and then demanded his signature. On this he requested to know
who were the partizans of Richard, before he promised
a general pardon. The first name on the list, announced to him, was that of John, his youngest son.
Treachery from that unexpected quarter filled him
with astonishment; he raised himself from his recumbent posture; his features were convulsed, and the
expression of his eyes became wild and haggard. " Is
it indeed true," said he, " that John, the child of my affections, for the love of whom I have brought all these
calamities on my head,—is it true that he has abandoned his aged father in his hour of trouble ?" It was
answered that nothing was more certain. " Then,"
exclaimed Henry, " life and its concerns are to me as

nothing : do what you please." At this moment
Richard approached, and demanded the kiss of peace;
it was granted, but the prince heard his father murmur
in an under-tone, " Would that God spared me, till I
was avenged on you ?"

A few days after this scene Henry the Second died.
To his last moment he groaned over his misfortunes.
" Shame," said he, " shame and dishonour to a vanquished king. Cursed be the day of my birth, cursed
be the sons I leave behind me." Nor could the prayers
and entreaties of the ministers of religion induce him
to retract this malediction.

The king expired on the 6th of July, 1189, after a
reign of thirty-five years, in the fifty-seventh year of
his age, at the castle of Chinon, near Saumur. His
body was treated with the same neglect and indignity
as that of his grandfather, William the Conqueror.
There was difficulty to find persons to wrap it in a winding-sheet. All that was valuable was plundered.
The funeral procession was met by Richard, as it
entered the church of the abbey of Fontevrault, about
five leagues distant from Chinon, where Henry had
ordered his body to be interred. The Count of
Poitiers, whose conduct had embittered the life of his
father and shortened his days, now affected the
warmth of filial affection. He threw himself on his
knees and prayed before the altar, and then quitted
the church with every outward demonstration of
sorrow.

The assistants wished to cover the body with the ap-
propriate insignia of royalty, but the guardians of
the royal treasure at Chinon refused their assent, and
the most urgent supplication could only procure a

damaged sceptre and a ring of small price. Instead of a crown, his head was covered with some gold fringe, taken from a woman's dress; and in this humble and grotesque style, Henry, son of Geoffrey Plantagenet, King of England, Duke of Normandy, Aquitaine, and Brittany, Count of Maine and Anjou, Lord of Tours and Amboise, descended to the grave.

# RICHARD CŒUR DE LION,

## ELEVENTH DUKE OF NORMANDY.

RICHARD succeeded his father without opposition, and immediately pacified the troubles which had raged for so many years in Anjou, Guienne, Poitou, and Maine. On the 20th of July, 1189, he received the ducal crown, mantle, and tiara, in the cathedral-church of Rouen, in presence of the nobles and the Archbishop of Canterbury. He confirmed his brother John in the possession of the province of Mortain, and gave him an annual pension of four thousand pounds sterling, to be charged on the revenues of England. After devoting three weeks to the general administration of Normandy, he crossed the Channel at Barfleur, and was crowned at Westminster, on the 3rd of September, 1189.

The King of France soon renewed the demand he had made on Henry for the restoration of the French Vexin,[1] which had formed the dowry of Margaret of France, and while some of the old writers pretend that Richard was compelled to pay twenty-four thousand

---

[1] The Norman Vexin is quite distinct from the French Vexin. The former includes the land between the Epte and the Andelle ; the latter contains the land between the Epte and Oise.

pounds, as a compromise, while others reduce the sum
to four thousand pounds, it is also affirmed that Philip
ceded the land on condition that Richard would marry
Alice, to whom he had been for many years affianced.
This last is the most probable opinion, for the King of
England wanted money, and never, on any occasion,
showed the least disposition to part with what he possessed.   At the same time the two monarchs confirmed
the ancient treaties, the Count of La Perche representing the King of France, and William de Mandeville,
Earl of Essex, representing the King of England.

When Richard opened the royal treasury at Winchester he found  nine hundred thousand pounds sterling of coined money, besides many vases and other
ornaments in gold and silver, with precious stones of
considerable value.   This sum he soon squandered
away in preparations for the crusade, and devised an
expedient for recruiting his finances, as lucrative as it
was dishonest.   He offered the crown-lands for sale,
and when remonstrated with by his council, openly
declared that he would sell London could he find a
purchaser.[1]   When he had disposed of very considerable properties, he pretended that he had lost his seal,
and ordered a new one to be prepared; and all the
buyers were told that no grant of land would be deemed
valid, unless a fresh instrument was drawn up and
regularly attested by the second seal; this was looked
upon as a mere formality, but when the purchasers
came before the king, he denied that they had any
title whatever, and made them pay their money a
second time.

[1] " Londonias quoque venderem, si emptorem idoneum invenissem."  *Guil. New-
brig.* p. 306.

On the 11th of December, 1190, Richard set sail from Dover with thirty thousand infantry, and five thousand cavalry, and landed in Flanders, where he was entertained with great magnificence  From thence he proceeded to Rouen, where he convoked the states of his duchy; all the chief vassals did him homage and swore fidelity during his absence.  On this occasion, an intrusive monk, named Fulk, Curate of Neuilly, near to Paris, whom indiscreet zeal had induced to travel to the capital of Normandy, advised Richard to get rid of three pernicious passions, which he called three loose women, pride, avarice, and luxury.  The king sharply answered; I cannot dispose of them better than by giving the first of these women to the knights of the Temple, the second to the Cistertian monks, and the third to the bishops of my dominions.

Having provided for the internal administration of Normandy, Richard repaired to Nonancourt, which Philip had appointed as the place of their meeting. The two monarchs solemnly pledged their faith to each other, and forwarded letters-patent to their respective governors and lieutenant-governors, which contained, in substance, the following articles:—First, that the King of France should aid the King of England to defend his dominions, as loyally as he would himself defend the city of Paris, were it attacked. Secondly, that King Richard would serve and aid Philip, as sincerely as he would Rouen, were an enemy at its gates. Thirdly, that in case of the death of either of them in the expedition to Palestine, the survivor should have the gold and silver of the deceased, and take the command of his army against the infidels. Fourthly, that all the earls and barons of France and

Normandy, as well as of other kingdoms belonging to
the contracting parties, should swear inviolable fidelity,
and remain at peace during the continuance of the
Holy War.  Fifthly, that the archbishops and bishops should excommunicate those who violated these
terms of peace, and also those who committed any
depredation on the property or rights of the crusaders.

The armies of France and England joined each
other in the plain of Vezelay, in the Nivernois, whence
they marched together to Lyons.  There they separated, Philip taking the road to Genoa, and Richard
that to Marseilles.  From these ports they respectively
embarked, reaching Messina, in Sicily, in which they
took up their winter-quarters.

Notwithstanding their outward professions of friendship, and the repeated oaths they had plighted to each
other, the amity of the two kings was hollow and in-
sincere ; each was jealous of the other; each was ambitious ; neither could brook a rival.  With such feelings, opportunity alone was wanting to throw them
into opposition, and this was soon afforded.  When
the crusaders arrived in Sicily, Tancred was king of
the island.  William, the last monarch, when dying,
had declared his sister Constance heiress to the throne.
Tancred had usurped the sceptre to the prejudice of
that princess, married to the emperor, Henry the
Fourth.  Henry was friendly with Philip, and Tancred
had to fear his resentment ; still more had he to appre-
hend from Richard, whose sister, named Jane, and
widow of the last king of Sicily, was detained by him
in prison.

Shortly after the arrival of the English fleet at Mes-

sina, the king seized on a convent, and expelled the
monks, his intention being to convert the building into
a military magazine.   In consequence of this outrage
the people closed the gates of the city against his soldiers, while the most infuriated of the mob attacked
his quarters; but they were repulsed, and Richard,
having carried the town by assault, planted his banner
on the ramparts.   Philip had not taken any part in
this tumult, but when he saw that Richard had displayed his own ensigns, in token of conquest, he was
highly incensed, exclaiming, "Does a prince, who is
my vassal, dare to exhibit his standard over a city in
which I am living?"   At the same time he gave orders
to tear it down, and hoist his own in its stead.

This was the signal for battle between the crusaders.
The bows were bent, the swords unsheathed, and the
carnage was about to commence, when Richard
begged the King of France to be reconciled, and reserve their strength for the infidels.   "I am ready,"
said he, "out of my respect to you, to take down the
banner that my victory placed on the walls; but what
I will thus do of my own will, you could only obtain by
force, with great efforts, even if at all; and I would
hold you responsible to the pope for all the blood that
might be shed in the conflict."   This submission,
haughty and insulting as it was, was accepted by
Philip: it was agreed that the two kings should remain joint masters of Messina until Richard had obtained satisfaction from Tancred for the wrongs done to
his sister Jane, and that the city should be committed
to the special guardianship of the Knights Templars and
Knights Hospitallers.

The compensation claimed by Richard is curious in

its kind.  He demanded for his sister a golden chair, a
golden table twelve feet long, and three feet and a
half wide, two golden tripods, on which the table was to
rest, a large silken tent, fit to accommodate two hundred gentlemen at dinner, twenty-four cups of silver,
and as many plates; he also demanded for his own
army sixty thousand measures of wheat, and as many
of barley and wine, besides one hundred armed gallies
fully provisioned for two years.[1]  With these demands Tancred not only complied, but, with the advice
of his council, gave Richard twenty thousand ounces of
silver, as a full acquittance of the claim of his sister for
dower; and it was further stipulated that Arthur,
Duke of Brittany, and nephew of Richard, should be
affianced to one of the daughters of Tancred.  Philip
was a party to this engagement, which was attested by
the Archbishop of Rouen, and several of the French
and Norman barons.

Shortly after these differences had been arranged,
Tancred sought Richard in secret.  "Distrust the
King of France," said he: "the Duke of Burgundy,
has brought me a letter from him, in which he accuses
you of breaches of faith and treason, and promises, if
I will join him, to attack your camp in the night."
Richard having answered that he could not credit such
perfidy, Tancred put the autograph into his hand.

Philip soon suspected that he was betrayed, as
Richard treated him with marked coolness: he demanded an explanation, when the King of England
sent him the letter he had written to Tancred, by the
Earl of Flanders.  Philip, as surprised as irritated, denied being the author of the letter: he declared the

[1] Dumoulin, p. 439.

whole transaction to be an intrigue of Richard's, to put an end to their treaties of friendship and evade his marriage with Alice; but he vowed that unless that union were completed, he would avenge the insult offered to his family, on his return from Palestine. Richard coolly told the King of France that he would never marry his sister, because she had had a child by his father, Henry, which he was prepared to prove by numerous and credible witnesses.[1] The fact was indeed certain, and was made so evident to Philip, that he at once and for ever waived the pretensions of Alice; but Richard agreed to pay her an annual pension and restore Gisors.

While these disputes were being carried on, Queen Eleonora arrived in Sicily with Bérangére, daughter of Sancho the Sixth, King of Navarre, intending that her son should marry that princess.   She attributed her ten years' imprisonment in great measure to Alice, and was anxious to avenge herself on the mistress of her husband.   Though Philip could not prevent this union, he felt indignant at its celebration in the very city where he was dwelling, but he stifled his resentment for the sake of conquering Jerusalem.   He abruptly quitted Messina for the Holy Land, after having made Richard promise that he would follow him as soon as he had solemnized his nuptials.

Regulations were enforced during the voyage to Ptolemais, or St. Jean d'Acre, which merit notice, as showing the spirit of the times.   With the exception of the clergy and the knights, no one was allowed to play for money at any game during the whole pas-

---

1 " Quia rex Angliæ eam cognoverat, et filium ex eâ genuerat... Et ad hoc probandum multos produxit testes." *Rog. de Hoeeden*, p. 688.

sage ; but the clergy and knights were permitted
to lose twenty halfpence in a day and night. On
board of the vessel which carried either king, the
royal sergeants-at-arms, if specially permitted, might
play to the amount of twenty halfpence, and the same
indulgence was extended to the sergeants of the archbishops, bishops, earls, and barons. But if any soldier or artificer played without leave, he was to be
scourged three times, on three succeeding days; if a
sailor offended, he was to be plunged three times into
the water, from the top of the mainmast.

The fleet of Richard encountered a violent storm
shortly after its departure from Sicily. A part of it
cast anchor at Candia, whence it proceeded to Rhodes ;
the remainder was driven on the coast of Cyprus, and
in this division were the two queens, the mother and
wife of Richard. Isaac Comnenus, who ruled in the
island, would not allow the shipwrecked voyagers to
come to Limisso, the capital ; he even had the inhu-
manity to imprison the sailors. As soon as Richard
received intelligence of this inhospitable usage, he
steered for Cyprus, and quickly made himself master
of Limisso. He seized Comnenus, who prayed for his
life, and begged not to be loaded with chains. " You
shall live," said Richard, " though you deserve to die ;
and as you seem alarmed at iron chains, you shall
carry chains of silver." The king completely conquered Cyprus, and appointed Robert de Twineham,
Senechal of Anjou, provisional governor. After this
achievement, he set sail, and landed under the walls of
Acre, which the crusaders were besieging.

Richard and Philip renewed their quarrels as
soon as they came in presence of each other. The

King of France insisted on having the half of Cyprus,
while Richard claimed half of the treasures of the Earl
of Flanders, who had recently died, and which Philip
had appropriated to his own use; for they had made a
bargain, before they set out on the expedition, to di-
vide all the plunder they might realize. Nor were these
the only causes of dispute. Conrad, of Montferrat,
and Guy of Lusignan, aspired to the throne of Jerusalem. Philip supported the claims of the former, who
numbered among his friends the Genoese, the Templars, the Germans, and the Duke of Burgundy.
Richard protected the latter, whose cause was espoused
by the Pisans, the Hospitallers, Henry, Count of
Champagne, and the Flemings. Though the common
interests of all engaged in the crusade induced them
to reconcile Montferrat and Lusignan, still the resentment between Richard and Philip was unappeased.

After a siege of five months Acre submitted to the
Christians. Leopold, Duke of Austria, who commanded the Germans, placed his standard on one of
the towers of the captured city. Richard and Philip
deeming this an insult, ordered it to be removed and
trampled under foot, an outrage which was sternly
avenged on the King of England after his return from
Palestine.

The glory obtained by Richard in this crusade far
exceeded that of any of his companions in arms.
The Saracen mother quieted an unruly child by tell-
ing him that King Richard was coming; and if a
horse started on the road, the rider would say, " Do
you think King Richard is concealed behind that
bush?" Such an accumulation of honour on the head
of his rival kindled the jealousy of Philip, who could

not conceal his chagrin. He resolved to return to
France, disgusted with a war in which success would
give him no additional power, and in which failure
would weaken his resources and diminish his reputation. He pretended that the air of Palestine enfeebled
his health, and that his presence in France was necessary, to take possession of Artois, which he claimed
on the death of Philip of Alsace, Earl of Flanders,
who, he affirmed, had made him a present of it, when
he married his niece, Isabella, daughter of Baldwin,
Count of Hainault; but the real motive to his conduct
was the increasing fame of Richard, and the desire of
humbling his rival, by invading his territories; for it is
certain, that when Philip arrived at Rome, on his
journey homewards, he beseeched Pope Celestine the
Third to absolve him from the oath he had taken not
to attack the possessions of Richard, so long as that
prince remained in Palestine. The monarch received
from the Pontiff a refusal as humiliating as it was merited. It would be pleasing to suppose that this imputation on his character was a calumny, but unfortunately the truth of it is fully confirmed by the subsequent conduct of Philip.[1]

The King of France, fearing that his departure
might be ascribed to cowardice, or lukewarmness in
the cause of Christendom, sent the Bishop of Beauvais and the Duke of Burgundy to Richard, with a
view to convince him that the engagement they had
entered into in Europe was fulfilled. "What!" replied Cœur de Lion, " does the king, my brother,
wish to leave our conquest incomplete? Did we only
bind ourselves to the capture of the town? Or did

[1] Segur. Hist. de France, vol. iv. p. 418.

we not undertake this long and perilous expedition
to recover the Holy Land from the infidels and
re-establish the kingdom of Jerusalem? Let Philip
fly the scymiter of Saladin; so long as Richard can
wield a battle-axe, he will continue a faithful soldier of
Christ." This answer was so just and noble, that the
bishop and the duke shed tears: Philip was touched
at the heroism of his rival, and suspended his departure.

But the influence of these better feelings was of
short duration. The King of France soon sent a second deputation to Richard, with a repetition of his
request, and it was granted on conditions. Before
they separated, it was decided that Lusignan should
hold the sceptre of Jerusalem, during his life, with the
provinces of Jaffa and Cesarea, but that, on his death,
Montferrat should succeed to the crown, guaranteeing
the two provinces to the children of Lusignan. Philip
engaged to leave ten thousand French soldiers in the
camp of the crusaders, under the command of the
Duke of Burgundy, and again swore that he would
not attack any part of the dominions of Richard
during his absence, nor before the expiration of forty
days after his return to England. These terms clearly
show what little confidence the two kings placed in
each other.

When Philip had embarked for Europe, Richard
resolved on the siege of Ascalon. His army consisted of one hundred thousand men, while the infidel
forces amounted to three hundred thousand, commanded by the skilful and indefatigable Saladin. The
advanced guard of the Christians was under the orders
of James d'Avênes, Lord of Guise, one of the bravest

captains of the age; this division was composed of
Danes and Flemings. The king led on the English,
Normans, and Germans: the French formed the rear-
guard, at the head of which was the Duke of Burgundy. James d'Avênes commenced the battle, and
twice pierced through the hostile squadrons: at the
third charge he was thrown to the ground, and one
of his legs was severed from his body; still he fought
bravely, till his right hand was cut off, when recognizing Richard, he exclaimed, " Valiant king, avenge
my death!" and expired. Cœur de Lion furiously
assaulted the enemy, and the plain was strewed with
the dying and the dead.

Saladin, with the flower of his army, had not yet
mixed in the fray. When he saw the discomfiture of
his troops, he made a circuitous movement, and fell on
the division of the Duke of Burgundy, who being
taken by surprise, and with very inferior forces, was
thrown into confusion; but he was soon relieved by
the king, when the battle became general. Saladin
and Richard performed prodigies of valour, and victory was long doubtful. They at length met in single
combat, when Richard struck the sultan so weighty a
blow on the head, that nothing but the temper of his
helmet saved his life; he was stunned, fell from his
horse, and would have been taken prisoner, had not
the desperate fury of his brave and enthusiastic followers repulsed the Christians. Saladin, quickly reco-
vering from the injury he had received, mounted a
fresh charger; but seeing that the fortune of the day
was against him, he ordered a retreat, leaving forty
thousand slain on the field of battle.

After this victory Richard deemed it prudent to

fortify the maritime ports in possession of the crusaders,
that he might the more readily obtain reinforcements from Europe. He strengthened Acre, Ascalon,
and Jaffa, and nearly lost his liberty, if not his life,
when sojourning in this last city. The king was pas-
sionately fond of hunting, and being one day much fatigued, he sought repose under a tree, and uncon-
sciously fell asleep. He was roused by the trampling
of horses, and soon surrounded by a Saracen detachment. Richard, with six attendants who had followed
him to the chase, rushed on his opponents sword in
hand; four of his companions were slain, and he must
inevitably have perished, had it not been for the generous devotion of one of them, who declared that he
was the king. At this announcement the Saracens
seized him, and led him to Saladin, paying no attention
to the remainder of their opponents, quite contented
with the prize they had secured. When brought into
the presence of the Sultan, he avowed the stratagem
he had practised; and Saladin, who knew well how to
appreciate real merit, ordered him to be treated with
all the respect and distinction due to his valour and his
fidelity. Richard ransomed his friend by the ex-
change of ten emirs, whom he had captured at the
battle of Ascalon.

The old writers are not agreed as to the name or
country, of this heroic man. Some call him Guilliame-
des-Pourcelets, and make him a native of Provence;
others call him Despréaux, and make him a native of
Normandy. If the former opinion be the true one, it
would be a remarkable fact, since the only person
spared at the Sicilian Vespers, was a Provençal, named
William-des-Pourcelets, and his life was saved on ac-

count of his rare probity. Thus, in the space of one hundred and ten years, two men of the same baptismal and family name, and born in the same province, would have manifested such extraordinary virtue as to be respected even by their most cruel enemies.

The crusaders, animated by the victory of Ascalon, now desired to attack Jerusalem, but the season of the year being unfavourable, Richard was indisposed to attempt this expedition before the spring. Hence arose dissensions in the combined army. The Duke of Austria, who had not forgotten the indignity put on his banner after the siege of Acre, made the postponement of the siege of the holy city, a pretext for his return to Europe; and the Duke of Burgundy, who had secret instructions from Philip, prepared to follow the example of Leopold; but he died at Acre: however, the French troops departed.

Shortly after these desertions, Richard received messengers from England, advising him of the intrigues of his brother John, who was secretly incited by Philip to seize on the throne, and promised men and money to aid the enterprise. Richard knew well the character of John and Philip, and gave full credence to the report: he assembled the crusaders, and pointed out the circumstances which rendered his return to Europe necessary, desiring them to elect a new generalissimo, and their choice fell on Conrad, Marquis of Montferrat.

While Richard was making preparations for his departure, Conrad was assassinated; and as Philip of France malevolently attributed this crime to the instigation of the King of England, the calumny requires refutation.

The history of the Old Man of the Mountain may
have been exaggerated, but that such a personage existed, and had immense power, is beyond doubt. This
despot occupied part of Phœnicia, and maintained
himself independent against the caliphs of Egypt and
the Kings of Jerusalem. His territory was small, but
he ruled over fanatics, whose zeal compensated the
want of numbers. Conrad governed Tyre, contiguous
to the fontiers of the assassin, who dreading the vicinity
of a prince whom Saladin himself could not subdue,
dispatched two of his emissaries to stab him, when un-
guarded. They waited for their victim as he came
from the house of the Bishop of Beauvais, where
he had been dining, and wounded him so severely
that he only survived a few hours. The murderers did
not attempt to escape, but underwent capital punishment with a fortitude and a cheerfulness that superstitious enthusiasm could alone have inspired.

They were put to the torture to declare by whom
their weapons were sharpened, but they made no answer; and Philip availed himself of their silence to fix
the deed on Richard, whose territories he was eager to
invade, and he knew well that if he could brand the
King of England with having contrived the assassination of a crusader, he would detach many warriors from
his standard. The open and chivalrous character of
Richard ought alone to exonerate him from so foul a
crime; to him dissimulation was unknown; a drawn
blade and a ready hand were the only arbiters of his
quarrels. The King of France was himself so fearful
of the Old Man of the Mountain that he sent him numerous valuable presents, and was the first French
monarch who surrounded his person with a body-guard,

though to slander Richard he pretended to disclaim any knowledge of the prince of the assassins. Moreover, when Conrad was dying, he expressly charged his widow to deliver up Tyre to the King of England, and to him alone; and she, though aware of the imputation sought to be cast on Richard, did so; a convincing proof of his innocence.

Richard was deeply chagrined at this calumny, and two years afterwards produced an autograph letter from the Old Man of the Mountain, which he had most probably forged, written in Hebrew, Greek, and Latin characters, and containing, among others, the following passages. " To Leopold, Duke of Austria, and to all the princes and people of the Christian faith, greeting. Having heard that several kings, in countries beyond the sea, impute to Richard, King of England, the death of Conrad, Marquis of Montferrat, I swear, by the God who reigns eternally and by the law we observe, that King Richard had no participation whatever in his murder. Know that we have given these presents in our dwelling and castle of Messiac, in the middle of September, and have sealed them with our seal, in the year 1505, after Alexander."[1]

The death of Montferrat compelled the crusaders to elect a new generalissimo during the absence of Richard. Their choice fell on Henry, Earl of Champagne, a nephew of Richard and Philip, and he married the widow of Conrad. Richard gave Cyprus to Guy de Lusignan, on condition of his surrendering Jerusalem to the Earl of Champagne. The king then concluded a truce with Saladin for three years, which secured to Henry

[1] Dumoulin. p. 464.

all the towns in Phœnica which Richard had conquered, and guaranteed the other Christian princes in
all they possessed in Syria, on condition that the
fortifications of Jaffa and Ascalon should be destroyed.
It was stipulated that pilgrims might visit the Holy
Land, and appoint priests in the churches of the Holy
Sepulchre, Nazareth, and Bethlehem.

Richard embarked from Acre with a small retinue
on his return to Europe. After passing Sicily, he was
captured by a pirate, but the valour of his resistance,
and the respect paid to his name, induced his conquerors to restore him and his companions to liberty : they
were safely landed at Zara, in Sclavonia. The king was
attended by two devoted friends, Baldwin de Bethune
and William de l'Etang. The governor of Zara was a
relative of Conrad of Montferrat, and it was necessary
to obtain his permission to pass freely through the
country. Richard sent him a ring, ornamented with
a beautiful ruby, to conciliate his favour; but the jewel
was known to the governor, who had formerly sold it
to some merchants of Pisa, who had bought it of him
expressly for Richard. "Who demands a free passage?" said he to the messenger. "Pilgrims returning
from Jerusalem." "What is the name of their master?" "One is called Baldwin of Bethune, the other,
Hugh, the merchant, who offers you this ring." The
governor examined the ring for some time with great
attention, without uttering a word : he suddenly broke
his silence, saying, "You do not speak the truth; this
ring does not belong to Hugh, the merchant, but to
King Richard ; but since he has been so generous as
to offer me a gift though he has no knowledge of me,

I will not arrest him : I return the ring, and allow him to depart in peace."[1]

Richard, astonished at this discovery, hastened his departure, but though the governor of Zara had allowed him to escape from his own jurisdiction, he wrote to his brother, who commanded the adjoining town, advising him that the King of England was in the neighbourhood. The brother had a Norman servant, whom he desired daily to visit houses in which pilgrims were lodged : he was ordered to spare no pains in pointing out Richard, and promised half the town if he succeeded. After an active search, the king was detected, but the Norman did not betray him; on the contrary, he procured him a fleet horse, and advised him to leave the country without delay. On returning to his master, he said that the information received from Zara was incorrect; that Richard was not in the country, but one of his subjects who resembled him, named Baldwin de Bethune, who had recently quitted the Holy Land. The governor was so enraged at losing the capital prize he hoped was within his reach, that he seized Baldwin and put him into prison.

The king reached the German territory, accompanied by William de l'Etang, and a single servant, who spoke the Teutonic dialect. Unfortunately he rested at Vienna on the Danube, then governed by Leopold, Duke of Austria, whose banner Richard had torn down from the walls of Acre, and trampled under foot. The servant, when he went to market, ostentatiously paraded some precious jewels, and indulged in imprudent conversation about the wealth of his master; these

[1] Radulph de Coggeshale, apud script. rer. fr. t. xviii. p. 72, cited by Thierry, t. iv. p. 67.

circumstances roused suspicion, and as it was known that Richard had disembarked at Zara, Leopold had vigilantly posted spies in every direction, hoping to secure the person of the King of England, not only to avenge the insult he had received, but also to extort a heavy ransom.   His emissaries seized the servant, and ordered him to lead them to the residence of his master ; this he refused to do, on which he was put to the torture, and confessed all.   The inn where Richard lodged was immediately surrounded by soldiers, who seized and confined him in prison, chosen men of approved fidelity guarding him night and day with drawn swords.

When the news of his captivity was made public, Henry the Sixth, Emperor of Germany, demanded Richard from Leopold, who was his vassal, on the plea that a duke could not, with propriety, detain a king, who was worthy of an imperial gaoler.[1]   Leopold yielded to this argument, and transferred his prisoner to his suzerain, pretending to be satisfied with the extraordinary reason assigned by the emperor, but he stipulated for a share of the expected ransom.   Richard was accordingly removed from Vienna to Worms, and Philip of France wrote to Henry, beseeching him not to release the King of England, whom he termed the disturber of the peace of Europe, at the same time offering to pay more than the ransom, if the emperor would confide Richard to his custody.

Philip thought that the favourable moment was arrived to strip his former friend of his continental

1 " Allegans regem non decere teneri à duce, nec esse indecens si ab imperatoriâ celsitudine decus regium teneretur." *Guillelmus Neubrigensis, apud script. re. Franc.* t. xviii. p. 35.

dominions, but he was still under the obligation of his
oath, and as Pope Celestine had refused to absolve him
from it, he had recourse to the following scheme to
evade the thunders of the church. He sent the Bishop
of Noyon to Denmark, who demanded from Canute
the Sixth his daughter Ingelburge in marriage for his
royal master, asking, as a dowry, the cession of that
nominal right of sovereignty which the Danish kings
claimed to the throne of England. Had this been conceded, he would have pleaded the pretensions of his
wife, and treated Richard as an usurper; but though
Canute was disposed to agree to these terms, his barons
refused their assent.

Disappointed in this quarter, Philip now pursued
a different line of policy. He offered Prince John his
sister Alice in marriage, and promised to aid him in
seizing the crown of England, provided he would give
up Gisors, the Vexin, Tours, and the whole of Normandy, except Rouen and its territory.

John, who was surnamed Lackland, because he never
received any independent estates from his father, gladly
listened to these overtures, and signed the treaty, after
having further exacted a portion of Hainault, thus
conspiring against his brother, and agreeing to marry
a woman who had been the concubine of his own
parent. John then did homage to the King of France
for all the domains he held in that country; after
which he collected troops, and made a descent on
England, but being opposed by the barons, he only
succeeded in capturing some few castles of little importance.

While these transactions were proceeding, Philip,
thinking himself bound, as most great culprits do, to

observe the current forms of justice while he was violating its substance, sent word to Richard that he
could no longer recognize him as one of his vassals,
and summoned the senechal of Normandy to place in
his hands all the fortresses of the province.   The misfortunes and the captivity of Richard made men forget
his vices; in his hour of trouble they thought only of
his dauntless courage.   This feeling made a friend of
each of his subjects.   The senechal resisted Philip in
the field; and the English territories beyond the Loire,
attacked by the partizans of the King of France, were
bravely defended by the King of Navarre, Sancho the
Sixth, father-in-law to Richard.

Philip, at the head of a numerous army, entering
Normandy, quickly made himself master of Gisors,
Eu, and Neufchâtel, and laid siege to Rouen; but the
Earl of Leicester threw himself into the metropolis,
and drove the French from the walls.   Philip retreated,
but captured Pacy and Ivry.   Meeting with a resistance he had not anticipated, the King of France granted
a truce to the English ministers, who put into his
hands four castles, as a guarantee that they would not
renew hostilities.   Philip did not make this concession
from want of courage, but Eleonora, mother of Richard,
in concert with the bishops of Normandy, had bitterly
complained to Pope Celestine the Third, reproaching
Philip with a violation of his oath, and inveighing
against the tyranny of the German emperor.   The
Holy See could not remain indifferent, when it saw
Christian princes leagued against the most heroic of the
crusaders, and Philip sheathed his sword rather than
encounter the thunders of the Vatican, the more ter-

o

rible on this occasion as they would have been pointed
by justice.

Henry was not so submissive to the orders of the
sovereign pontiff. He assembled the diet, before whom
Richard appeared as a criminal. He was accused of
having unjustly captured Cyprus,—of having insulted
the Duke of Austria,—of having assassinated the
Marquis of Montferrat; moreover, he was charged
with attempting to gain possession of Sicily, corresponding with Saladin, and with having concluded a
truce of three years with the Saracens.

The answer of Richard was dignified and worthy of
a great man: certainly he could have recused the
competency of his pretended and self-elected judges;
but he preferred to justify his conduct and establish
his innocence, less indeed with a view to convince those
who assumed the right of trying him, than to satisfy
his cotemporaries, and perhaps posterity. When the
accusation had been read, he thus addressed the diet:—

"I am born in a rank which recognizes no superior
but God, to whom alone I am responsible for my actions; but they are so pure and honourable that I
voluntarily and cheerfully render an account of them
to the whole world. The treaties I have concluded
with the King of Sicily contain no infraction of the
law of nations. I do not understand how I can be reproached for the conquest of Cyprus. I avenged my
own injuries and those of the human race, in punishing
a tyrant and dethroning an usurper; and by bestowing
my conquest on a prince worthy of the throne, I have
shown that I was not prompted by avarice or ambition;
so much so, that the Emperor of Constantinople, who
alone had any right to complain, has been wholly silent

on the subject. In reference to the Duke of Austria, he ought to have avenged the insult on the spot, or long since to have forgotten it; moreover, my detention and captivity by his orders should have satisfied his revenge. I need not justify myself against the crime of having caused the assassination of the Marquis of Montferrat; he himself exonerated me from that foul charge, and had I my freedom, who would dare to accuse me of deliberate murder? My pretended correspondence with Saladin is equally unfounded; my battles and victories alone disprove the false assertion: and if I did not drive the Saracen prince from Jerusalem, blame not me, but blame the King of France, the Duke of Burgundy, the Duke of Austria himself, all of whom deserted the cause, and left me almost single-handed to war against the infidel. It is said that I was corrupted by presents from the sultan, and that I joined the crusade from the love of money; but did I not give away all the wealth I seized in capturing the Bagdad caravan, and what have I reserved out of all my conquests? Nothing, but the ring I wear on my finger. Do you, then, render justice to me; have compassion on a monarch who has experienced such unworthy treatment, and put more faith in my actions, than in the calumnies of my deadly foes."

The address of Richard to the diet, supported by the indefatigable exertions of Queen Eleonora at the court of Rome, determined the assembly to release their prisoner, and his ransom was fixed at one hundred thousand marks of silver. When the King of France, and Prince John, who was then styled Earl of Mortain, heard of this resolution, they sent ambassadors to the emperor, who offered, on behalf of the former, fifty thousand marks of silver, and, on the part of the latter, thirty thousand marks, if he would detain Richard till Michaelmas, 1194; or, if he preferred it, they agreed to pay him one thousand marks monthly, for every month that he guarded the prisoner; but if he would consent to place the person of Richard at once in the custody of Philip, then he was promised one hundred and fifty thousand marks in ready cash.[1]

These tempting offers shook the resolution of the emperor, who strongly inclined to accept the bribe proffered to him, and even showed Richard the letters of his two enemies. The unfortunate monarch now deemed his fate inevitable, and, for a moment, the courage of the lion-hearted hero failed him; but he soon regained his presence of mind, and told Henry that the matter did not rest with him alone,—that the assembled diet had pledged their honour for his liberty, and that he appealed to them. To this demand the emperor yielded, feeling confident that he could corrupt his vassals by gold, and thus gain his point, while he loaded the diet with the odium which ever must attach to a violation of good faith. The archbishops of Mayence and Cologne, the bishops of Worms, Spire, and Liege, the dukes of Suabia, Austria, and Louvain, the Palatine of the Rhine, and other nobles, were accordingly assembled, and they boldly and generously taxed the emperor with avarice, injustice, and cruelty, and firmly insisted on the liberation of Richard. They compelled Henry to receive that portion of the ransom remitted from England, and accept as hostages for the remainder the Archbishop of Rouen, the Bishop of

[1] Dumoulin, p. 468.

Bath, and the sons of several earls and barons, who were placed in charge of the Duke of Austria.[1]

Richard regained his liberty on the 4th of February, 1194, but fearing to traverse France or Normandy, then in great part occupied by French soldiers, he travelled through Germany, and reached Antwerp in safety. He was there detained a month by contrary winds, during which time the offers of Philip and the Earl of Mortain to Henry were renewed and urgently pressed. The avarice of the emperor now triumphed over every feeling of honour, and he sent orders to arrest Richard, but this scheme was discovered by the Archbishop of Rouen, and he found means to advise his sovereign of the meditated treachery. Richard immediately embarked on board a small trading vessel, belonging to a Norman merchant, named Alain Tranchemer, and landed safely at Sandwich.

When the king arrived in London he ordered the ceremony of his coronation to be repeated. It is difficult to understand what motives of policy could have prompted him on this occasion, for neither his imprisonment nor the revolt of the Earl of Mortain had rendered his claim to the throne for a moment doubtful. His first act of administration was one of gross injustice ; he cancelled all the sales of land he had made prior to his departure for the crusade, pretending that they were not absolute transfers, but merely pledges or mortgages for loans of money. The purchasers, in reply, produced their deeds, regularly signed and at-

---

[1] Connected with the captivity of Richard is a romantic story of his having been discovered by a minstrel named Blondel. This is entirely fictitious. The emperor and the Duke of Austria made no secret of his imprisonment. He received the visits of the English and Norman prelates openly. All that his gaolers wanted was money ; they made no attempts on his life, which, indeed, would have defeated their mercenary policy.

tested by the royal seal, but the plea was not admitted.
The king answered them thus: "What pretext can
you have to hold property that belongs to me? Have
not your advances been fully reimbursed by the rents
and revenues received out of my domains during my
long absence? If you pretend to claim more than a
fair equivalent, remember that it is a deadly sin to
exercise usury towards your sovereign, and that I have
a bull from the pope which prohibits such practices
under pain of excommunication. If what you have
received falls short of what you have paid, and any
balance is justly due to any of you, I will make up
the deficit from my treasury, and thus you will have no
just cause of complaint."

No one had courage to remonstrate, and all was restored without compensation.   Richard thus again
entered into possession of the castles, boroughs, and
lands he had alienated, and such was the first benefit
that the Norman race of England derived from the
return of their chief, without whose presence the court
flatterers pretended that they could no more live than
if their heads were removed from their bodies.   As to
the English race, after having been pressed to the
death under the weight of the taxes levied for the
royal ransom, they were to be again assessed for the
redemption of the hostages left in Austria, and for the
cost of the war which was denounced against Philip.[1]

The Earl of Mortain, alarmed at the return of his
brother, fled to the court of France.  All the strong-
holds he possessed in England soon fell into the power
of Richard.   The parliament accused John of high-
treason, and summoned him to appear before them

[1] Thierri, t. iv. p. 104.

within forty days, or forfeit all claims to the regal
succession. They then voted subsidies for the invasion of France. Richard took an oath that he would
make neither peace nor truce with Philip, till he had
restored all that he had plundered him of during his
captivity; he further swore that he would not take
his eyes from the soil of Normandy till he had given
battle to his enemy. He made an opening in the walls
of Westminster-hall, in the direction of Normandy,
through which he looked every day to remind him of
his oath, and through this aperture he walked before he
set out on his expedition. He embarked at Portsmouth
with one hundred vessels, and landed at Barfleur in 1194.

The King of France was already in the field, and had
captured Verdreuil, Neufbourg, and Evreux. When
Richard landed in Normandy, he was besieging Verneuil, but in consequence of a perfidious act of treachery
and cruelty committed by the Earl of Mortain, he suddenly quitted that city with a chosen body of men,
leaving the main army to continue the blockade.
Philip had appointed the Earl of Mortain governor of
Evreux; but that prince, uneasy at the approach of his
brother, determined to regain his confidence by betraying the King of France. The garrison of Evreux was
composed of three hundred gentlemen; these John invited to a banquet. As soon as they were seated at table,
he gave the signal to a band of assassins, who were secreted
in an adjoining apartment, and the whole were merci-
lessly massacred. This worthless prince had the barbarity to place the heads of his victims on pikes, and
range them on the walls of the town. Detestable as
this crime was, it was accepted as a peace-offering by
Richard, and the two brothers were reconciled. It is

difficult to pronounce on their relative turpitude, and say which was the greater criminal, the perpetrator of the deed or the applauder of it.

It was to avenge this outrage that Philip quitted his army, and marched on Evreux, in the hope of seizing John, but the criminal had escaped. The King of France set fire to the town, which he reduced to ashes; thus punishing the innocent inhabitants for a deed of which they were guiltless.

In the mean time Richard advanced to the relief of Verneuil, and the French, dispirited at the absence of their monarch, were seized with a panic; they abandoned their lines, and fled. Richard pursued them with vigour, committed great slaughter, and took possession of Verneuil, which he had been on the point of losing. Philip met his fugitive soldiers, but no persuasion could induce them to return to the encounter.

A negociation for peace followed these transactions, and it was proposed to grant a truce for one year, during which time the terms should be arranged. The Archbishop of Rheims, the counts of Nevers and Bar, and Anselm, Dean of Tours, represented the King of France. The Archbishop of Rouen, and the Senechal and Constable of Normandy, represented the King of England. They proposed the following conditions:—

1. That Richard should retain all the territories of which he was in possession, and Philip all the towns that he then occupied.

2. That either party should be permitted to strengthen by additional fortifications any castles actually in existence, but the construction of new ones was prohibited.

3. That all church property and personal property belonging to the clergy, which might have been seized during the troubles should be restored to the original holders.[1]

These articles were agreed upon, and were about to be signed, when Philip proposed an additional clause, to the effect that all his partizans, as well as those of Richard, should be included in the truce for one year, and be restricted from fighting against each other. This clause Richard rejected, because the ancient laws of Poitou and Aquitaine gave a privilege to all gentlemen to settle their private differences by the sword; and had this right, founded on immemorial usage, and cherished as a distinctive mark of honour, been invaded, the whole of the higher classes would have broken out into revolt.

The negociation was accordingly broken off, and hostilities were immediately renewed. The rival princes met at Vendome, but Philip, being inferior in numbers, attempted to retreat: the impetuous Richard fell with fury on his rear-guard, seized the baggage of the King of France, his military chest, his royal seal, and all the national archives, which, according to the strange custom of those times, invariably accompanied the army where the sovereign commanded in person. Those precious registries were lost, which England, though frequently solicited, would never restore.[2]

---

[1] Dumoulin, p. 471.

[2] Every exertion was made to remedy the inconveniences which resulted from the loss of the royal papers and titles. A keeper of the archives, named Walter, supplied, by a wonderful effort of memory, almost all the most important deficiencies. A treasury of charters was established under the charge of a treasurer, whose office, in 1582, was united to that of the king's procureur-general. These were at first deposited at the Temple, afterwards at the Palais de Justice, and finally at the Sainte Chapelle of Paris. After the defeat of Philip, the archives were never exposed to the chances of war.

Philip, more incensed than discouraged at this disaster, eagerly sought an opportunity for revenge. The English army were besieging Vandreuil: they were taken by surprise, and suffered immense loss. Several battles were fought on either side, with varied success, but they only present horrible and monotonous pictures of cruelty and ambition. No national interest, no ennobling passions animated the scenes of these frightful tragedies, which were marked by dogged and obstinate valour, but were deficient in all that was chivalrous or heroic. Neither party gaining any material advantage, while the lands were desolated and the prelates and nobles impoverished, the conditions of a truce were at length signed, as the preliminary step to a general pacification.

"1. In consequence of the prayers of the cardinal legate, and the abbot of Citeaux, the King of France grants a truce to the King of England and his adherents.

"2. The King of England may fortify, if he please, Neubourg, Driencourt, Conches, and Breteuil; the other fortresses dismantled, or partly destroyed, by the King of France, shall remain in their actual state, until a definitive peace is signed.

"3. The King of France shall remain in possession of Val-de-Rueil, Louviers, Aquigny, Laire, and the adjoining territory, up to Haye-Malherbe, and Pont de l'Arche.

"4. The King of France, during the truce, may fortify, dismantle, or burn all the fortresses in his possession up to the day of signing the truce, and do what he pleases with all the lands he may have acquired antecedently to such signature.

"5. The King of England shall have the same right over the fortresses now in his hand, but he shall not be at liberty to fortify any of those which the King of France may have dismantled, except the four above mentioned.

"6. The King of France stipulates that all the parties who attached themselves to him before the war, shall be included in the truce, with those of Arques, Driencourt, Eu, Mortemer, the subjects of the Earl of Boulogne, Hugh de Gournay, the people of D'Aumale, de Baveu, de Neufmarché, Gisors, the Norman Vexin, Vernon, Gaillon, Pacy, Illiers, Marcillac, Loye, Nonancourt, Tilliers, La Nuë, and Fraiteval; also the Earl of Angoulême, John de Rouveray, Baldwin D'Aquigny, and the Count of Meulan.

"7. The truce shall continue from the day of All Saints next ensuing to the day of All Saints, 1195.

"8. As the King of France has named those whom he desires to be included in the truce, the King of England shall be bound to name those whom he desires to include, within fourteen days, otherwise the King of France will not recognise them; nevertheless, all who are publicly known to be partisans of the English shall have the benefit of the truce.

"9. The kings have each elected and named two sovereign judges to decide on the indemnity which shall be paid within forty days, if either of the said kings, or any one of their subjects, violates the articles of this treaty, which judges shall swear on the Gospels, that neither friendship, hatred, fear or bribes shall influence their minds, but that they will give sentence according to equity.

"10. If any hostile enterprise is undertaken beyond

the Loire in the direction of Berri, the judges shall meet between Issodoun and Chateauroux. The ordinary judges in the locality where the enterprise is undertaken shall give notice of the same to the two sovereign judges, who shall, without delay, assemble at the appointed place, and there assess the indemnity. But if the enterprize is undertaken on this side of the Loire in the direction of Normandy, the place of meeting shall be between Tillieres and Verneuil. In case the two judges cannot agree, then the legate of his holiness, as the best referee, acting with good faith and at the peril of damning his soul, shall investigate the truth of the facts, and without favour shall launch the thunders of the church against the party who has undertaken the enterprise, and refuses to pay the indemnity, and moreover shall put his lands under an interdict.

" 11. If the wrong doer be a subject of France, then the King of France shall use all his efforts to enforce the payment of the indemnity; if he be a subject of England, then the King of England shall be under a similar obligation.

" 12. If the King of France attacks the English, or if the King of England attacks the French, the cardinal legate shall put the kingdom of the aggressor under an interdict, should either party refuse to pay the indemnity awarded by the judges.

" 13. Richard, King of England and Duke of Normandy, with those of his party, shall remain in possession of what they hold on this side of the Loire, in the direction of Normandy, at the date of the agreement to make the truce; and as to what concerns lands or castles beyond the Loire, they shall continue in the state in which they may be on the day that the truce is signed.

. "14. The King of England wills that all who, before the war, were attached to him and not to the King of France, shall be included in the truce.

"15. The prisoners of the King of France shall return to their houses, giving such bail as his majesty may require: if not, the judges shall compel them to swear that they will voluntarily return to prison, in fifteen days before the expiration of the truce; the King of England shall have a similar right over his prisoners.

"16. The two kings shall swear to observe the said truce, by placing their hands within the hands of the legate, and shall give each other letters binding themselves to observe all the clauses. Now Gervaise of Chatillon, as representative of the King of France, has sworn to observe all the articles above recited, and maintain the truce. Those whom the King of England may appoint, whether clerks or laics, shall swear for him in the manner prescribed by the judges. And be it known to all men, that we who have sworn to keep this convention sacred, have taken such oath after having received letters from their majesties, by which they promise to ratify and confirm all that we may do for the maintenance of the truce, in testimony of which we have affixed our seals to these presents. Done between Verneuil and Tillieres, on the 23rd day of July, one thousand one hundred and ninety-four."[1]

This truce neither accorded with the personal wishes of Richard or Philip, but was extorted from them by

[1] Dumoulin, p. 474.

their prelates and barons. Richard indeed very soon disclaimed its validity, on the plea that it was not attested by his true ducal and royal seal, which he affirmed had been lost when his Vice-chancellor, Roger Mauchien, was drowned at Cyprus. But though both the kings were eager for war, a dreadful famine in France and Normandy prevented immediate hostilities, but they were only postponed for a short' season. The intervention of a third party soon roused the rivals to battle.

On the death of Tancred, Henry, Emperor of Germany, rapidly conquered La Pouille, Calabria, and Sicily, and conceived the extravagant hope of equalling the power and glory of Charlemagne. Knowing the hatred that Richard entertained against Philip, he sought to ingratiate himself into his favour by conferring on him the Viennois and Burgundy, with the towns and territories of Lyons, Arles, Marseilles, and Narbonne, to the sovereignty of which Henry pretended, as forming part of the ancient empire of the German Cesars. Richard was to hold these as a feudatory, though the people of those countries had never acknowledged the imperial authority, nor ever accepted a ruler of his nomination ; and, in return for this barren gift, which conveyed only the shadow of power, he promised to aid Henry in the conquest of France. Had this insane project succeeded, Richard must have ultimately shared the fate of his rival, but he was blinded to all views of sound policy, and sought only to gratify his personal revenge.

Philip, informed of this league, anticipated the menaced attack, armed his subjects, and razed all the fortresses which the truce had placed in his hand.

Richard carried fire and sword through the provinces of France, burning whole villages, slaughtering the inhabitants, cutting down trees, and rooting up vines ; the cruelties of Philip were equally atrocious, and the war became a scene of fierce extermination.

An unexpected event led to another truce.  Boyac, Emperor of Africa, having heard of these constant battles between the Christian princes, landed in Spain, at the head of an immense army, routed Alphonso, King of Castille, and laid siege to Toledo.  This invasion alarmed both Richard and Philip ; they dreaded the ascendancy of the Saracens, and agreed to a suspension of arms, lest their continued quarrels might endanger the safety of Christendom.

It was agreed between them that Louis, heir to the French crown, should marry the sister of Arthur, Duke of Brittany, and niece to King Richard, who covenanted to give up to them and their heirs, Gisors, Neaufle, Baudemont, with the Norman Vexin, Vernon, Ivry, Passy, and pay them, as a marriage portion, twenty thousand pounds in silver. The King of France, on his part, engaged to surrender to the King of England all that he claimed in the province of Angoulême, the entire provinces of Aumale and Eu, the castle of Arques, and several other fortresses that he had seized in Normandy and elsewhere.

The ratification of this peace was deferred till Richard had time to communicate with the emperor, for he had bound himself not to conclude any treaty with the French, till he had obtained his sanction.  During this interval Richard restored the princess Alice to Philip, not from any good feeling of his own, but at the request of his mother, Eleonora, who detested her.

She was shortly afterwards married to the Count of Ponthieu.

When the Norman Chancellor returned from Germany, he announced that the emperor refused his consent, considering the terms dishonourable to the King of England, who ought never to recognize the right of Philip to any conquest which he had made when Richard was in prison, because Philip had engaged on oath not to attack his dominions till forty days after his return from Palestine; and Henry offered to pay back to Richard out of his ransom seventeen thousand marks of silver, to enable him to regain what he had lost. However, when the day of All Saints arrived, (the time fixed for signing the treaty,) the two kings repaired to Verneuil, and when the hour struck for their meeting, Richard went into the hall of audience, and declared himself ready to perform his share of the contract; but the Archbishop of Rheims begged him to wait a short time, as Philip had not yet left his council. To this he consented, and after some delay the Bishop of Beauvais accused him of perfidy and perjury, and handed him a cartel of defiance from the King of France.

The fiery Richard eagerly accepted the challenge, and both parties rushed to arms with equal fury. Philip, however, gained the advantage; he compelled his rival to raise the siege of Arques, and captured Dieppe. An English fleet, which attempted to recover the port, was totally sunk, and thus France triumphed by land and sea. But Philip feared to penetrate into the interior of Normandy, and meditated an invasion of Berri, when Richard offered to settle their disputes by single combat, or by a battle of six on each

side, on condition that the King of France was one of
the party ; but this was rejected by the French barons,
on the plea that Richard was the vassal of Philip, and
consequently that his suzerain could not place himself
on an equality with his inferior.

The French army marched into Berri and besieged
Issodoun :  Richard hastened to its relief; an engagement seemed inevitable, when suddenly the two kings,
advancing in front of their respective lines, embraced
each other with seeming friendship.   The old writers,
always fond of the marvellous, attribute this reconciliation to some supernatural agency, but it was owing
to the interference of the pope, who was justly alarmed
that these wars would depopulate the finest provinces of Christendom.   They quitted each with apparent cordiality, and agreed to meet at Louviers, in
January, 1196, when they concluded the following
treaty.[1]

" 1. We, Richard, King of England, Duke of Normandy, &c., give to Philip, King of France, as a perpetual inheritance, Gisors, Neufle, and the Norman
Vexin, on condition that Stephen of  Longchamp
holds Baudement and its territory, as a fief from the
King of France.

"2. Hugh de Gournay, during his life, shall do homage to the King of France, unless he prefers returning
into our service ; and after his death, his entire fief
which is in Normandy shall revert to us and our
heirs.

---

[1] A curious circumstance occurred at this interview, not unworthy of record.  The
two kings were seated under a tree, from the trunk of which a huge serpent issued
forth.  They drew their swords to kill it, but their soldiers witnessing the fact,
without perceiving the cause, rushed to arms, and it was not before many men
were slain on both sides, that the tumult was appeased.  *Segur. Hist. de France*,
t. iv. p. 442.

"3. Richard de Vernon, exchanging with the King of France the castle of Vernon, for eight hundred Parisian livres of annual rent, shall hold all the land that Hugh de Gournay held in England, and if such is not of equivalent value to the land of Vernon, then the king shall be obliged to make up the difference. Richard de Vernon, and his son, with our consent, and by our command, have abandoned to the King of France and his successors the rights and privileges of *chatelains* of Vernon, and have sworn never to make any further demands for compensation

"4. We consent to, and ratify, the donation of Pacy, as well in fief as in demesne, its dependencies and rights, as the Earl of Leicester transferred the same to the King of France for his ransom.

"5. We make over to the King of France, to be enjoyed in hereditary right, Neufmarché, Vernon, Gaillon, Pacy, Ivry, and Nonancourt, with their castle-wards and seignorial jurisdictions, and we ordain that boundaries shall be placed between Gaillon, and Val-de-Rueil at Merrille, which boundaries shall stretch from the Eure to the Seine, and all on the side of Gaillon shall belong to the King of France, and all on the side of Val-de-Rueil shall belong to us.

"6. We yield to the King of France all that we hold, or pretend to hold, in Auvergne.

"7. If the Earl of Leicester, Richard de Vernon his son, or any other of our subjects, on account of fiefs or demesnes, that we have ceded to the King of France by this treaty, do injury to him or his, we bind ourselves to put their land into possession of the King of France, and give him also full satisfaction for all damages, and banish them from our dominions.

" 8. In order that this peace may be permanent between us and our suzerain the King of France, the said suzerain yields to us and our heirs for ever, Issodoun, Grassey, in Berri, and all the fiefs depending on them, the fiefs of Chastre, of Saint Chartier, of Chastelet, as Andrew de Chavagny used to hold them of the Kings of France, and the fief of Castle Meliand, with its appurtenances, excepting those parts which the Count of St. Gilles, and his people, and the Count of Turenne, and his people, were possessed of in Michaelmas last.

" 9. We permit the King of France, if he chooses, to fortify Ville-Neuve on the Cher.

" 10. By this treaty the provinces of Eu, Aumale, Arques, and Driencourt, remain to us, and the lands of all the gentlemen who hold of Hugh de Gournay, and have entered our service, shall be restored to them, but they are at liberty to do homage and service to the said De Gournay, though without prejudice to the fidelity they owe us.

" 11. The King of France gives up to us Beauvoir, and all the other lands belonging to us and our subjects, which we lost when imprisoned in Germany, except the lands specified above, which shall remain to him and his heirs for ever.

" 12. The Count of St. Gilles shall be included in this treaty, by which we are to retain all the lands we held on the eve of St. Nicholas, in the province of Toulouse, which we may dispose of as our own, and which we may fortify as we please ; and the Count of St. Gilles shall have the same privileges. But if the said Count shall refuse to be included in this treaty, the King of France shall not give him any succour, and we shall be allowed to do him every possible injury by fire and sword; but as we wish to be at peace with him, should he accept this treaty, we agree to restore to him all the places we have taken since last Michaelmas.

"13. The Counts of Perigord and Angoulême, and the Viscount de la Brosse, and their subjects, shall be put into possession of their lands, and they shall do us homage and service as heretofore.

"14. The Viscount of Turenne shall hold jointly from the King of France and from us, as it is reasonable; and in reference to Fortunat de Gorde, if we succeed in proving, by thirty irreproachable witnesses, that we have held and possessed for a year and a day the castle of Perville, which we desire to place in his hand, the King of France shall not interfere in the matter.

"15. In reference to the new castle, which we desire to build at Tours, we shall follow the advice of the Archbishop of Rheims, and Drogon de Mellot.

"16. Neither the King of France nor ourselves claim any thing from the fief of Andely; but should the Archbishop of Rouen put the King of France under an interdict or excommunicate him, his majesty may send two priests or deacons to Andely, or any other place dependent on the archbishop, and they shall there remain till they have decided, with two other priests and deacons, we shall send, whether the interdict, or excommunication, be just. If they find it just, the King of France shall be bound to restore Andely and its dependencies, and all that he may have taken from it, to the archbishop, and indemnify him according to the decision of the arbitrators. But if, on the contrary, they shall decide against the archbishop, then he shall remove the interdict or the excommunication, and we will indemnify him; and if the archbishop dies, the revenues of Andely and its dependencies shall be held in trust by the chapter of our Lady of Rouen, till his successor is appointed, but no one shall be allowed to fortify Andely.

" 17. All that has been plundered from the clergy on either side shall be faithfully restored; and should war again break out, nothing shall be taken from them, and they shall enjoy all their properties and privileges as in time of peace.

"18. We have renounced, and do hereby renounce all pretensions over the subjects of the King of France and the fiefs that belong to them, and the King of France is bound by the same obligations to us.

"19. We have mutually promised not to give refuge to the liege subjects of each other.

" 20. It is agreed that the Earl of Leicester, and all prisoners and hostages on both sides, shall be set at liberty.

"21. We have mutually sworn to observe this treaty, and faithfully maintain it; and to give it greater formality and solemnity, we have signed it with our royal seals, at Louviers, between Gaillon and Val-de-Rueil, in the year one thousand one hundred and ninety-six."[1]

We have given this treaty at length, as it illustrates the peculiar features of the times, particularly in reference to the royal prerogatives. It is clear that the kings were rather the heads of a baronical aristocracy, than independent or absolute monarchs, as many of the nobles were parties to the contract, stipulating for express provisions entirely personal to themselves,

---

[1] Dumoulin, p. 482.

and having, as in the case of De Gournay, an option to choose either Philip or Richard as suzerain. It also shows the immense power of the clergy, who received back all their lands, with a special guarantee against future losses.

Shortly after the ratification of the treaty of Louviers, Leopold, Duke of Austria, died, and the German prince, in his last moments, ordered the liberation of the hostages, and the remission of the balance due for the ransom of Richard. This concession did not spring from any generous feeling, but was wrung from Leopold by an excommunication levelled at him by Pope Calixtus the Third, which he heeded not when in health, but which produced its effect, when he became sensible that his last hours were approaching.

The treaty of Louviers was broken within six months after it was executed. Richard summoned to his court the Lord of Vierzon in Berri, and Duke of Aquitaine, on which Vierzon was a dependency, but he refused to appear; on which Richard razed his castle to the ground. The refractory baron appealed to France; Philip gave him his protection, and entering Normandy through the frontier of Berri, seized on Dangu. He next laid siege to Aumale. Richard advanced to its succour, but was defeated and wounded severely by Alain of Dinan. Nevertheless, having received a reinforcement of three thousand Welsh soldiers, he once more tried the fate of arms, and was again unsuccessful.

While the King of England was sustaining these disasters, his brother John, Earl of Mortain, had penetrated into the Beauvoisis, and captured the Bishop of Beauvais, cousin to the King of France. It was this

prelate who had been sent on a mission to the Emperor of Germany, with a request that he would never
liberate Richard, and at whose entreaty the prisoner
was loaded with chains.   The English prince now determined to wreak his vengeance on his persecutor;
he shut the prelate up in a strong tower, and fettered
him with iron.   Philip applied to the pope for the release of his relation, and the pontiff wrote to Richard
demanding the liberty of the bishop, whom he called
his dear son.   In answer, Richard sent to his holiness
the armour of the prelate, who as frequently wore a
helmet as a mitre, with these lines: " Do you recognize the robes of your dear son?"   This silenced the
pope, and the bishop only regained his freedom, after a
detention of many years, by paying two thousand
marks of silver.

The Bretons and the Toulousains declared against
Richard.   The first insisted that he should confide to
their guardianship their Duke, Arthur, nephew of
Richard; the second were apprehensive of some attack on their national independence, so frequently
menaced by the dukes of Guyenne.   The king satisfied the Bretons by restoring their prince, and reconciled himself with the Count of Toulouse, by giving
him his sister in marriage.   Profiting by the discontents
and jealousies of the great barons of France, who were
alarmed at the ambition of Philip, he formed a
league with the Counts of St. Gilles and Champagne,
and this was strengthened by the adhesion of Baldwin,
Earl of Flanders, formerly Count of Hainault, and father-in-law to Philip.   Baldwin pursued this hostile
policy, because Philip claimed the province of Artois
as the dowry of his wife Isabella, and which he had

forcibly seized, as well as a considerable part of Flanders.

Richard opened the campaign by marching into Picardy and capturing the town of Saint-Valery-sur-Somme. Baldwin made himself master of Douai and laid siege to Arras. Against this latter Philip directed his attacks, but he fell into an ambuscade, was compelled to capitulate, and received the law from his vassal. As the price of his liberty, he bound himself to restore all that he had taken from Baldwin and Richard. But when the King of France was called upon to execute the terms of the treaty he had signed, he positively refused to do so, pretending that, as the Count of Flanders was his vassal, he could not force his suzerain to fulfil his engagements, as that would have involved a confession of inferiority. This pitiable sophistry shows the marked bad faith of Philip. Baldwin most clearly had him in his power; he could have made him a prisoner, and marched on to Paris, in the event of which, supported as he would have been by Richard, he might have seated himself on the throne of France. Moreover, the feudal obligation never compelled a vassal to surrender his rights, or allow his lands to be invaded by his suzerain; but as Philip had no moral or legal plea to justify the violation of his contract, he sought to shelter himself under a pretext, which he well knew was unfounded. Richard and Baldwin, incensed at this perfidy, at once renewed hostilities; the latter seized on Aire and St. Omer in Artois, and the former captured all the fortresses that Philip possessed in the French Vexin.

The King of France displayed his usual activity,

and collecting an army of forty thousand men, he
marched against Richard, in full confidence of victory,
as the forces of his rival were much inferior in number.
He pushed forward with five hundred cavalry, not
thinking the enemy so near at hand, and was suddenly
surrounded, between Gisors and Courcelle, by the English troops. His capture seemed inevitable, but he
bravely cut his way through the hostile lines. In crossing
the bridge of Gisors, it broke down; the king was precipitated into the river Epte, but his horse swam to the
shore, and he landed in safety. Twenty noblemen
were drowned; many perished on the field of battle,
and a hundred prisoners of the first rank, among
whom were a Montmorency and a De Mailli, fell into
the power of the victor.

The main body of the French army, which Philip
had imprudently quitted in the plain of Courcelle, soon
joined their discomfited monarch, who marched on
Evreux, and, to satiate his vengeance, gave that city
a second time to the flames. After this disgraceful outrage, he advanced to Beaumont-le-Roger; but suddenly changing his policy he returned to Paris, dis-
banding his troops and leaving the French Vexin and
the Beauvoisis at the mercy of Richard. He had,
however, written to Pope Innocent the Third, imploring his intercession to prevail on Richard to
agree on terms of peace; and the sovereign pontiff
succeeded in appeasing the wrath of the English monarch, by pledging himself to use all his spiritual influence in the elevation of his nephew, Otho, Duke of
Saxony, to the imperial throne of Germany.[1]

---

[1] Otho was the son of Matilda of England, sister to King Richard, by her marriage with Henry the Lion, Duke of Saxony.

In 1198, the Cardinal of Capua, holding the functions of apostolical legate, arrived in France, and a conference was held between Andely and Vernon. Philip rode to the bank of the Seine, and continued on horseback; Richard remained in a boat on the river. The latter insisted that Baldwin of Flanders should be included in the peace, to which the former positively objected. Under these circumstances no definitive settlement was effected, but the two kings agreed on a truce for five years on the following conditions :—

1. That the King of France should restore to Richard all his conquests, excepting Gisors ; and as a compensation for holding that city, Philip gave Richard the right of nominating to the Archbishopric of Tours.

2. That Prince Louis, son of Philip, should marry the Princess of Castile, niece to the King of England.

3. That the King of France should promise and swear to assist with all his power the election of Otho, nephew of Richard, to the imperial throne of Germany.

4. That King Richard should give to Prince Louis, on his marriage with his niece, the castle of Gisors, and twenty thousand marks in silver.[1]

This treaty was never signed, that formality being postponed till the return of Richard from Poitou, where he met his death. A vassal of Vinomar, Viscount of Limoges, had discovered, buried in the ground, a valuable treasure. It was a golden group of figures, representing an Emperor, his wife, his sons and daughters, seated at a table, and round the table was an inscription declaring the names of the parties and the times in which they lived. Vinomar claimed this

[1] Dumoulin, p. 491.

prize from his vassal, but his vassal refused to surrender it; while Richard, as suzerain of Limousin, by
virtue of his ducal rights over Guienne, demanded the
whole, as treasure-trove.   Thus menaced, Vinomar
and his vassal agreed to settle their own disputes, and
unite in resisting the claims of the king; for which
purpose they fortified the castle of Chalus, which
Richard besieged.   As he was reconnoitring the place,
Antoine de Gourdon shot an arrow at him, by which
he was severely wounded.   The injury, however, would
not have been fatal, had Richard treated himself with
prudence, but he continued to live intemperately, as
he was wont to do: gangrene followed, and the monarch died on the 6th of April, 1199, twelve days after
he received the wound.

Before his death, he ordered the citadel to be assaulted, and it was carried.   Gourdon was taken prisoner, and reserved for a cruel punishment.   He was
brought before the king, who asked him why he had
singled him out for a mark.   Gourdon sternly answered, " You have put to death my father and two
brothers; I wished to avenge their deaths by slaying
you with my own hand; avenge yourself in turn, by
taking my life."   " I pardon you," replied Richard,
" I prefer that you should live an example of my clemency, than that you should die an example of my
vengeance."   He also gave him a sum of money, and
commanded his restoration to liberty; but Marcado,
chief of the Brabançons, a man of ferocious character,
seized him and flayed him alive.

Richard made a will, by which he divided all his
personal estate between the poor of his dominions,
his domestic servants, and his nephew Otho, Empe-

ror of Germany. He also directed that three hundred
measures of wine, of sixty gallons each, should be
annually presented to the cathedral of Rouen ; one
hundred for the archbishop, and two hundred for the
canons; and this grant was continued till 1553, when
a judicial order of the Court of Rouen commuted each
measure of wine into a money payment of forty
sous.[1] He desired that his body should be buried
at Fontevrault, at the feet of his father, that this humiliation might atone for his filial disobedience:
his entrails were deposited at Poitiers, and his heart
in the church of our lady of Rouen, in a vase of
silver, which was afterwards sold to contribute to the
ransom of Saint Louis, of France, and the heart transferred to a vase of stone.[2]

Richard was rather an adventurer than a king.
Brave as a soldier, undutiful as a son, a perfidious
ally, and an ambitious and grasping tyrant, his character scarcely exhibits any traits of virtue. His personal courage has gained him the admiration of those
who are dazzled by the false glitter of military glory,
but in the eye of the moralist, he was a ruthless murderer. Harsh to his subjects, cruel to his enemies, he
was only beloved by his soldiers, who conferred on
him the title of Cœur de Lion. His desire of vengeance was equal to his love of fame, and he was only
generous to the enemy who slew him. He lived as an
heroic barbarian and died as a Christian.

[1] Dumoulin, p. 493.     [2] Ibid, p. 494.

# JOHN,

## TWELFTH DUKE OF NORMANDY.

On the death of Richard, the ducal and royal thrones
were usurped by the Earl of Mortain, brother of the
deceased monarch, to the prejudice of Arthur, Duke of
Brittany, his nephew, then a youth fourteen years of
age. This young prince was son of Geoffrey, second
son of Henry the Second, by his marriage with Constance of Brittany; and as the laws both of France and
England recognized representation in the first degree,
Arthur was, without doubt, legitimate successor to his
uncle Richard, who had died without offspring. Moreover, Cœur de Lion had publicly proclaimed him his
heir, before he embarked for Palestine, and in that
capacity he had been acknowledged by the barons and
prelates: his rights had been further guaranteed by
the treaty signed between Richard and Tancred at
Messina. But the validity of his claims, though based
on truth and justice, being unsupported by money or
soldiers, proved unavailing, and Arthur neither inherited England nor any of the continental possessions
of his ancestors.

John was in Normandy when intelligence arrived of

the death of Richard in Limousin, and he at once determined to seize the throne.  The first measure of the
usurper was to possess himself of the royal treasure
deposited at Chinon, which was readily given up to
him by Robert de Turneham, the governor, and he
made use of it to corrupt the troops, who swore allegiance and fidelity to his person.  His mother, Eleonora,
secured the adhesion of Aquitaine; but Anjou, Maine,
Touraine, and Poitou, separating themselves from the
cause of Normandy, recognized Arthur as their chief,
and formed among themselves a league offensive and
defensive, at the head of which were the Bretons.  This
confederacy, however, was weak, its nominal head
being a child; and though he was under the protection
of France, yet it suited not the policy of King Philip
to render him such efficient aid as would have secured
his independence, but simply to use him as a check on
John, whom he resolved, if possible, to expel from the
Continent; not indeed with any view to assert the
rights of Arthur, but to seize on all the English dominions, and incorporate them with France.

Walter, Archbishop of Rouen, favoured the cause of
the usurper, to revenge himself on Richard, who had
prevailed on the pope to transfer the revenues of Andely to the ducal exchequer, contrary to the sixteenth
article of the treaty of Louviers, although the metropolitan received, as an equivalent, the mills of Rouen,
the town and seignory of Dieppe, with the seignories
of Bouteilles and Louviers, and the forest of Alier-
mont.[1]  The prelate knew the intentions of Richard
towards his nephew, nor was he ignorant of the detestable character of the Earl of Mortain, who, after con-

---

[1] Dumoulin, p. 485.

spiring with the King of France to dethrone his brother
when absent in Palestine, sought to be reconciled to
him by massacring the garrison of Evreux in cold
blood.   None of these considerations, however, influenced the prelate; he sacrificed honour and justice to
avenge himself on the dead, and, opening the gates of
Rouen to the usurper, installed him with the usual
formalities.

Hubert, Archbishop of Canterbury, was equally instrumental in seating John on the throne of England,
and he was crowned at Westminster by that prelate on
the 26th of May, 1199.   But the speech which Hubert
delivered on that occasion bears internal evidence that
he was himself convinced of the injustice of his own
conduct, for, to excuse himself, he declared that the
succession to the crown was elective, and not hereditary, and that it belonged to the most worthy, and not
to the most legitimate; those points to be determined
by the barons.   "John," said Hubert, "holds his
crown from the free will of the nobles and commons,
and not from his birth.   I shall anoint him as a
monarch called to the government of the state by Providence and the suffrages of the nation : in the exercise
of his authority he must always remember that the
sceptre is a sacred deposit, entrusted to him by God
and the people, and not a patrimony which descends
to him by a full and clear title from his ancestors.   Such
indeed was originally the institution of anointing kings;
thus Saul and David were first chosen by God, and
afterwards consecrated by his ministers.   As archbishop, I do not feel myself bound to place the crown
on the head of the nearest heir, nor do I hesitate to
prefer the *more worthy; the greater worthiness I dis-*

*cover in the person of John,* brother of the deceased King Richard; therefore it is that I pronounce his election legitimate." After this address Hubert said, " I am ready to proceed with the ceremony of anointing, as soon as the voice of the people has declared itself."

The spectators applauded this speech, and accepted John, who was duly consecrated, amid the acclamations of the multitude.

It is certainly true that legitimacy, as the basis of hereditary right, was not a settled principle as in modern times; and many instances have been adduced, in the course of this history, to establish that fact. Rufus was preferred to Robert, who was again set aside by his younger brother, Henry; and Stephen of Blois swayed the sceptre to the prejudice of Henry the Second. The same form of procedure was adopted, in the earlier ages, in Germany and Italy, as well as in the Peninsula. At the council of Valence, for instance, held in 890, Louis, son of Boson, was elected King of Arles, and the principal reason assigned was that he descended from the imperial family. The kingdom of Arles (as were all the other petty states which were fragments of the empire of Charlemagne) was elective and hereditary; elective, because the kings could only ascend the throne through the choice of the national representatives; hereditary, because the electors always chose a member of the reigning family.[1] But although Hubert could plead this custom in favour of his decision, it is equally true that he put a gloss on the usage to suit his own purpose. He knew well the character of

---

[1] Introduction aux Memoires sur la Revolution Française, par F. Grille, tome i. p. 19, in notis.

John, already steeped in crime, and he was not justified in pronouncing him *more worthy* than Arthur, an
innocent youth, whose moral conduct was unblemished.
The appeal to the people to sanction his choice was an
artful and impudent trick, to give colour to the usurpation he advocated, for the people in those days were
mere "hewers of wood and drawers of water;" and
even at a subsequent date, when Magna Charta was
wrested from John, the "liberi homines" alone received the benefits of that palladium of aristocratic
liberty, all the inferior classes being excluded from its
provisions.

John, having thus secured possession of England,
crossed over to Normandy, with a view to dissolve the
league formed by Brittany, Anjou, Maine, and Poitou,
nor was he without serious alarm as to the future
policy of the King of France, at whose court Arthur
resided.   Philip had received the homage of the young
prince for all the continental territories he claimed, and
constituted himself his guardian; but instead of protecting his interests, his first measure was to raze all
the strong fortresses in Poitou; and when the young
prince remonstrated against this act of perfidy, Philip
angrily answered, " Am I not your suzerain? Have
you not done me homage? Shall a vassal, dependent
on my protection, question my conduct?"   Constance,
mother of Arthur, saw at once that her son was rather
the prisoner than the guest of France, and they both
fled to Angers and threw themselves on the mercy of
John.   That wily and unprincipled monarch pretended
the greatest friendship to his nephew, but his artifice
was soon discovered; and Arthur, being assured that

P 5

his uncle intended to imprison him, once more returned to the court of Philip.

Though John was resolved upon the ruin of his nephew, he was not disposed to allow Philip to incorporate his inheritance with France, and he accordingly prepared himself to resist force by force. War would have been inevitable, had not the Cardinal of Capua, the papal legate, interposed, and by his mediation a treaty of peace was drawn up at Andely, in 1200. The terms were highly advantageous to Philip, and equally disgraceful to both parties. John abandoned all the conquests of Richard on the Loire, and surrendered Issodoun, and the strongest places in Berri. He also yielded the province of Evreux, and the Norman Vexin. In addition to this large sacrifice, he consented to pay twenty thousand pounds for Brittany; by which bargain John became suzerain of his nephew, with the power of crushing him, under the colour of feudal sovereignty. It was further stipulated that Blanche of Castille, niece of John, should marry Louis, son of Philip.[1]

History records few transactions more disgraceful than this treaty. It is an indelible stain on the memory of Philip that he should have abandoned Arthur to his uncle, for he knew his character, and could not have forgotten the treacherous murder of three hundred of his subjects at Evreux. The eagerness which John displayed to have a hold on his nephew, and the immense sacrifices he made to carry his point, must have convinced so shrewd a politician as Philip of the sinister intentions of the King of England. Horrible as

[1] The historian Rigord affirms that John declared Louis his heir, in case he died without issue. He has been copied by most writers; but De Segur seems to doubt the fact, as he states that Rigord gives no proof for his assertion.—*Hist. de France,* tome iv. p. 459.

the imputation is, it is difficult not to believe that
Philip speculated on the criminal designs of John, as
the murder of Arthur would have furnished him with
a pretext to confiscate Normandy, an event which actually followed shortly afterwards.

The marriage of Louis, though he was only thirteen
years of age, with Blanche of Castille, was celebrated
on the day after the treaty of peace was signed. Arthur
went to Vernon, and did homage to his uncle for Brittany. The two kings repaired to Paris, where John
was entertained with royal magnificence, but their
friendship was hollow and insidious. The ambition of
Philip could not brook the English domination over
the fairest provinces of the Continent, while the King
of England, more powerful than his suzerain, spurned
at the humiliation of being a vassal of France. They
concealed their mutual hatred of each other under the
mask of cordiality, each waiting for some plausible opportunity to renew hostilities.

John was married to Isabella, daughter of the Earl
of Gloucester; but becoming enamoured of Isabella,
daughter of the Earl of Angoulême, he determined to
repudiate his first wife, and a divorce was pronounced
by the Archbishop of Bordeaux, on the ground of consanguinity. But this was not the only difficulty he
had to surmount; Isabella of Angoulême had been
affianced to Hugh de Lusignan, Count of La Marche,
and he insisted on the completion of the contract.
John, however, defeated his pretensions through the
aid of Philip, who was cousin to Isabella, she being
the grand-daughter of Peter of France, brother to
Louis the Seventh. Lusignan was compelled to submit, but he prepared himself for vengeance.

Accompanied by his bride, John repaired to England, and his consort was crowned with great pomp at Westminster, on the 8th of October, 1201. He soon returned to Normandy, and, heedless of the intrigues of his enemies, abandoned himself to pleasure. The Count of La Marche had interested his brother, the Count of Eu, in his cause; and William and Savary de Meuleon joined his party, while the sequel proved that Philip secretly encouraged the plot of the discontented. The confederates soon broke out in open revolt, and when cited before the tribunal of John, they refused to obey the summons. The King of England forthwith attacked the castle of Dancourt, which belonged to the Count of Eu, who appealed to the King of France, as his suzerain, for protection. Philip affected the character of a friendly mediator, but, at the same time, he delicately hinted to John, that if he denied justice to his vassals, he should be reluctantly compelled to render them the assistance they required. John had sense enough to penetrate the real views of Philip, and replied that the rebellious barons must first be tried in his court before their peers; "then," added he, "if my sentence is illegal, you yourself will have the right to judge me, assisted by your peers, the great vassals who hold immediately from France." This answer, strictly in accordance with the feudal system, admitted of no refutation nor evasion. Philip was compelled to acknowledge its justice, and sent back the complainants to the tribunal of their liege lord, the King of England.

Had John possessed any principle of honour, he might have dispelled the storm ready to burst on his head, by pursuing even a prudent line of conduct; but

he had neither worldly tact nor moral rectitude. When
Lusignan and his friends found themselves obliged to
obey the summons of John, they demanded safe conducts, but these were refused, and the confederated
barons again appealed to Philip to guarantee them
their personal safety. He accordingly commanded
John to show cause why he withheld the feudal securi-
ties always customary on such occasions, but his answers were evasive and unsatisfactory; on which the
King of France assembled his troops to avenge an insult which had become personal to himself.

The favourable moment seemed now to have arrived
for realizing those vast schemes of ambition which
Philip had so long and so anxiously cherished, and he
determined again to bring Arthur on the scene, to embarrass his uncle, and promote his own views. He
conferred on the young prince the order of knighthood,
and affianced him to his daughter, Mary of France,
whom he had by his marriage with the unfortunate
Agnes de Meranie. Arthur was honoured with a guard
of two hundred horsemen, and marched into Poitou,
attended by the Counts of La Marche and Eu. The
Bretons had promised a reinforcement of five hundred
cavalry and four thousand infantry, but the youthful
impetuosity of Arthur, who was only in his sixteenth
year, would not brook delay; he laid siege to Mirebeau, and captured the town. But the castle was
strong, and defended by a numerous garrison, who
were animated to resistance by the presence of Queen
Eleonora, mother to John, and they held out so effec-
tually that the King of England had time to advance
in person to their relief. William Desroches, a gentle-
man of Poitou, who acted as Arthur's general, was

surprised by the arrival of this unexpected succour, and fearing to place the prince in peril, he concluded a peace, which John readily granted, and by virtue of the treaty he entered the town.　But the unprincipled monarch at once displayed his habitual perfidy, by imprisoning Desroches and all the gentlemen of his army. He sent Arthur to the castle of Falaise, from whence he was transferred to the tower of Rouen, and placed under the custody of Robert de Vieux Pont.

When John returned from this campaign he visited Arthur, professed a warm friendship towards him, offered him the highest honours subordinate to his own, and, after pointing out the insidious policy of Philip, urged him to dissolve his alliance with France; but his nephew rejected all his overtures with indignation, demanding the throne of England, and all the continental territories, by virtue of his paternal rights, and by virtue of the repeated declarations of his uncle Richard.　John was staggered by a display of spirit so determined in one so young, and he resolved to remove a competitor whom he could neither cajole nor intimidate; but his mother, Eleonora, penetrated his views, and forbade him to imbrue his hands in the blood of her grandson.　He could not disobey a parent who had made so many sacrifices on his behalf, but her death, which occurred within a few months after the imprisonment of Arthur, gave full scope to his criminal desires.　Unprincipled as he was, John felt some qualms of conscience at murdering his nephew with his own hand, and he requested William de la Braye, the captain of his guards, to commit the assassination; but that noble-minded soldier recoiled with horror from the cowardly and detestable act.　Thus disap-

pointed, the king resolved to perform the office of
executioner.   He entered the prison of his victim in
the night, dragged him into a boat, and plunging\ a
sword through his heart, threw the body into the Seine,
and returned to his palace.  The murder was perpetrated on the 3rd of April, 1203.

Such, according to the French historians, was the
tragical death of the unfortunate Arthur.   D'Argen-
tré, in his history of Brittany, states that the prince,
wishing to escape from Rouen, leapt from the wall into
the river, and being unable to swim to the bank was
drowned.   Matthew Paris ascribes his death to mental
grief, when in prison.   It is stated by other writers
that the murder was committed at Cherbourg, on a
rock close to the margin of the sea ; and that after John
had there slain his nephew, he threw the body into the
water, which was drifted away by the tide, and never
afterwards seen.[1]

Intelligence of the murder soon reached Brittany,
and the whole population of the province, from the
highest to the lowest, clerks and laymen, united in one
generous burst of indignation.   Constance, mother to
the unfortunate prince, invoked the aid of Philip to
avenge the death of her son ; and all the Breton nobles,
sharing her grief, implored him to punish this fearful
violation of divine and human law.  The King of
France was not slow to answer this appeal, not moved
indeed by any generous or ennobling feeling, but
prompted by policy and ambition.  He seized with
alacrity the favourable opportunity that presented
itself to restore to France those rich and extensive
provinces, which the imprudence of his father had

[1] Dumoulin, p. 514.

lost by the repudiation of Eleonora, and cited John before his tribunal to answer the charge preferred against him by the duchess and the barons of Brittany.

"When the King of France," says the Flemish chronicle, "heard the complaints which reached him from all quarters against the King of England, he was deeply incensed: he summoned his peers and explained to them the injuries he had personally received, and asked them their advice, when they decided that two of their members should repair to England, and have an audience with John. They accordingly selected the Bishop of Beauvais and the Bishop of Noyon, who saw the king at a castle called Windsor, and delivering their letters said, "Sire, the peers of France have decided to summon you, on the demand made by their king; and we, who are peers of France, now cite you before this tribunal."

On this John dispatched the Bishop of Ely to Paris, to demand a safe conduct. "I grant it," said Philip, "he may come securely." "And return?" rejoined the English envoy. "Yes, if the sentence of his peers allow him," replied the monarch; "for I swear by all the saints in France, that he shall never return unless he is acquitted." "But remember that he is a king," remarked the Bishop of Ely, "and that the English barons will never allow him to expose himself to captivity, or perhaps death." "What matters that to me?" said Philip. "John, Duke of Normandy, is my vassal: I know that he seized the crown of England by violence; but a suzerain never loses his rights over a vassal because a vassal has increased his power." In consequence of this answer, which placed his personal safety in peril,

John refused to appear before the tribunal of Philip; but the peers, proceeded to try him, found him guilty, and confiscated the duchy of Normandy.

It is a remarkable fact that no authentic details have been preserved of this memorable process; and Segur observes that the names of the peers are unknown, with the exception of Odo, Duke of Burgundy, who was president, the counts of Nevers, Boulogne, St. Paul, and Dampierre. The sentence convicted John of parricide and felony, condemned him to death, and stripped him of all the lordships and fiefs dependent on the crown of France.

This judgment would have been nugatory had it not been carried into execution by force of arms. Philip soon took the field at the head of a powerful army; and such was the contempt into which his rival had sunk, that when the King of France displayed his standard on the frontier of Poitou, all the inhabitants voluntarily joined him, and delivered up the castles. Thus successful even beyond his hopes, Philip was equally well received by the people of Maine, Anjou, and Touraine; and thus strengthened he invaded Normandy, already attacked by the Bretons, who had captured Mont St. Michel, Avranches, and all the country between that town and Caen. The French, advancing into the eastern frontier of the duchy, took Andely, Evreux, Domfront, and Lisieux, and effected their junction with the Breton army in the neighbourhood of Caen. Instead of making head against this confederacy, John passed his time in pleasure; and when the extent of conquest was made known to him, he carelessly answered, " Let Philip proceed; I will recover more in a day than he can gain in a year."

The French proceeded from victory to victory, and in twelve months Rouen, Verneuil, and Chateau Gaillard alone remained to the English monarch.

Chateau Gaillard stood on an eminence, overhanging the Seine, whose waters bathed its base. Richard Cœur de Lion, knowing its importance as a military position, had fortified it at great expense. He considered it the rampart of Normandy, and gave it the strange title of Gaillard, because he was wont to say that behind its shelter he could laugh at all the efforts of France. The citadel was built on a steep rock, surrounded with precipices, defended by a double trench cut out of the solid stone, and by two arms of the river, so that it became a peninsula: it could only be approached by a narrow causeway. The garrison was secure against the shock of the battering-ram, and the command was entrusted to the Earl of Leicester, one of the ablest captains of the age.

Unintimidated by these obstacles, Philip resolved to obtain possession of the castle, then deemed almost impregnable. As soon as it was invested, heedless of the flights of arrows incessantly discharged from all parts of the fortress, he succeeded in throwing a bridge across the river, and on this he erected lofty towers which overtopped the citadel. Elated with this success, he rashly attacked the trenches, but was repulsed with great slaughter. Compelled to retreat, after having lost many of his bravest soldiers, he changed his tactics, hoping to reduce by famine those whom he could not expel by force. The siege was converted into a blockade. The cowardly John, who had only courage to perpetrate crime, sent William the Marechal, an experienced warrior, to the re-

lief of Chateau Gaillard, with three thousand cavalry
and four thousand infantry. A large flotilla conveyed these troops down the Seine. The movements
of the English general were so prompt and secret,
that Philip had no suspicion of the danger which
menaced him. His army, surprised and attacked in
the night, was seized with a panic; in the disorder,
many were slain, and others drowned. But after the
first shock, the French rallied. The king gallantly
threw himself into the thick of the fight; his nobles
followed his example; the ardour of the soldiery was
rekindled, and they repulsed the assailants. The
English flotilla, in the mean time, attempted to destroy the bridge, but most of the vessels were sunk by
huge beams of timber; the remainder fled, and victory
remained with the besiegers.

A few days after this encounter a famous diver,
Gobert of Mantes, swam across the river, below the
bridge, and landed on a spot not guarded.[1] He took
with him some iron pots filled with inflammable materials. With these he ignited the palisades; the flames
spread to the neighbouring buildings. Philip, availing
himself of the disorder and alarm produced by the fire,
attacked and secured the houses without the walls of
the citadel, on which the town capitulated, but the
fortress still resisted.

The scantiness of provision had reduced the gallant
Earl of Leicester to great extremities, and he applied
to John for assistance. The king, in reply, thanked
the earl and the garrison for their courage, and earnestly implored them not to surrender; but he observed
that, if food failed them so as to produce famine, then

[1] Segur. Hist. de France, t. iv. p. 475.

Leicester was to follow the orders of Pierre de Preaux, William de Mortemer, and Hugh de Huelles.[1]

In the meanwhile the French engineers had been undermining a tower, which fell to the ground, and this was the signal for a general assault. Philip had in his pay a corps of Brabançons, and their chief, Cadoc, first planted the French banners on the rampart. The intrepid governor, defeated but not discouraged, retreated behind his last entrenchment, after having set fire to all the works which surrounded the demolished tower.

A house built by King Richard still remained standing in the midst of the ruins, and on the edge of the ditch. A young French hero, Pierre Bogis, descended into the ditch, with some of his comrades, under cover of the night. Raised on their shoulders, he reached the window of King Richard's house, and by the aid of ropes, which the party had carried with them, he drew up his associates; two hundred men were thus brought to bear on the garrison, who were not more than equal in number to their assailants. The combat was long and bloody, but while victory still hovered doubtfully between the besiegers and the besieged, the last sheltering front of the wall fell to the ground. Philip at once rushed through the opening with a fresh body of chosen troops, and the gallant Leicester, after a desperate resistance of six months, was compelled to surrender Chateau Gaillard.[2]

The capture of this fortress, deemed impregnable, greatly raised the military reputation of Philip; and his troops, inspired with unbounded confidence in his skill and resources, marched boldly to Rouen, eager to

[1] Dumoulin, p. 517.          [2] Segur. Hist. France, tome iv. p. 477.

plant their standard on the capital of Normandy. But the garrison and the burgesses resolved to imitate the heroic bravery of the defenders of Chateau Gaillard, and bury themselves in the ruins of their metropolis rather than acknowledge a foreign ruler. During a whole year the attacks were incessant and furious, and the resistance steady and determined ; but the want of food to sustain so large a population compelled the Rouennois to request a truce, which Philip granted on the following conditions :—

" 1. The governor, men-at-arms, the mayor, jurats, and municipality of the city and town of Rouen, oblige and bind themselves to surrender to King Philip Rouen with all its castles, within thirty days, counting from the first of June, 1204, unless within that time peace is concluded between the King of France and King John, Duke of Normandy, or unless the duke raises the siege by force of arms.

" 2. They put in the hands of the king the Barbachanne, or tower at the end of the bridge, and yield to him ten feet frontage of the water of the Seine, with permission to fortify it with boats or vessels, if such should be his pleasure.

" 3. They also agree to demolish, if required, four arches of the bridge.

" 4. The King of France, on his part, binds himself to guarantee the lands, lordships, and immoveable property of the nobles, burgesses, and soldiers, now present in Rouen, and of which they were legally seized on the first of June, provided they do him homage and service, as they have been accustomed to do to the Dukes of Normandy ; this clause to take effect only on condition that they are compelled to surrender.

"5. The nobles, burgesses, and soldiers of the Count of Eu, at present in Rouen, shall be put into possession of their property, and shall recognize the Count of Eu as their lord.

"6. The burgesses of Drincourt, Eu, and Aumale shall also be put into possession of their lands, doing the services to which those lands are subject, and provided they return to, and live on, their estates.

"7. The nobles and vassals of Robert, Earl of Alençon, at present in Rouen, shall be put into possession of their estates, on rendering the services they owe to the said count.

"8. The King of France, after the full accomplishment of all the conditions above prescribed, and the surrender of the town and city of Rouen, binds himself to preserve all their liberties and customs, both by land and water, throughout Normandy, Anjou, Poitou, Maine, Brittany, and Gascony, excepting the province of Evreux, the Norman Vexin, and the lands and lordships of Hugh de Gournay.

"9. The king also binds himself to give a safe conduct to those nobles and soldiers now in Rouen, who refuse to be included in this treaty, and that within thirty days, whether they should choose to retire by land or water.

"10. The King of France may navigate his vessels on the Seine, in such manner as he pleases, provided he commits no act of traffic, except of what he now possesses ; and if any of his people on board such vessels take any thing from the Rouennois or others included in this treaty, the king binds himself to make

full compensation within thirty days, provided the
claimants can prove by credible witnesses what property
they have lost.

" 11. The nobles and soldiers now in Rouen shall
be at liberty to go to the lands that belong to them,
and if they choose to do homage to the king, he shall
receive them as his lieges.

" 12. All the merchants of Rouen, during the thirty
days' truce, may export and import their merchandize,
with the exception of corn, both by land and water,
into or from the territories of the King of France, on
payment of the usual tolls and customs.

" 13. If the people of Verneuil and Arques, who
still hold out for King John, wish to be included in
the present treaty, and to make peace with the King
of France, they will signify such intention on the Sunday after Ascension ; but in any case they are to enjoy
the truce of thirty days."

Such were the terms of this memorable treaty, for
the guarantee of which the Normans gave hostages,
and which was signed by all the principal officers on
both sides, that it might bear the strongest and the
most solemn character. These formalities concluded,
the Rouennois sent deputies to England, to acquaint
the duke with their position, and requiring aid. They
found the contemptible monarch playing at chess, and
such was his indifference that he dismissed them till
he had finished his game. His only answer was that
he could not give them assistance in the time required,
and he advised them to make the best terms they could
for their own safety. When this cowardly message
was communicated to the soldiers and burgesses of

Rouen, they resolved to deliver the keys of the city to
Philip, and Verneuil and Arques followed their example.    Thus the province of Normandy, ceded by
Charles the Simple, in 912, was reunited to the crown
of France by Philip Augustus, in 1204, after a separation of two hundred and eighty-two years.

# APPENDIX.

# APPENDIX.

## I.—THE TAPESTRY OF BAYEUX.

THIS curious and venerable specimen of ancient Norman manufacture is a piece of linen cloth, nineteen inches high, and two hundred and ten feet eleven inches long, on which various figures are traced, and worked into the cloth. It forms one entire piece, and is exhibited in the nave of the cathedral of Bayeux on the eighth day after the festival of Nuns. It appears never to have been completed; the extremities are beginning to crumble away, and with a view to prevent the total loss of so precious a document of antiquity, the chapter of that church have recently resolved on making a duplicate of it, and have deposited in their archives a copy of the inscriptions it contains. The country people in the neighbourhood of Bayeux familiarly call it "The Toilette of William the Conqueror." It is supposed by some that Matilda of Flanders, Queen of England, Duchess of Normandy, and wife of the Conqueror, weaved this tapestry, with her attendant ladies, while her husband was engaged in his wars. The Abbé de le Rue, professor of history at the College of Caen, and several English antiquarians, attribute this tapestry to the Empress Matilda, daughter of Henry the First. M. Delauney, in consequence of many indecent emblems that appear in the border of the tapestry, denies that it is a female production, and ascribes it to Bishop Odo: M. Le Prevost inclines to this latter opinion; he considers that a work of this description could only be accomplished by persons who lived at the time when the events recorded happened, and that its special destination was to ornament the church of Bayeux, the bishop of which was brother to William the Conqueror. In the eighth volume of "Memoires de l'Academie des Inscriptions et Belles Lettres," there is a learned disquisition on the tapestry, by M. Lancelot, and the following account is translated from his papers :—

"The first figure in the tapestry is that of a king seated on a throne, with a crown on his head, and a sceptre in his hand, and appearing to speak to two men who are standing before him. It is intended to represent King Edward the Confessor, who orders or permits Harold, son of Earl Godwin, to journey into Normandy. Above these figures are inscribed the words, '*Edvardus Rex.*'

"At the spot where the next inscription begins, there was a hole in the cloth, which has been rudely patched up, and this patch has not only obliterated a letter of the first word in the second inscription, but has also disturbed four other letters, which are quite awry. The letters B I are legible, and the letter effaced seems to have been U, and on this supposition the second inscription runs thus :—'*Ubi Harold dux Anglorum, et sui milites equitant ad* Bosham.' The meaning of this is that Harold, after his audience with the king, set out on his expedition : he is on horseback, a hawk on his wrist, and his dogs running before him. Bosham is a small village in Sussex, near to Chichester ; it was formerly a frequented sea-port.

"The next object represented in the tapestry, is a chapel or church, and the word "*Ecclesia*" is inscribed. Harold appears in the attitude of a man who prays to the Almighty for a prosperous voyage. The church is followed by an apartment in which persons are seated at table ; some drink out of cups, others out of horns. The repast finished, Harold goes down to the beach and embarks, as explained in the next inscription :—'*Hic Harold mare navigat, et velis vento plenis, venit in terram Widonis comitis.*' The Count Guy, on whose coast Harold landed, or, according to some, was wrecked, was Wido, or Guy, Count of Ponthieu, who imprisoned the English prince, with a view to obtain a ransom, as was customary in those days. The inscription states the fact : '*Hic apprehendit Wido Haroldum, et duxit eum ad Belrem, et ibi eum tenuit.*' Belrem was the modern Beaurain sur la Canche.

"Harold being now the prisoner of the Count of Ponthieu, it was necessary that they should fix the terms of his liberation. The bargain they were striking is indicated by the inscription : '*Ubi Harold et Wido parabolant.*' This Guy was a vassal of William's, and when the duke heard of the captivity of Harold, he dispatched two ambassadors to the Count of Ponthieu, demanding the

release of the prisoner; the inscription anounces their
arrival: ' *Ubi nuntii Willelmi ducis venerunt at Widonem.*'

"The next figure is that of an officer, or domestic, who
holds two horses by their bridles, and above his head is
the word 'Turoldus.' Who this Turoldus was, it seems
impossible to determine; the name was a common one in
those days, and the tutor of William in his boyhood was
called Turoldus. But he was slain soon after William
obtained the dukedom of Normandy, therefore he could
not be the person denoted by the tapestry who accompanied the ambassadors to the Count of Ponthieu. Guy
refused to surrender Harold on the first summons, on
which William dispatched a second deputation. The
tapestry represents them on horseback, with an inscription
showing who they were: ' *Ubi nuntii Willelmi.*' This embassy prevailed on Guy to liberate the captive. A courier
brought the news to William; the tapestry thus describes
the event: William is seated on his throne, holding his
sword in his left hand, and directing his right hand towards
a man who trembles with fear; this is supposed to be Count
Guy. The inscription runs thus: ' *Hic venit nuntius ad
Willelmum ducem.*'

"After this meeting the tapestry exhibits a castle;
above the gate are seen two men, one of whom carries a
lance; they appear to be sentinels on duty. It is probable
that this was intended to represent the castle of Beaurain,
whence the Count, after having released Harold, set out
to deliver him into the hands of the Duke of Normandy.
Guy is at the head of a troop of horsemen; he caries a
hawk on his thumb, and with his right hand he points out
Harold to William, who is also on horseback, and who,
now being free, has resumed the customary badges of distinction, holding his hawk on his wrist. Behind Harold
are seen two files of cavaliers, accoutred with lance and buckler; they are the retinue of Count Guy. William, Harold,
and Guy are the only persons who wear mantles fastened
at the right shoulder; all the rest have plain short dresses.
Here the inscription is, ' *Hic Wido adduxit Haroldum ad
Willelmum, Normannorum ducem :*' 'Here Guy conducts
Harold to William, Duke of the Normans.'

"Eadmer, Roger de Hoveden, and many other English
historians say, that Count Guy contented himself with
releasing Harold, and that he did not accompany him to
Normandy. The tapestry, however, is more exact, and in
this particular it accords with the statement of William

of Poitiers, a cotemporary historian of the reign of Duke
William, and also with those of William of Malsmbury
and Matthew Paris, all of whom declare that the Count of
Ponthieu personally delivered up the prisoner to William.
William of Poitiers even mentions the very place where
this event happened, ' *apud Aucense castrum,* ; that is, at Eu,
which is in fact on the frontier between Normandy and
Ponthieu. Count Guy was handsomely rewarded by the
duke, and received presents of various kinds as an equivalent for the ransom he had demanded : the chronicle of
Normandy relates that he acquired a noble manor on the
bank of the river Eaulne, and other property.

" William immediately conducted Harold to Rouen.
' *Haroldum veró sufficientissime cum honore in urbem sui prin-
cipatus caput Rothomagum introduxit,*' says Matthew Paris.
The inscription on the tapestry, however, is more general :
' *Hic dux Willelmus cum Haroldo venit ad palatium suum :*'
' Here Duke William came with Harold to his palace,'
without mentioning Rouen. The procession was conducted
in the following manner :—William on horseback, a
mantle on his shoulders, is at the head ; Harold follows
him, holding a hawk on his wrist, while his dogs run before him ; he is only attended by a single cavalier. In
front, and in advance of all, is another horseman, one of
the esquires of the duke, who precedes the rest, to open the
gates of the palace, and who appears speaking to a sentinel
who stands under the wall of the castle.

" We next see an apartment or saloon, in which a man
is seated, his hand resting on a sword, listening to the conversation of another who is standing ; behind the latter
are several persons armed with lances and bucklers. This
scene is supposed to represent the interview in which
William announces to Harold his intention to succeed
Edward the Confessor in the throne of England, and
requires him to aid the enterprise. Harold pledges his
word to give the assistance requested, and William engages
to bestow on him his daughter Adéle, in marriage. There
is no inscription in this part of the tapestry, and there
never was any, the elevation of the saloon, which is represented, filling up the whole space from the top to the
bottom. It is followed by another, where we see an
unarmed man, a mantle hanging from his shoulders, who
stretches out his hand, and appears to be speaking to a
female. We read : ' *Ubi clericus et Aelfgyva.*' This is all
that appears on this part of the tapestry. It is complete

in itself, having no connexion with what precedes or
follows, for it is terminated right and left by a portion of
the house and castle, which throughout the whole of the
tapestry, serve to distinguish one event from another.
It is difficult to say precisely what is intended by these
two figures and the words of the inscription; however,
Aelfgyva was a common name in those days in England
and Normandy.

"The tapestry next alludes to the expedition which
William persuaded Harold to undertake against Count
Conan, in Brittany. This Count had sent a defiance to
the duke, and announced the day on which he proposed
to invade Normandy. William was not the man to slum-
ber when he was menaced; he marched at once against
his enemy, and knowing the valour of Harold and his
associates, he asked him to undertake the campaign on his
behalf, as affording an opportunity of signalizing his
prowess. The tapestry here represents William and Harold marching with their cavaliers towards Mont St.
Michel. They have no longer their birds nor dogs, as
they always had when they journeyed for amusement;
they are now equipped for war. It may be well in this
place to describe the military accoutrements of the
period.

"The body dresses were of two sorts. One was quite
plain, consisting of a common habit which fitted closely
to the person; those who wore this dress had only a cap
of cloth or leather on their heads, but no casque or helmet.
The men armed in this simple way were the troops who
always followed the principal leaders noticed in the
tapestry; they were a species of subaltern militia, who
attended the banner of their lords. The other dress was
a coat-of-mail, covering the body from the shoulders down
to the knees. The exhibition of this description of armour
is exactly painted in that division of the tapestry which
represents the carriage of ammunition and provisions on
board the Norman vessels, for the invasion of England,
under the Conqueror. The soldiers had then no iron
head-pieces, which were introduced after the time of
William. In the place of them they had certainly a sort
of covering, but not at all resembling that which appears
in the Prayer Books of Charles the Bald, ancient as they
seem. The old head-pieces of Normandy were narrow,
and terminated at the top in a sharp point; they fell
over and covered the back of the neck, and in front they

had a projection to protect the nose against wounds in battle. This projection formed a solid part of the head-piece, and in this respect was quite different from the "nasal" of later times; the latter was flexible and move-able at pleasure, so as to admit freely of respiration, but the projection depicted in the tapestry of Bayeux is fixed and immoveable; nor indeed was it required to be flexible, as the greatest part of the face was uncovered, and breath-ing in no respect impeded. Among the cavaliers thus armed, some had leggings, others none: these leggings were of the same material, and corresponded with the body part of the accoutrements. The bucklers were slightly convex, somewhat oval at top, and terminated at the bottom in a point: there are, however, three or four in the tapestry which have a different form; they are round, more concave, and have in the centre a sharp point, suffi-ciently long to serve as a weapon of attack and defence. As Duke William and his followers never used a similar weapon, it is fairly to be inferred that the tapestry, in this particular, intended to designate the warlike instruments of Harold and his companions, to whom this species of arm was indeed peculiar. All these bucklers, whether round or oval, were passed through the left arm, by means of a leathern strap to which they were fastened; on some of these bucklers are painted the figures of lions, dragons, and of other fierce beasts; such, in general, were the de-fensive weapons.

"The offensive consisted chiefly in swords, axes, lances, javelins, and arrows. The swords were long and broad, nor did they taper downwards from the hilt, but kept all through the same breadth, except at the very extremity, which was a narrow and sharp point; the guards were heavy and strong; the swords were suspended on the left side. There was nothing peculiar, or worthy of remark, about the axes. The lances were very long, and the iron points were just one-sixth of the length of the wooden handles; the soldiers hurled them in the air, as is proved by many parts of the Bayeux tapestry, more especially in those sections of it which describe the raising of the siege of Dol and the battle of Hastings; and we also see arrows flying through the air. In the border which skirts that part of the tapestry which represents the first embassy from Duke William to the Count of Ponthieu, we observe a man throwing a stone at some birds from a sling. The sling was of common use in the chase; but there is not a single instance in the whole of the tapestry, in which this weapon was used in military operations. We find, however, *bâtons* or sticks, which, being much heavier at one end than at the other, may be called staves or clubs; these arms were only wielded by the serfs and peasants; the sword and the lance belonged to the freemen. Almost all the horsemen had stirrups: some, however, had them not; and this exception indifferently applies to those who wore coat-of-mail and those who wore the common plain dress. The spurs at that time were very short, but fashion, in later days, greatly extended their dimensions. This diversity in the accoutrements of the cavaliers, some wearing stirrups and spurs, and some riding without either, is further proved by the seals used in this period. The saddles of the horses were heavy and rude, and closely resembled the modern pack-saddles still used in many parts of the country, for the rider was wedged in between two upright pummels. There is only one sort of standard or banner, described in the tapestry. It terminated in three points or pennons, and was always fixed to the end of a lance; this was called the ' *gonfanon*,' or ' *gonfalon*,' which sovereign princes, or those who represented them, were alone permitted to carry.

" We left William and Harold on their expedition into Brittany. The tapestry represents a troop of six or seven cavaliers; in the middle of the group we see two armed with coats-of-mail and casques, marching in front of the others. The one on the left, holding a lance, is Harold; the one on the right, carrying the gonfanon, which rests on the stirrup, is William. The horseman in the centre has no coat-of-mail, but is dressed simply, and wears a cap. Behind them follow two men on horseback, wearing the common dress; these figures designate the ducal army. In front of the three cavaliers already mentioned is another horseman, who wears a coat-of-mail; but, instead of a casque, he has simply a cap, and his only weapon is a club; he is evidently not one of the villains, because he wears the coat-of-mail, a privilege only enjoyed by those of noble condition. This is a proof that the weapons usually confined to the serfs and peasants were occasionally borne by persons of higher degree. Who then can this man be, so singularly accoutred with the coat-of-mail of the nobles, but no casque, and carrying a simple club instead of a sword or lance? The most probable conjecture is that he was the mace-bearer of Duke William, or

some other officer attached to his more immediate household, and therefore permitted to wear accoutrements intermediate between the two ranks, by virtue of his office.
The inscription on the tapestry in this place is the following :—' *Hic Willelm dux et exercitus ejus venerunt ad Montem
Michaelis :*'—' Here Duke William and his army arrived at
Michael's Mount.' Mont St. Michel is represented by
a castle built on a rock. We next see the soldiers fording
a river :—' *Et hic transiérunt flumen Coesnonis ;*' 'and here
they crossed the river Coesnon.' This river separates
Normandy from Brittany. The flood-tides from the sea,
and the shifting of the sands, frequently change the course
of the bed of this river, and render the passage dangerous.
The tapestry represents the army of William crossing it
with great minuteness; we see the men on foot holding
their bucklers above their heads; one horseman is figured
raising his legs on the saddle ; others appear thrown down
by the moving sands. We observe a man drawing out a
companion from the stream with his hand, and another
lifting an associate on his shoulders: it is Harold, who is
specially named in the inscription on the tapestry, as
rendering these services :—' *Hic Haroldus trahebat eos de
arenâ.*' Indeed, Ordericus Vitalis describes him as a man
of extraordinary strength and stature. The tapestry
further seems to indicate that many lost their lives on this
occasion, for on the skirt of the lower border we remark a
dead man, extended on the bank of the river.

" The army of William having entered Brittany, the
duke and Harold marched upon Dol, which Conan was
besieging. A crowd of cavaliers, who are represented as
in the act of hurling their javelins, seem running rapidly
towards a castle, which is placed on an eminence. The
most advanced of these cavaliers is already on the bridge,
or rather on the steps by which they ascend it. On the
opposite side, we observe a warrior, with a helmet on his
head, hanging on to a rope fastened to the battlements;
but it is doubtful from the tapestry whether he is scaling
the castle or endeavouring to escape from it, for his attitude admits of both interpretations. At some little distance the horsemen are fleeing at full speed, some holding their lances in their hands, others carrying them under
their arms, and all appear most anxious to escape the fury
of those who are pursuing them. Under this point of
view the tapestry describes the raising of the siege of
Dol, the entrance of William into the town, and the

retreat of Conan; — a series of actions thus expressed
by the inscription : ' *Et venerunt ad Dol, et Conan fugâ ver-
titur.*'

" The tapestry next represents the castle of Rennes, to
which Conan pushed forward part of his forces, when he
received intelligence that William had entered Brittany.
This castle is described as raised on an eminence ; it is divided into battlements and surmounted by a tower, or
donjon, in the centre, with the inscription ' *Rednes.*' The
true inscription was doubtlessly ' *Redones ;*' in the tapestry
the name is cut in two thus, ' *Red*' and ' *nes,*' and between
these two syllables is the painting of the castle, in consequence of which the letter O is lost or omitted.

" The capture of Dinan, a small town in Brittany, at six
leagues distance from Dol, is next represented : no historian of the time has noticed this event. Cavaliers, armed
in the manner hereinbefore stated, present themselves before a lofty castle, and are in the act of hurling their javelins, and on the gate and ramparts are other cavaliers similarly accoutred, who resist the entrance of the attacking
party, and also hurl javelins ; on all sides these weapons
may be seen darting through the air. At the foot of the
castle walls we remark two men armed, but on foot, each
with a lighted torch in his hand, with which they fire the
palisades : the inscription in this place is, ' *Hic milites Willelmi ducis pugnant contra Dinantes,*' that is, ' Here the soldiers of Duke William fight against Dinan.' This mode
of expression leads one to suppose that William was not
personally present at the siege, and that it was undertaken by a detachment of his troops, probably commanded
by Harold ; and this supposition corresponds with the remark of William of Poitiers, who observes that the Duke
of Normandy did not think it prudent to advance with his
whole army into Brittany, as the whole population had
retired into strong fortresses, and the corn was not yet
ripe. Dinan was compelled to surrender, which is shown
in the tapestry, by representing Conan himself standing on
the gate of the castle, opposite to the side on which it is attacked, and holding out his lance, to which his gonfalon is
attached : at the end of the lance are the keys of the castle ; these are received by one of the Norman cavaliers at
the end of his lance ; he is accompanied by two others, and
if Harold had the command of the expedition, it is he
most probably who received the submission of Conan.
' *Et Conan cl aves porrexit :*' ' And Conan stretched forward

the keys.' This section of the tapestry teaches three
things; first, the siege and capture of Dinan in 1065,
which has not been mentioned by any of the old chroniclers.
Secondly, the mode of surrendering a town in those days, by
presenting the keys on the end of a lance to the besiegers,
who received them on a similar weapon. Thirdly, that
the town of Dinan was anciently called Dinantes, although
M. de Valois declares that he has never found it called
among ancient authors by another name than Dinanum.
With this conquest the tapestry concludes the expedition
into Brittany.

"William now desired to confer on Harold some token
of his gratitude, and reward him and his followers for the
courage they had displayed in the war. According to the
inscription on the tapestry the duke gave the English
prince some military weapons : ' *Hic Willelm dedit arma
Haroldo.*' William is standing up, armed from head to foot,
his sword at his side; he puts one hand on the helmet of
Harold, and the other on his arm. Harold, who is also
standing up and armed, rests on his lance, to which his
gonfalon is attached, and wears his sword at his side. From
this ceremonial, it would seem that William then created
Harold a knight, as the expression ' *arma dare*,' in this passage, seems to import, for the bare gift of warlike weapons
would have been unworthy of the generosity of the duke;
and indeed the Roman de Rou expressly states, that William conferred knighthood on Harold. We may here remark, that this ceremony was almost the same as observed
on similar occasions at a later date. They girded on the
sword, placed the helmet on the head, wore the coat-of-
mail, presented the lance, and placed the hand on the right
arm of the knight. The Roman de Rou states that this
honour was bestowed on Harold, at Avranches, *before* the
expedition into Brittany.

"William and Harold next went to Bayeux, and according to the tapestry, Harold there swore upon the relics of the saints, that he would inviolably fulfil the promise he had made to William, as to his succession to the
English throne. Almost all the old authors differ as to
the place where this oath was pledged. William of Poitiers says that it took place at a public meeting purposely
convened by the duke, before the expedition into Brittany,
' *Apud Bonam Villam.*' It is not easy to discover this town,
as there are many called Bonneville in Normandy. Ordericus Vitalis affirms that it took place at Rouen, and the

Chronicle of Normandy, at Sainte Marguerite, near Jumièges. These contradictory statements seem to be all erroneous, for the tapestry and the Roman de Rou both agree in fixing Bayeux as the place, and their evidence is decisive of the locality. It may be further remarked that Odo, uterine brother of William, was then Bishop of Bayeaux, and it is highly probable that the Duke of Normandy would select the cathedral of that town to give the increased solemnity of a religious sanction to a promise so important to his interests. The Chronicle of Normandy states that William employed some trickery in the administration of this oath, which it would have been much easier to effect at Bayeux than at any other place, as his brother was disposed to use all his efforts to aid his ambitious views.

"According to the chronicle, William devised the following stratagem to give additional solemnity to the oath of Harold: he made him swear on a greater number and a better assorted choice of relics than the Saxon prince was aware of. These were placed in a box, which was covered over with an embroidered napkin, and on the top, visible, an ordinary relic was deposited, the sanctity of which was not peculiarly remarkable. Harold took the oath in the usual form : ' *Ita me Deus adjuvet, et sancta evangelia* ;' ' So may God help me, and the holy gospels.' William, in order to inspire his dupe with greater feelings of reverence, and impress upon him more forcibly the religious obligation of his promise, then removed the napkin, and exhibited the concealed relics on which Harold had unwittingly sworn. The truth of this story, as narrated above, is, however, doubtful, at least it appears to be exaggerated ; none of the cotemporary historians mention it, nor can any influential evidence be deduced from the tapestry, to justify the statement; the inscription simply announces that William came to Bayeux : ' *Hic Willelm venit ad Bagias.*' Bayeux is designated, as are all other places described in the tapestry, by a castle seated on an eminence, and which could only be ascended by flights of steps.

" William is next represented as siting on his throne, wearing a mantle over his shoulders ; he holds his sword in his right hand, and stretches out the left to Harold ; behind him are standing two of his officers or courtiers. Harold, also covered with a mantle, is standing between two shrines, designed for the reception of holy relics, which shrines are painted in the form of an oratory or small chapel; he places one hand on each of these shrines: the inscription is, '*Ubi Harold sacramentum fecit Willelmo duci :*' 'Where Harold pledged his oath to Duke William.' Beyond the further shrine are seen two men armed with lances: the covering of their legs is made of small fillets, which was unusual with the soldiery, from which circumstance it would seem that they were thus purposely distinguished from the rest of the attendants, to represent the chief lords and vassals of the court, carrying their weapons on account of their dignity, but otherwise apparalled in what is now called a 'court-dress.' These fillets, which also encircle the legs of William and Harold, formed the usual coverings of princes and nobles under the second race, as appears from the old paintings of Charlemagne, Lothaire, and Charles the Bald. According to the tapestry, it seems that they were still in use in the time of the Conqueror, with, however, this difference ; in times anterior to his, they extended to the extremity of the foot, but in the reign of Duke William they did not cover the foot, which was protected by what we may call a modern slipper. It appears, moreover, that this part of the dress belonged exclusively to the chief lords, so far at least as the tapestry is instructive on this point, for it is only seen on the Count of Ponthieu, William, and Harold, and a very limited number of persons, who are clearly the principal barons.

" By his oath Harold engaged, if we are to believe William of Poitiers, who declares that he received his information from many credible persons who were present, to act as the vicar or attorney of William, at the court of Edward the Confessor, so long as that king lived; that he would do all in his power, both by his recommendation and by bribes, to guarantee and secure the sceptre of England to William after the death of Edward; and moreover, that he would not only give up Dover Castle, but such other fortresses as the duke might wish to have garrisoned by Norman troops, and at the same time supply them with provisions. This promise of surrendering Dover is also attested by William of Malmsbury, by Eadmer, and his copyist, Roger de Hoveden. Ingulphus, Ordericus Vitalis, William of Jumièges, Matthew Paris, and other historians are silent as to this part of Harold's engagement; they only agree in admitting that he covenanted to accept William's daughter in marriage. The Chronicle of Normandy calls her Adéle and Aéle, and William of Jumi-

èges, Adelize. None, but Ordericus Vitalis, call her
Agatha; he says that she had a sister named Adelaide,
who consecrated herself to God, and lived in holiness with
Roger de Beaumont. Probably he confounded the names
of the two sisters. However this may be, notwithstanding
the solemn oath pronounced upon the most sacred relics,
'*super sanctissimas reliquias*,' says Ordericus Vitalis, '*super.
reliquias sanctorum multas et electissimas*,' says Henry of
Huntingdon, Harold did not keep his promise. No sooner
had he repeated his vows of fidelity to William in private
conversation, than he passed over into England. The tapestry represents a vessel with a single mast, a sail extended, and some sailors on the deck; it seems just ready
to take the ground. The castle which follows the painting of the voyage serves both to separate one event from
the other, and to designate the port at which Harold disembarked. We see two cavaliers holding their lances,
dressed as simple travellers, though one of them wears
a mantle; this latter is Harold, who having landed in
England, proceeds to join king Edward; the inscription
expresses this event; '*Hic Harold dux reversus est ad An-
glicam terram, et venit ad Edvardum regem.*' Edward is
seated on his throne, his mantle on his shoulders, and the
crown on his head. It appears to have been the intention
of those who gave this design for the tapestry, to represent
the monarch as bent with years and enfeebled by debility,
as his long beard and the drooping attitude of his head
clearly indicate. Behind him stands one of his officers,
armed with a battle-axe: Harold, who stands in the fore-
ground, also wears a mantle, and is attended by a man
armed with a battle-axe. He speaks to Edward, and
appears to be giving an account of his journey. Ordericus
Vitalis says that, at this interview, he disguised the truth,
assuring Edward, whose life was daily despaired of, that
William had promised him his daughter in marriage, and
had abandoned to him all his pretensions on England, by
way of dowry. Eadmer, on the contrary, and his continuators, and other English historians who have followed
their statements, affirm, in order to preserve the honour
and integrity of Harold, that he gave a statement of all
that had happened to him in Normandy, and of the artful
measures resorted to by the duke, to compel his co-operation in effecting the annexation of England to the duchy,
and that Edward replied that he had clearly foreseen
what would happen, and had expressly warned Harold

of the consequences of his journey to Normandy. The historians of the two countries give such versions of the fact as suited their national predjudices. The Norman chroniclers affirm, not only that Harold violated his oath, but also that Edward declared William his successor, and that the sole object of the mission of Harold was to notify this arrangement to the Duke of Normandy. The English, on their side of the question, declare that William, who had no legal claim to the throne of England, had extorted the pledge from Harold by violence and fraud.

"There is here an irregular disposition in the tapestry, for which it is not easy to account. Immediately after the audience of Harold with Edward, just described, we see the burial of the Confessor, after which the king is represented speaking to his officers and courtiers in bed, and lastly we see him at the moment of death. We imagined at first that this irregular disposition of the tapestry was caused through the carelessness of those who were charged to put the several compartments together, but on mature reflection we found this conjecture untenable, because there is no seam or juncture of any kind. Might it not have been done for some private object, of which we have lost the clue? Or might not the embroiderer have proceeded some way in the work, before the error was discovered, and not thought it worth while to correct a fault that was so palpaple as to correct itself? It is somewhat in favour of this last supposition that the figures in the representation of the death of Edward are reversed, that is to say, they run from right to left, contrary to the usual practice observed in the tapestry, where the figures except in this instance, always run from left to right. We shall presently offer another conjecture on this irregularity, but as we do not feel ourselves justified in deviating from the order of the tapestry, we shall commence with the section descriptive of Edward lying sick in his bed. His beard is long, the crown is on his head; a man raises him up from his recumbent posture, and supports him in his arms; two others stand by the bed, who are mourning. At the foot of the bed is another figure, which seems to be that of a female weeping; the inscription marks the farewell interview: ' Hic Edvardus rex in lecto alloquitur suos fideles.'

" It was at this meeting given by Edward to his principal subjects and most intimate friends, that he declared Harold his successor, being goaded into this nomination

by the friends of the English prince. Below this scene
the tapestry represents Edward dead, and laid out in a
winding-sheet, while two men, one at the head, the other
at the feet, arrange the body. At the side is another
man standing upright, elevating two of the fingers of the
right hand; both his attitude and dress seem to indicate a
priest pronouncing the last benediction. The inscription
announces his death : ' *Et hic defunctus est.*' He expired
on the 5th of January, 1066. Six days afterwards the
corpse was carried to the church of St. Peter, at Westminster : ' *Hic portatur corpus Edvardi regis ad ecclesiam Sancti
Petri.*' Edward rebuilt this church, and the monastery
attached to it, from the bottom to the top, and the dedi-
cation only took place eight days before his burial. In the
tapestry, the church appears large and spacious. The
principal entrance is flanked by two large gates, and two
small ones; at the extremity is a tower, by the side of
which appears a man, standing on the roof of a church;
he puts one hand on the summit of the tower, and the
other hand on a vane which carries a cock. Above the
church is seen a hand, issuing out of the clouds. The
hand is frequently found on the medals of the last emperors of Constantinople. It is also figured above the head
of Charles the Bald in the superb Bible which that monarch gave to the church of Metz, and in his book of
prayers.

"It is generally supposed that the hand placed above the
head of these emperors, was intended to signify that they
held their crowns from the gift of God, but that explanation is quite out of place in reference to the tapestry. It
is not above the head of the king, but above the roof of
the church. It is most probable that the image was here
intended to denote, in a more solemn and impressive form,
the sanctity of the building. The bier is carried by eight
men ; it is nearly square, intersected with stripes or sec-
tional divisions, and loaded with small crucifixes, and
other holy ornaments. Of these eight men, four are in
front and four behind ; they carry the bier on their shoulders with the aid of long poles, two men to each pole;
such was the ancient mode of conveying the dead, for
hearses are a very recent invention. Formerly in France
certain people had the privilege of carrying the body of a
deceased king to the grave, or his effigy, and this happened
in 1610, to Henry the Fourth, who was conveyed to the
tomb on poles, as Edward was. At each side of the bier

we observe two men who hold a bell in each hand. The custom of having bell-carriers in funeral processions, is very ancient. At the close we see a crowd of persons, clearly mourners, and all the historians admit that Edward was sincerely lamented by his subjects.

"Harold lost not a moment in seizing on the throne. Scarcely was the corpse of Edward deposited at Westminster, than he caused himself to be proclaimed king. This fact has not been omitted in the tapestry. We observe Harold, his mantle on his shoulders, leaning on his battle-axe; two men, also wearing mantles, stand before him; one presents him with the crown, while the other seems to say that it is the crown of Edward. The moment of the late king's sickness, owing to the irregular disposition of the tapestry already noticed, is placed alongside of the section in which Harold is proclaimed: was this the reason (in order to connect these two circumstances, in the view of showing that Harold seized the throne even *before* the Confessor was buried,) why Matilda and her ladies purposely caused the irregularity which exists? If so, the tapestry differs from the statements of most of the historians, who declare that the crown was not given to Harold till *after* the burial of Edward. The other man who stands before Harold, holds a battle-axe. The inscription explains that they gave the crown to Harold :—' *Hic dederunt Haroldo coronam regis.*'

"The section immediately following represents Harold seated on the throne. He wears a mantle, the crown on his head ; in his right hand he holds a sceptre, and in the left a globe surmounted by a cross. ' *Hic residet Harold, rex Anglorum.*' At his left side is a man stretching out his arms ; his dress is long, and sweeps the ground ; underneath is a representation of the *pallium*, and of the *chasuble* or cope, which the priests wore when celebrating the mass ; above the head of this man is the inscription, ' *Stigand, archiepiscopus:*'—' Stigand, archbishop.' Ingulphus and his copyist, Florentine of Worcester, say that it was Aldred, Archbishop of York, who crowned Harold ; William of Poitiers and Ordericus Vitalis, on the contrary, assert that it was Stigand, Archbishop of Canterbury, although the other prelates had not given their sanction to the election, and that this archbishop himself was under an interdict pronounced against him by Pope Alexander the Second, he having been accused of simony, and other breaches of ecclesiastical discipline. The testimony of these two last historians, corroborated by the tapestry, appears the preferable, more especially if we take into account the conduct of William towards Stigand, after the battle of Hastings, which shows that he was highly displeased with that prelate. After his victory, he refused to be crowned by him, although that privilege was part of his sacerdotal prerogative, as Ingulphus remarks, but conferred the honour on Aldred or Albert, Archbishop of York. William did more, for he deposed him in a council held at Westminster, two years afterwards, in 1668, and gave his diocese to Lanfranc, the first Abbot of St. Stephen's, at Caen.

"On both sides of the throne Harold sees his new subjects, who seem by their gestures to be recognizing him for their sovereign : on the right are two men, wearing mantles on their shoulders; one of them holds up his sword in the air, and appears to be the representative of the chief nobility.   On the left are a crowd of persons presenting their hands and bowing their heads in token of allegiance.   This ceremony is followed by a remarkable event, narrated by all the old chroniclers : we allude to the comet which appeared in the month of April, 1066.  The ancient historians differ as to the day on which this comet appeared, and also as to the length of time that it was visible.  The Saxon Chronicle fixes it on the 14th of the kalends of May, or the 18th of April.    Florentin of Worcester, and Bertoldus of Coutances, (who continued the Chronicle of Hermannus Contractus up to the year 1100, when he died,) fix it on the eighth of the same kalends, which corresponds with the 24th of April.  Pére Labbe, the learned Jesuit, corrects Bertold, who is the only author he quotes, and insists that the comet was first seen on the evening of the 23rd of the same month.   According to Florentin of Worcester, it was visible during seven days ; according to the Roman de Rou, fourteen ; according to Ordericus Vitalis and William of Jumièges, fifteen ; according to Bertold, and after him Labbe, thirty days.

"The credulous of those days did not fail to attribute the overthrow of Harold, and all the changes in the form of government effected by the Conqueror, to this celestial phenomenon, *after* the event.  The following verses from an old chronicle published by Labbe, commemorate the superstition of the times:

> " Sexagenus erat sextus millesimus annus
> Cum pereunt Angli stellâ monstrante cometâ."

*f*

As well as these two leonine verses :—

> " Anno milleno sexageno quoque seno
> Anglorum metæ flammas sensere cometæ."

In the same spirit this comet is spoken of by Ingulphus, Ordericus Vitalis, the Roman de Rou, and Matthew of Westminster.

"This comet was first seen in the west, and travelled towards the south. It is represented in the tapestry as a large star, from the rim of which rays dart out, which form a bright circle. We observe people looking at it attentively, one of whom is turning away his head. Perhaps this was intended to denote the alarm it had created among the great mass of the people. The inscription is, ' *Isti mirant stella.*' Two lines drawn, one above the letter *t*, in *mirant*, and one above the letter *a*, in *stella*, induce us to read, *Isti mirantur stellam*, ' They are wondering at the star.'

"It is difficult to say positively what the next section means. Harold is on the throne, resting on a lance, the crown on his head ; he bends his head so as to listen to some one who is speaking to him. The inscription is simply, ' *Haroldus*,' but as the lower border seems to paint the sea covered with vessels, and as we know that Tosti, Harold's eldest brother, discontented at being refused his share of the inheritance of Godwin, their father, had formed a party with the Norwegians, and made a descent on the northern counties of England, there is every probability that Harold was listening to the news of this invasion, an invasion that compelled him to march precipitately against those enemies, by which he was detained so long as to be unable to attack William, when he was landing at Pevensey.

"Intelligence of the usurpation of the crown of England by Harold soon reached the Duke of Normandy. This circumstance is marked in the tapestry by a vessel on the beach : the anchor is dropped ; the sailors are furling the sails, and one of the crew is seen walking over the sand ; the inscription is : ' *Hic navis Anglica venit in terram Willelmi ducis :*'—' Here an English ship comes into the country of Duke William.' If we believe Ordericus Vitalis, it was Tosti himself, the brother of Harold and the brother-in-law of William, (for he had married the sister of the duke's wife,) who had persuaded William to cross over to England to claim the crown which had been promised to him, and for the guarantee of which Harold had pledged his oath. The Roman de Rou and the Chronicle of Normandy give a copious account of several councils held on this occasion ; as also of the different expedients to which the duke resorted to raise an army and supplies among his own subjects and his allies. We shall not here enter into details, not only because William of Poitiers and Ordericus Vitalis take no notice of them, but because the tapestry passes at once to the orders which the duke gave to build ships, and make all necessary preparations for this expedition. The inscription is,—' *Hic Willelmus jussit naves ædificare :*'—' Here William ordered vessels to be built.' He is seated on his throne, his mantle thrown entirely across his shoulders, his arms hanging by his sides ; on his left is a man, also wearing a mantle and seated, in the act of stretching out his hand to an artizan, who holds an instrument which seems to be an axe or hatchet, and issuing the orders of William. He apparently is Robert, Earl of Mortain, uterine brother of the duke, and also brother of the Bishop of Bayeux, who took a very considerable part in the invasion, and whose birth, moreover, gave him great influence at the ducal court. It is most probable that Matilda and her ladies have represented him here as partaking of the anxiety which the duke must have felt in building and provisioning his fleet. At the right hand of William is a man standing up ; he wears a mantle ; this dress denotes that he was a powerful baron, or one of the principal officers of William's army.

"The next section of the tapestry represents the execution of the orders of William : two men are represented felling trees with axes, a third lops off the branches, a fourth planes the timber and squares it ; others are engaged in the construction of vessels. We have already remarked that the smiths' tools, used in those days for these purposes by the carpenters, resembled a wooden axe or hatchet ; the handle was short, with iron projecting on both sides, slightly curved at the extremities, corresponding to the implement called in England a twy-bill. One of the builders leans with both hands on a tool, which seems to be an auger. All this compartment, descriptive of the labours of the workmen, is without any inscription ; just afterwards is the following: ' *Hic trahunt naves ad mare.*' ' Here they draw the ships to the sea.' Next is a representation of men drawing the vessels into the sea

with ropes, the masts not being fitted ; the labourers are up
to the middle in the water ; it appears from this part of
the tapestry that the people knew no other method of
launching a ship than this rude contrivance. All these
vessels appear very low in the hull.

"We next observe persons carrying ammunition and
provisions to put on board the armament. The men, two
and two together, carry coats-of-mail on their shoulders,
and in their hands axes, casques, swords, clubs, and lances;
others carry sacks and barrels. A carriage on four wheels,
loaded with military weapons and wine, is pushed forward
by two men. The inscription explains their movements :
' *Isti portant armas ad naves, et hic trahunt currum cum vino
et armis.*' This is not the only passage in old records
where the Latin word ' *arma* ' is made feminine. Many
authors, in the middle ages, committed the same inac-
curacy.

"All being now ready for the embarkation of the troops,
William repairs to the port of Dive, which seems to be
that of Saint Sauveur, where that river empties itself into
the sea ; this was the rendezvous of the forces. We see
the duke on horseback, his mantle thrown over his left
shoulder ; in the right hand he holds his lance, at the end
of which floats his gonfalon ; behind him follow a train of
cavaliers, armed with spears and bucklers. It may here
be remarked that William and his retinue are not fully
accoutred in their warlike costume, because, in this passage, the tapestry merely describes their approach to the
place of meeting, where the main army expected them.

"The voyage across the Channel is prosperous ; it is so
described in the tapestry by a fleet of vessels all sailing
under full canvass ; some appear to be small, others large ;
in the first are men only ; in the latter, men and horses.
The ship in which Duke William embarked is in the
middle of the armament, and distinguished from all the
others by a banner on which a cross is figured. This was
intended to represent the consecrated standard sent to the
duke by Pope Alexander, as a mark of his approbation of
the enterprise.

"The tapestry next represents the disembarkation of
the horses : ' *Hic exeunt caballi de navibus.*' We see a vessel
without sails, and the masts lowered on the deck ; it is dry
on the beach ; a man on the shore leads two horses by the
bridles. From the manner in which these horses seem to
get out of the vessels, they must have been nearly flat-bot-

tomed; several others, resembling barges, are unloaded, and ranged in tiers along the shore. In the following section we observe four men on horseback, gallopping at full speed; they are accoutred for battle, having the coat-of-mail and the buckler, and the lance in the rest; two of them carry pennons at the end of their lances. The tapestry has not sufficiently distinguished the two different sorts of standards, so as to enable us precisely to discriminate between the baron and the simple knight. The inscription in this place, however, announces what these horsemen were about: *'Et hic milites festinaverunt ad Hastingas ut cibum raperent:'* 'Here the soldiers hastened to Hastings, that they might seize provisions.' William of Poitiers says, that the vessel on which the duke embarked, being the swiftest in the fleet, arrived at Pevensey first, and fearing that those who accompanied him might be panic-stricken at being alone on a hostile country, he resolved to dissipate their terrors by amusing them with a festival.

The presence of mind and the tact of William have not been forgotten in this part of the tapestry, where the preparations for the merry-making are minutely described. After the representation of the horsemen who gallop towards Hastings, a small town about three miles from Pevensey, we next see a number of men on foot, who return with the captured booty: one leads a pig, another a sheep, a third raises an axe with which he is about to fell a bullock, and a fourth appears to carry on his back a quantity of dinner-utensils and some linen.

The next section is not so easy to decipher. We see a man on horseback fully armed, having an iron casque on his head, carrying his buckler on his left hand, and a long stick in his left hand, his legs being encircled with fillets similar to those worn by William and Harold, and the principal officers of the Norman court. Before him stands another man, wearing spurs, and resting his battle-axe on his shoulders. The inscription here is simply *'Hic est Wadard.'* The most attentive examination of this part of the tapestry makes it certain that no more than these three words were ever marked in this place. But they do not clearly indicate their own meaning. Some have supposed that this Wadard was the senechal of William, who was giving orders to recall all stragglers to the encampment; others have imagined it to represent one of the military barons, who was about to reconnoitre the enemy. These suppositions, however, are purely conjectural, nor is there a single

remark in any of the cotemporary writers to clear up the
difficulty; but from this passage, as well as from others,
wherein the tapestry records facts and mentions names
unknown to the historians of the conquest, it is certain
that the tapestry, not borrowing its details from any preceding document, must be deemed in every sense an original, composed at the time of this celebrated expedition.

"Immediately after this representation of Wadard, we
see people seated at table. We may here remark their
mode of cooking meat, and the culinary implements then
in use. They are even more rude than those described in
the regulations which James the Second, King of Ma-
jorca, ordered for his household, and which have been
printed at the head of the third volume of the Acts of the
Saints and the Bollandists; whether the age of William
had really not made more progress in the art of cookery,
or whether, in his peculiar situation, the attendants of the
kitchen were obliged to make shift with whatever they could
lay their hands upon; however this may be, the tapestry
exhibits two forked sticks upright in the ground, on which a
third is laid horizontally, from which is suspended a cauldron
over a fire. The inscription, '*Hic coquitur caro,*' denotes
that they are cooking meat. Another man, who stands
near to the cooks, holds a hooked instrument with which
he is drawing out cakes, or some other pastry. We next
see other servitors who present meat to the officers at the
table, by whom it is arranged on the table: '*Et hic minis-
traverunt ministri.*' Among these officers or attendants,
who are all standing up round the first table, there is one
drinking from a horn. He apparently is tasting the quality
of the liquor. The table of the duke next follows, on
which some peculiarities are observable. Firstly, its shape
is circular. Bernard de Monfaucon has remarked that
this shape was almost universal among the ancients, and
the object seems to have been to prevent any querulous
disputes as to precedency, which frequently arise at square
tables having a top and bottom. Secondly, it is laden with
a variety of different articles, fish, bread, cakes, cups,
small bottles, and cruets for oil. Thirdly, before the table
is a person on his knees, holding a sort of covered porringer. Above this compartment of the tapestry is the following inscription: '*Hic fecerunt prandium, et hic episcopus
cibum et potum benedixit.*' The prelate here alluded to is
Odo, Bishop of Bayeux. He is in the ct of blessing the
repast; he places two of his fingers on the top of the cup

or porringer; on his right hand is the duke, easily recognizable by his mantle. The meal being finished, and the whole fleet of William having arrived, the duke then deliberates on the plan of hostilities most prudent to pursue. William of Poitiers relates that a Norman nobleman, whom he calls Robert, the son of Guimare, a lady of high birth, then living on the Sussex coast, fearing that the duke, his natural sovereign, for whom he entertained the highest esteem, had undertaken a rash and dangerous expedition, dispatched a courier to advise him of the forces and popularity of Harold.

"William then held a council of war. To denote this event, the tapestry represents an apartment in which three persons are seated, and in conversation. No doubt this meeting was more numerous, for the duke would certainly have consulted all the principal officers of his army; but the tapestry, in order that this section should not be overcrowded, merely puts forward the three principal characters, whose names are written above their heads. In the centre is William; he wears his mantle thrown over his shoulders, and holds his sword above his head, the point upwards, as a mark of his ducal supremacy. The inscription is 'Willelm.' At his right hand is another man, who also wears a mantle; the inscription is 'Odo, eps.' that is, Bishop Odo; 'eps.' being a contraction of 'episcopus.' The one on his left is without a mantle, and rests the point of his sword on his knee; the inscription is 'Rotbert,' Robert, Earl of Mortain, also uterine brother to the duke. We have already had occasion to speak both of Odo and Robert. The decision of the military council was, that the army should entrench itself near to the place of disembarkation. Hastings, a small village, with a trifling harbour, which was close at hand, was pitched upon as the most eligible spot. William lost no time in executing this project. We see him standing up, wearing his mantle, and the fillets round his legs, and leaning on his lance, from which his gonfalon floats, surmounted by a cross; he seems to be giving some orders to a man who carries tools with him to excavate the ground. Others, having similar instruments, march towards Hastings. Two men appear striking against each other with clubs; this might have been a martial exercise of the times, or perhaps it was intended to shew a skirmish between a straggling party of the invaders and some of the inhabitants of Hastings or the neighbourhood. None of the old authors, however, support the last conjec-

ture; on the contrary, they unanimously declare that
William encountered no opposition whatever from the
country people.

"The tapestry next represents the entrenchments constructed at Hastings. The duke superintends all the arrangements, habited in the same costume as described
above, when he gives his first orders. Among the labourers some hollow out the earth with tools resembling a modern pick-axe; others throw up the loosened earth with
shovels, not much dissimilar from those in modern use, but
narrower; we also observe the common spade of our days,
which the men handle as diggers do at the present time.
Above these workmen appears a castle surrounded with a
palisade; the inscription is the single word ' *Castra,*' 'the
camp.' While William is thus entrenching his troops, he
receives intelligence that Harold is advancing with his
army. The tapestry thus announces his approach: '*Hic
nuntiatum est Willelmo de Haroldo.*' The duke, seated on a
chair with a curved back, listens to a man who speaks with
violent gesticulation; the speaker is evidently above the
common rank, because he wears a mantle, carries a sword,
and supports himself on a lance. At the termination of
this audience we see in the tapestry a house burning; two
men set fire to it with torches, and a terrified mother,
holding her child to her breast, rushes out from the flames;
the sleeves of this woman's gown are remarkably full and
large. The inscription denotes the event: '*Hic domus
incenditur.*'

"The Duke of Normandy was too brave a soldier, and
too able a tactician to await the attack of Harold in his
entrenchments: scarcely had he heard of his advance than
he determined to sally forth and meet him; the tapestry
represents this onward movement immediately after the
fire just mentioned. We now see the duke giving orders
for the march: he is no longer in his ordinary dress; his
mantle and the fillets round his legs are thrown aside; he
is accoutred in a coat-of-mail, his casque on his head: he
seems to issue forth from the gate of a fortress, lance in
hand, to which is attached his gonfalon, surmounted by the
cross: he speaks to a footman who holds his horse by the
bridle; this attendant is unarmed, and no doubt is one of
the grooms leading the war-charger.

"We next observe the order of battle, which is denoted
by the following inscription: '*Et venerunt ad prælium
contra Haroldum ducem.*' All the combatants are mounted

on horseback, and advance in the following order :—the duke wears his coat-of-mail, his war-helmet with the projecting 'nasal,' and holds in his hand his ducal *bâton :* the person immediately behind him also carries a *bâton,* but not of a military character; it is the Bishop of Bayeux, the warlike priest : the third has a buckler and lance ; this is Robert, Earl of Mortain. A fourth also carries a lance, at the end of which is a circlet from which rays seem to dart out. It is not easy to determine what this design intended to personify ; it certainly was not a weapon of attack or defence, for of what use in battle would have been the addition of the circlet of rays ? The probability is that it was a badge of honour, or, perhaps, a hieroglyphic of the ducal crown of Normandy. The learned Du Cange has proved that similar symbols were in use long before this period, but he leaves it doubtful whether they were exhibited in military expeditions. There is another conjecture that may be hazarded. By this mark of distinction the embroiderers might have wished to designate the *senechal* of the duke, an officer who was always present at the head of the army, in the courts of law, and the royal palaces. At the battle of Hastings this post of honour was conferred by the duke on William, the son of Osbert, one of his maternal relations ; Ordericus Vitalis speaks of him in terms of high praise. The remainder of the troop of cavaliers who follow William are not peculiarly distinguished : they march in the van, three a-breast ; their dress, their casques, their bucklers, their lances, are such as we have frequently described in this article.

"During the march a horseman, who had been sent forward to reconnoitre the enemy, is seen returning at full gallop to report what he had observed : '*Hic Willelmus dux interrogat Vital, si vidisset exercitum Haroldi.*' 'Here Duke William enquires of Vital if he had seen the army of Harold.' The cavalier, by way of answer, points with his left hand towards the direction in which he had seen the Anglo-Saxon troops. The tapestry calls this person Vital; this designation of names is peculiar to this ancient record, and the minute exactitude thus observable is a proof that it was composed at the time when these events happened, and when every particular was well known. In front of this Vital we see two other horsemen, one of whom carries an ordinary standard without a cross; he is armed, and on his head is a casque with a 'nasal ;' the other is also armed, but instead of a casque he wears a mailed cap, such as that

worn by Wadard. They stand on an eminence, and from
the following inscription it is evident that they are observing the disposition and array of the English army: '*In-
terea exploratum directo ducis jussu probatissimi equites hostem
adesse citò nuntiant.*'

"Harold, on his side, equally curious to learn the number
and the equipment of the invaders, dispatched several spies
to collect intelligence. The tapestry represents one on
foot, armed in coat-of-mail, carrying a lance, a sword, and
a buckler: he stands on an eminence, displaying the action
and manner of a person who regards his object with deep
attention; he raises his right hand, as though he were astonished, whether at the discipline of the Normans, their
warlike aspect, or their great numbers: he is next seen
descending the hill, and running towards the camp of
Harold, to whom he relates what he has observed, and announces, by a movement of the arm, that the Duke of
Normandy is advancing to the attack, as we learn from the
inscription: '*Iste nunciat Haroldum de exercitu Willelmi
ducis.*' Immediately after this interview between Harold
and his spy, we notice William haranguing his troops. He
is armed in the mode already described, holding the *bâton*
or truncheon of command in his right hand, and stretching
out his left in the attitude of a speaker; the single cavalier
who is in front of him turns his head to listen, while all
the rest of the troop charge the enemy at full gallop. Here
the battle commences.

"William of Poitiers, Ordericus Vitalis, and others,
state that the duke drew up his forces in the following
order. He placed his archers on foot in the first rank.
In the second he formed another line of footmen, but better armed and covered with cuirasses. The cavalry were
in the third division, under the duke's immediate command. The tapestry seems to have observed the same
order of battle. We first see the archers on foot, who
have no cuirasses; behind them are other archers wearing
coats-of-mail; these are followed by the cavalry. The
same authors, above cited, also remark that the English,
having got possession of a height, dismounted from their
horses and formed a dense and compact body. William of
Malmsbury, who enlarges on the facts narrated by preceding chroniclers, says that they so disposed their bucklers,
as to resemble the tortoise of the Romans. In the tapestry we observe a crowd of English closely wedged together,
armed in the same general manner already noticed; they

cover their front, which is exposed to the enemy, with
their bucklers; the majority carry battle-axes; there is
also seen a single archer on foot, without a buckler; the
air is filled with lances, darts, and arrows. The ground is
covered with the dead and wounded. The lower border
of the tapestry is thronged with different scenes of battle;
among those stretched on the plain is a man who grasps a
round buckler, convex, and armed with a sharp projecting
point in the centre. We have already stated that this
form was peculiar to the Anglo-Saxons, for the troops of
William invariably carried oval bucklers, pointless, and
slightly concave.

"The tapestry does not omit the death of Leofwin and
Gurth, brothers of Harold, who perished in this combat;
their death is marked among the memorable events of the
day. Nothing, however, particularly distinguishes them
but the inscription: '*Hic ceciderunt Lowrine et Gurde, fra-
tres Haroldi ducis.*' We merely see two armed men
stretched on the field. It is here to be remarked that the
tapestry, in fixing the death of these princes at the commencement of the battle, totally differs from all the historians, who relate that they were not slain till after the
death of Harold.

"The next section represents a part of the Norman
army, entangled among the grass and brambles, which
covered an old entrenchment, where they were vigorously
repulsed by the English; great numbers of them were
slain: the tapestry graphically describes the onslaught;
we see the grass and brambles, and men and horses thrown
to the ground, while others are precipitated from the hill
into the fosse: '*Hic ceciderunt simul Angli et Franci in
prælio.*'

"The discomfiture of the Normans had nearly thrown
the whole of William's army into complete confusion and
rout. The Bishop of Bayeux rendered most essential service on this occasion; he stopped the fugitives, rallied
them, and exhorted them to return to the conflict. We
see the prelate, holding a crosier in his hand, speaking to
a horseman whose back is turned to the enemy, and who
has flung his lance over his shoulder, as if he were in the
act of running away. '*Hic Odo episcopus baculum tenens
confortat pueros:*' 'Here Bishop Odo, holding a stick or
crosier, encourages the youngsters.' After much examination this appears to be the real inscription, though the letters are so decayed as to be scarcely legible.

"The exhortations and entreaties of the prelate produced the full effect he desired; the Normans rushed back with fury to the assault. We observe them riding at full gallop, rage depicted in their countenances, all sword in hand, to rejoin the duke. William knew that a report of his death had been spread through the army; he had, indeed, been wounded, and had had two horses killed under him; he rides to different parts of the field, takes off his casque, and shows himself, bareheaded, to the troops. This event is described in the tapestry immediately after the harangue of the Bishop of Bayeux. We behold William showing himself to his followers, to satisfy them that he is yet alive, the intention being expressed by the inscription: '*Hic est Willelm dux.*' By his side is his standard-bearer, displaying the ducal gonfalon, who points to the prince as still prepared to fight for victory.

"The Normans, animated by the presence of their sovereign, fell with such fury on the Anglo-Saxons that they totally routed them, and penetrated to the spot where Harold had planted his standard. The English prince had been wounded early in the battle by an arrow which struck him in the eye. His death is the last event clearly noticed in the tapestry: '*Hic Haroldus interfectus est:*' 'Here Harold was slain.' We see him falling to the ground; near to him are three men on foot, one of whom holds the standard, to which is attached the image of a dragon or some other fierce animal, for the character is not clearly delineated. The two others have bucklers, slightly convex, with a sharp point projecting from the centre. These men were probably intended to represent the body-guard of Harold, whose special duty it was to protect his gonfalon. Immediately after this scene, we observe a cavalier who cuts off part of the thigh of a man stretched dead on the ground. The action thus represented agrees with what William of Malmsbury relates respecting the death of Harold: he says that a cavalier having found the body of Harold among the slain, cut off his thigh, for which ignominious deed he was expelled from the order of knighthood. Throughout the remainder of the tapestry, we merely observe slight outline touches of various form and figure; perhaps nothing more ever existed, as the paintings and the inscriptions might have been discontinued at the death of Matilda, who designed the whole work; or perhaps time and different casualties have defaced the extremities of the tapestry, or rotted the wool; nevertheless, we may still observe men fighting with swords and battle-axes, and distinguish the pursuers from the pursued. The inscription, explanatory of the closing section, though very faint, may still be deciphered : ' *Fugâ verterunt Angli.*' This certainly is not pure Latinity, but it suited the taste of those who worked at the tapestry.

" It is probable that Matilda had not intended to close her labours with the defeat of the Anglo-Saxons, but purposed continuing them to the coronation of her husband. It is a fair and reasonable conjecture that the extremity of this famous tapestry was destroyed by the ravages of time."

Such is the description given by Lancelot of this venerable and instructive tapestry, and as it must ever possess the most lively interest for the student of the early annals of English history, a few additional remarks may not be here misplaced.

M. de Boze, secretary to the " Academie des Belles Lettres," found among the manuscripts of the celebrated Foucault, an illuminated design of part of the tapestry, which he communicated to Lancelot ; he at once investigated the subject to which it alluded, and deemed it sufficiently important to become the theme of a dissertation which he read to the academy on the 21st of July, 1724. He then announced that he was ignorant from what original the design was copied, and, assuming it to be a picture, he could not pronounce whether it was a bas-relief, or a painting on glass ; but he conjectured, from several motives he assigned, that it did not coincide with the event represented.

The indefatigable ardour of the famous Montfaucon did not permit him to rest satisfied with this fragment of the tapestry. He wrote to every man of letters in France, in the hope of obtaining more copious information ; at length discovering that Foucault had been intendant of Normandy, he suspected that the design must have been borrowed from some relic preserved at Caen, or Bayeux. He was confirmed in this opinion by an answer he received from Mathurin Larcher, prior of St. Vigor de Bayeux, who informed him that the original of the illuminated design was a long piece of tapestry, or embroidery then preserved in the cathedral church of Bayeux ; that the fragment seen by Lancelot was only a copy of thirty-feet in length by eighteen inches high ; but that there was another piece, being a continuation of the same history, which

was two hundred and thirty-two feet long, having the same
height as the fragment. This tapestry, added he, was exposed in the cathedral, on certain festivals; and the most
ancient document which mentions it, was contained in the
inventory of the ornaments belonging to our Lady of Bayeux, drawn up in the year 1476, wherein it is thus described :—

"Item, une tente tres longue et tres etroite, de telle à
broderie de ymages et escripteaulx faisans representation
de la conquest d'Angleterre, laquelle est tendue environ
la nief de l'eglise, le jour et par les octaves des re-
liques."

Montfaucon obtained a design of this second part of
the tapestry, which he published with the first in his
".Monumens de la Monarchie Francaise," with some remarks, and this induced Lancelot to revise his first Me-
moir, and greatly enlarge it. It was read in its complete
state by him, before the Academy, on the 9th of May,
1730.

An account was also given of the tapestry by Ducarel in
his Anglo-Norman Antiquities, in 1767, but it is very
meagre. It has recently (1823) been translated into French
by M. Léchaudé d'Anisy, and enriched with some valuable notes. We shall notice some of his conjectures on the
points that Lancelot leaves doubtful; and first, as to the
inscription "*Turoldus.*" M. D'Anisy considers this person,
who is represented in the tapestry as of very diminutive
size, to be the court buffoon of the Count of Ponthieu.
That baron, alarmed at the menaces of William, for not
delivering up Harold on the first summons, could not have
sent a better ambassador than this dwarf, whose humour
might put the duke into a good temper: and his success
may be inferred from the embroidery, for William appears.
to be talking to him with great familiarity, while one of
his guards, or chief officers, places his hand sportively on
the head of Turold. This seems also to have been the
opinion of Montfaucon on this character.

One of the most obscure passages in the tapestry is the
introduction of the woman with the inscription "*Aelfgyva* ;"
it is the only occasion on which a female is mentioned.
When Edward sent the younger sons of Earl Godwin, into
Normandy, as hostages for the good conduct of their father, M. D'Anisy assumes, although all the historians are
silent on the point, that he at the same time sent his Queen,
Editha, whom he had repudiated on the plea of her hav-

ing countenanced the treasonable designs of her father, Earl Godwin, and he thinks that Aelfgyva is a corruption of Editha. When Harold arrived, Godwin was dead, and he claimed back the hostages by the order of Edward, who at this time, as M. d'Anisy conjectures, might have pardoned Editha; for he thinks this supposition borne out by the " *clericus*," or priest, who puts his hand on the head of the female, as if absolving her from some crime.

When the battle commences, Lancelot alludes to one of the persons who carries a lance, at the end of which is a circlet of rays, on which he offers some conjectures. On this M. d'Anisy observes, that some antiquarians have supposed it to represent the dragon, carried both by the Dukes of Normandy and the Kings of England; but in his own opinion, its clearly defined semicircular appearance makes it much more closely resemble that species of banner, or gonfalon, which was formed of one piece, instead of three pieces, such as Charlemagne bore in battle, and such as is seen on the shield of the old French families of Auvergne and Clinchamp.

The last account of the tapestry which we have seen, is by H. F. Delauney, of Bayeux, in which he chiefly seeks its date from its internal evidence, and he ascribes it to Odo. His pamphlet was published in 1824. It is full of learning, and will repay perusal by those who are fond of such researches. It is entitled "Origine de la Tapisserie de Bayeux, prouvée par Elle Meme."

---

## II.—LIST OF THE NORMAN BARONS WHO FOUGHT AT HASTINGS.

ROBERT WACE, in his Roman de Rou, has given a most copious narrative of the battle of Hastings, and he specially mentions all the principal followers of William. The edition of M. Pluquet is enriched with numerous notes by Auguste Le Provost, elucidating the history of these adventurers who, from the condition of houseless vagabonds, became suddenly possessed of lands and castles in the country they had conquered. We shall endeavour in this appendix to give a true account of the ori-

R 5

gin of many of our ennobled families, taking the list of Wace
as the genuine one ; and as his father accompanied the
expedition and communicated many particulars to his son,
who also had access to the best possible information in all
quarters, from his clerical functions and station, we con-
ceive the authority of the old troubadour to be of the highest value.

The first person mentioned is Raoul de Conches, or,
de Fosny. He was the second of his family, and was hereditary gonfalonier, or standard-bearer, to the Dukes of
Normandy. William desired him on this occasion to carry
the gonfalon, but he refused, saying that he preferred mixing in the thick of the fray :—

> " Mais li gonfanon, par ma fei
> Ne sera hui parté par mei
> D'Altre chose serviral
> En la bataille od vos irai,
> Et as Engleiz me combatrai
> Tant ke jo vis estre porral."    Vers. 12,736.

This baron lived till 1102, according to Ordericus Vitalis,
l. x. p. 809, but no record exists to show what lands he received in England.

The gonfalon was next offered to Walter Giffard, Lord
of Longueville in Caux, descended from a sister of the
Duchess Gonnor, wife of Duke Richard the First ; but he
also declined the honour, wishing to signalize his prowess
in the heat of the battle. According to Duchesne, he received from the Conqueror, in 1170, the county of Buck-
ingham, and was the stock of the first earls of that
title.

The standard was then entrusted to a knight of the
*Pays de Caux*, named Toustain, who became the founder of
an illustrious Norman family, which, according to Auguste
Le Prevost, commemorated the deeds of their ancestor at
Hastings by taking, as supporters to their coat-of-arms,
two angels, each holding a banner.

Roger, second of the name, Lord of Montgomeri, and
Count of Alençon and Bellême in right of his wife Ma-
bile, is next mentioned. As a reward for his services, he
received Shropshire, the town of Chichester, and the castle of Arundel, in Sussex. He died in 1094.

Wace, next speaks of Roger de Beaumont; but this is an
error, for William of Poitiers, a cotemporary historian,
asserts positively that he remained in Normandy, as

prime minister to the Duchess Matilda. Wace confounds the father with the son Robert, who made his first essay in arms at Hastings, and having subsequently inherited the estate of Meulan, took the title of Count of Meulan.

Malet de Graville, founder of an illustrious family not yet extinct in France, is mentioned by our poet, as well as William of Poitiers and Ordericus Vitalis, the two latter stating that he attended the funeral of Harold. He was appointed by the Conqueror, in the third year of his reign, to the office of sheriff of Yorkshire. His son Robert obtained from the same prince immense possessions, chiefly situate in Suffolk, in which county he established a monastery of Benedictines, at Eye. The charter of its foundation sufficiently attests the riches of this establishment, till the disgrace of the chief under Henry the First, who had raised him to the office of grand chamberlain.[1]

Hugh de Montfort was born at Montfort-sur-Rille, near to Brionne. Four barons of this district having successively been called Hugh, it is difficult to determine which of them fought at Hastings. Auguste Le Prevost thinks it was the second of the name, son of Hugues à-la-Barbe, and he corrects an error in Collin's Peerage, in which he is confounded with his ·father. It was the son who received one hundred lordships from the royal munificence dispersed over different counties. When William left England, in 1067, Hugh de Montfort was one of the Norman barons, to whom he confided the administration during his absence on the Continent.

Robert of Vieux-Pont distinguised himself at Hastings. In 1073, he was eminent among the Norman warriors sent to the aid of Jean de la Flèche. He remained as commanding officer in Maine, and according to the testimony of Ordericus Vitalis, was one of the first victims of the insurrection of 1085. But this fact is contradicted by a charter ·of Henry the First, in favour of St. Pierre-sur-Dive, in which religious house this Vieux-Pont is said to have assumed the frock. His descendants had large possessions in England. Robert de Vipont, a corruption of the old name, was one of the favourites of John Lackland, and is frequently mentioned in the reign of that prince and of his successor.

We may doubt whether Néel de Saint-Sauveur, was pre-

---

[1] Monasticon Anglicanum, vol. 1. p. 356.

sent, though Wace includes him in the list, for no other
writer mentions his name. In the Brompton Chronicle
we find the name of Sauzaver, but that is not a corruption
of Saint-Sauveur, but of Saunzavier, Sans-Avoir, a family
which established itself in England at the conquest, with
many others bearing more sounding names, but equally
pennyless.

Henry, Lord of Saint Hilaire de Ferrieres near to Bernay, was son to Vauquelin de Ferrieres, whom we have
noticed as one of the disturbers of the minority of William.
The site of the ancient Norman castle of this family is
still visible, surrounded with deep moats. The lords of
Ferrieres took the title of first barons of Normandy, on
account of their extensive forges, from which their name is
derived; for the power of working iron in a barbarous age,
and among a people not advanced beyond the threshold of
civilization, was a great title to distinction. This family
became extinct in Normandy during the seventeenth century;[1] but it still exists in England, in the earldom of
Ferrers. Henry de Ferrieres received from the Conqueror the castle of Tutbury and several lordships. His
descendants were the first earls of Derby and Nottingham.

Roger de Roumare took his title from an estate of that
name near to Rouen. He married Lucia, sister and heiress of the English Earl Morcar. He was distinguished
during the reigns of the two Williams, and his son William was created Earl of Lincoln, by King Stephen.

Hugh de la Mare was the ancestor of the family of that
name, which was formerly very numerous in England
and Normandy, though it was soon changed, in the former
country, into Delamere. The name is still very common
in the Channel Islands. Auguste Le Prevost derives the
stock from the fief of La Mare, situate in the commune of
Autretot, near Yvetot.[2]

Robert Balfou, or Beaufou, was descended on the fe-
male side from Raoul, Count of Ivry, uterine brother of
Duke Richard the First. The principal residence attached
to this ancient barony was in the neighbourhood of Pont
L'Eveque. This Robert, who displayed great valour at
Hastings, died at the abbey of Bec, as did his two sons.
His descendants founded the abbey of Belle Etoile, and

[1] Auguste Le Prevost.
[2] A "commune" in France is a district presided over by a mayor.

held an eminent rank in Normandy, England, and Ireland, in all which countries they had vast establishments in the twelfth century. The Norman barony of Beaufou passed into the possession of the Tilly family in the fourteenth century, and from them into that of the Harcourts, to whom it now belongs.[1]

Wace next mentions the Lord of Tancarville, the hereditary chamberlain of the dukes of Normandy; but he is the only author who says that this baron was at Hastings. He was indeed too old to have taken part in the expedition, and there is every reason to believe that he remained as one of the counsellors of the duchess.

The Lord of Estouteville was Robert, surnamed Grand Bois. There are two places of this name in Normandy, but this baron came from Estouteville, in Caux. The family had large possessions in England. They held the barony of Cottingham, and the estate of Skipwith, in Yorkshire.

Geoffrey, Lord of Magneville, near Valognes, frequently spelt Mandeville, and Mannerville, was after the conquest, appointed constable of the Tower of London, and created Earl of Essex.

William Crespin, first of that name, was Lord of Bec-Crespin, in the arrondissement of Havre. His family descended from Gislebert, Chatelain of Tillieres. William Crespin, second of that name, was distinguished for his bitter hatred against Henry the First, whose life he put in imminent peril at the battle of Brenneville, or as it would be more correctly written, Bremulle. It appears from Domesday-book that Milon-Crespin held eighty-eight manors in England, and was created Earl of Wallingford, in Berkshire. He died without issue in the reign of Henry the First.

Walter, of Saint Martin, was brother to William Martel. There are so many districts of this name in Normandy, that it is difficult to fix the exact locality in this instance. The best opinion, however, seems to be, that it was either in the Pays de Caux or the Pays de Bray. The Martels are still numerous in the Channel Islands, though the ennobled family is extinct in England. They founded the old abbey of Pont Robert, in Sussex, in 1176.

William, Lord of Moulines-la-Marche, in the arrondissement of Mortagne, was not only present at Hastings,

[1] Auguste Le Prevost.

but, in 1073, was appointed one of the generals of the Norman troops, sent to the succour of Jean de la Flèche. He died at an advanced age, in 1099. There was formerly an ennobled family of his name in England, but Auguste Le Prevost traces them from Limousin, and not from Normandy.

In a charter in favour of Saint Pierre sur Dive, Fulk Du-Pin is mentioned as a cotemporary of William the Conqueror. Ordericus Vitalis also notices a Morin Du-Pin as existing in 1060, under Robert and Henry the First. The Lords of Du-Pin were vassals to the Count of Meulan, and one of them was stripped of his estates and banished for having implicated himself in the revolt of 1124. The branch of this family which obtained estates in England, came from Du-Pin-au-Haras, in the arrondissement of Argentan.

Hugh de Grentemesnil, now written Grandmesnil, belonged to the arrondissement of Lisieux. He had been banished in 1063; but, being afterwards pardoned, he fought at Hastings, and narrowly escaped with his life. He received from the royal munificence the title of Viscount or sheriff of Leicestershire, the government of Hampshire, and upwards of one hundred lordships. He was moreover associated with bishop Odo and William Fitz-Osbern in the administration of judicial affairs. He died towards the close of the eleventh century, and was buried at Saint-Evroult, which abbey he had restored and largely endowed.

Humphrey, Lord of Bohun, took his name from that place, situate two leagues to the south of Carentan. The remains of the moat of the old castle are still visible. In this family the hereditary constableship of England long remained, and from it sprang the first Earls of Hereford, Essex, and Nottingham.

Carteret is in the arrondissement of Valognes. This family has long been extinct in Normandy. The Thynne family, who enjoy the Marquisate of Bath and the Barony of Carteret, descend, in the female line, from Humphrey de Carteret. A branch from this stock was settled in Jersey, and were highly eminent during the great rebellion, adhering to the cause of Charles the First with unshrinking fidelity, and serving it with extraordinary zeal and talent.

William de Warenne, the first of that name, related to Duke William on the side of his mother, who was niece to the

Duchess Gonnor, took his name from the fief of Varenne, or Warenne, in the district of Saint-Aubin-le-Cauf. He received from the Conqueror two hundred and ninety-eight manors, and in 1073, he was adjoined to Richard de Bienfaite, as grand justiciary of England. Created Earl of Surrey, by William Rufus, in 1089, he died shortly afterwards, and was buried in the abbey of Lewes in Sussex, which he had founded. His descendants, Earls of Warenne and Surrey, held the very highest rank in England and Normandy. In the latter they possessed, among other domains, the splendid estate and castle of Bellencombre.

Hugh de Gournay, the first of that name, is also called Hugh the Old, (Hugo Senex,) in a charter of Henry the First. He was one of the chiefs of the ducal army at Mortemer, in 1054. Becoming disgusted with the world, he retired to the abbey of Bec, in which he finished his days. He had received ample possessions in England from William. King John, when Normandy was separated from England, gave to the descendants of this Hugh de Gournay, the barony of Wherewhelton in Yorkshire, and the office of sheriffs of Buckinghamshire and Bedfordshire, as an indemnification for the loss of their Norman patrimony.

Engenufe de l'Aigle, was the son of Fulbert, who founded the castle of L'Aigle. He was slain in pursuing the fugitives after the battle, when the Anglo-Saxons, taking advantage of their original entrenchments, rallied for a short time, and made head against the invaders. As the reward of his services, his children received several estates from the Conqueror, among others, that of Pevensey in Sussex.

According to the English genealogists, William D'Aubigny, cup-bearer to the Duke of Normandy, and brother to the famous Néel de Aubigny, passed over to England at the conquest, and exercised his office at the coronation of William, from whom he received the barony of Bokenham, to which the title of cup-bearer remained attached. By his marriage with Avitia he became brother-in-law to Roger de Mowbray. But Wace is wrong in saying that he held the office of cup-bearer, (*pincerna regis;*) it was his eldest son, William, ancestor of the Earls of Arundel and Sussex. We need not here record the circumstances which transferred into the hands of Néel D'Aubigny the immense possessions of his cousin Robert de

Mowbray, and empowered his descendants to assume the rank and style of Barons Mowbray.  Several of the most illustrious English families, and, among others, the Dukes of Norfolk and Lord Arundel of Wardour, pride themselves on their descent from the seigneurs d'Aubigny.  The district from which they took their name is situate in the arrondissement of Coutances, near to Periers.[1]

Walter de Lacy received from the Conqueror the castle of Pontefract, in Yorkshire, and one hundred and sixty-three lordships, the major part of which were in that county.  Roger, son of Walter, also held one hundred and twenty lordships from the royal munificence ; but he lost them, and was banished in 1093, for having attached himself to the party of Robert de Mowbray.  In 1102 he was at the head of the army of Robert Courte-Heuse, Duke of Normandy.  The name of Lacy is derived from Lassy, on the road from Vire to Aulnay.

Turgis de Tracy, who signalized his valour at Hastings, commanded the Norman troops, in 1073, in Maine. Henry de Tracy, cotemporary with King Stephen, was distinguished for his unshaken attachment to that prince, from whom he received the barony of Barnstaple, in Devonshire.

Hugh d'Avranches, surnamed the Wolf, obtained, as the reward of his services, the county of Cheshire in 1070, on condition to hold it as freely by his sword as the king held England by his crown.  After a life almost entirely passed in military exploits, he died in August, 1101, in the abbey of Chester, which he had restored, and where, in his declining years, he had taken the frock.  He also founded, in 1085, the abbey of St. Sever, in Normandy.

Hubert du Port, received the barony of Basingstoke, in Hampshire, and fifty-four lordships in that county.  He took the frock at Winchester, in the reign of William Rufus.  His son Henry founded the priory of Sherborne, a dependency on the abbey of Cerisy, in Normandy.  The name of this family is from Port in Bessin, near to Bayeux.

Robert de Courcy, father of Richard, who fought at Hastings, was one of the six sons of Baudry, the German, and grand-nephew of Gislebert, Count of Brionne.  Rich-

---

[1] Recherches de M. de Gerville sur les Anciens Chateaux du Département de la Manche, No. 46.

ard de Courcy received from the Conqueror the barony of Stoke, in Somersetshire, and other lordships in Oxfordshire. His family held a distinguished rank in England and Normandy, for several centuries. It has been perpetuated in Ireland, to modern times, from John de Courcy, who, under Henry the Second, was among the foremost of its conquerors. Lord Kinsale, the premier baron of Ireland, descends in the male line, from this John, and consequently through him from the Courcys of Normandy. The family name is taken from Courcy, in the arrondissement of Falaise.

Baldwin de Meules, or de Brionne, otherwise called Baldwin of Exeter, and sometimes " The Viscount," was, on his paternal side, great-grandson of Richard the First, and consequently cousin-germane to the Conqueror, and he had the same relationship through his wife. He had passed his youth at the court of the Earl of Flanders, and contributed greatly to the marriage of William with the daughter of that Earl. The duke gave him Meules and Le Sap, in compensation for his father's property, which was alienated during his minority. In 1067 he was charged with the erection and the defence of Exeter Castle, where he chiefly resided. He received from the Conqueror the title of Viscount of Devonshire, with one hundred and sixty-nine manors in that county. He died in 1090.

William de Moyon, was Lord of Moyon, three leagues to the south of Saint Lo. The remains of the castle belonging to this family, one of the most distinguished in England under the Norman dynasty, may still be seen. William de Moyon, with several manors, received Dunster Castle, in Somersetshire, which became the principal abode of his successors. His grandson, also called William, was created Earl of Dorset, by the Empress Matilda, on account of the services he rendered her in the war against King Stephen. The Barons Mohun, of Okehampton, were descended from him, and this branch was not extinguished before the commencement of the eighteenth century.

Raoul de Gael, Lord of Gael and Montfort in Brittany, is the same person who is called by the English and Norman chroniclers, Raoul de Guader. This baron, after having received from the Conqueror the county of Norfolk, became displeased with the duke for refusing his assent to his marriage with the daughter of William Fitz-Osbern; when the king was absent, he solemnized his nuptials, and then conspired against him with his brother-in-law, Roger Fitz-Osbern. Besieged in Norwich, he evaded the anger of William by flight, and sought shelter in his patrimonial estates of Gael and Montfort, which he only quitted to take part in the crusade.

Paisnel, Anglicé, Pagnel, Lord of Moutiers-Hubert, founded the celebrated abbey of Hambie, which is about thirteen miles distant from Coutances. The more ancient chroniclers have spoken but little of this family. Ordericus Vitalis merely mentions William Paisnel, as the first of that name, among the distinguished barons who died about the same time as the Conqueror. He probably fought at Hastings, and certainly was the father of Raoul Paisnel, sheriff of Yorkshire. When Domesday-book was compiled, he possessed forty-five manors. In the reign of William Rufus, he founded the priory of the Holy Trinity, at York. His descendants possessed the castle of Dudley, and founded the priory of that name, as well as the priory of Tikford. A branch of the Pagnels of Hambie added its name to the town of Newport, in Northamptonshire. The English branch of this family became extinct in the commencement of the fourteenth century, and the Norman line failed about a century afterwards. In the island of Jersey a marvellous and romantic tradition is preserved of the knight of Hambie, who there slew a huge dragon and was poisoned by its breath. The Hougue-Bie, or Mount of Hambie, is one of the most picturesque spots in the island, and on it the Prince of Bouillon, during the last war, built a tower for his residence, called Prince's Tower.

Robert Bertrand, called Le Tort, Lord of Briquebec, founded, before the conquest, the priory of Beaumont en Auge, and gave large donations, *imminente morte*, to the abbey of Saint Stephen, in Caen. Although this baron lived at the date of the conquest, he is not the person usually designated as having taken a part in it, but William Bertrand, who probably was his brother, a grandson of Turstin de Bastenbourg, the common stock of the families of Briquebec and De Montfort. William Bertrand alone figures in Domesday-book. He founded the priory of Brickburn, in Northumberland, and was the head of the Bertrands, Barons of Bothall, which line became extinct at the close of the fourteenth century.

Wace next mentions a Lord of Saint-Sever, as present at Hastings, but he alone gives this title to a baronial family. Saint-Sever always belonged to the Viscounts of Avranches.

The Seigneur de Cailly was Osbern, son of Roger, who, in 1080, largely endowed the abbey of Saint Ouen. This family formed establishments in England. Thomas de Cailly was summoned to parliament in the reign of Edward the Second, but he died without issue, and his estates passed into the hands of the Cliftons. In Domesday-book Cailly is written Cailgi, and he is therein declared to be proprietor of several manors in Berkshire.

Martel of Bacqueville was one of the six sons of Baudry, the German, by a niece of the Duchess Gonnor. In 1143, William Martel, cup-bearer to King Stephen, was made prisoner, by the Earl of Gloucester, at Caen, and compelled to surrender the castle of Sherborne, for his ransom. Bacqueville is in the arrondissement of Dieppe.

The Praels, or Préaux, were a younger branch of the Lords of Cailly, from whom they were separated about the time that Wace wrote. They held a distinguished rank in the fourteenth and fifteenth centuries, being allied to the royal families of France and England, but they certainly were not at the battle of Hastings, as Wace affirms, for they did not become a distinct family till a much later date. Préaux is in the arrondissement of Rouen. In 1070, its castle belonged to Odo, called Dapifer, son of Hubert of Rye; not Rye in Sussex, but Rye in Normandy, three leagues to the north-east of Bayeux.

Drogon de Monceaux was the second husband of Edith, widow of Gerard de Gournay. This baron, or his son, who bore the same name, signed the foundation charter of the abbey of Dunstable, in Bedfordshire, in the reign of Henry the First. His descendants are frequently named in the Monasticon Anglicanum. There are several communes in Normandy bearing the name of Monceaux, but the one from which this Drogon derived his baronial title is in the vicinity of Bayeux.

Robert D'Oiley, who accompanied William to Hastings, received the appointment of constable of Oxfordshire. Néel D'Oiley, his brother and successor, gave large donations to the abbey of Saint-Pierre-Sur-Dive. Robert D'Oiley, second of that name, founded in 1129, the old abbey of Osenay, in Oxfordshire. The eldest branch of these powerful barons became extinct in the reign of Henry the Third, and their estates passed into the family of the

Earls of Warwick. The junior branches were numerous, and were established at Chislehampton, in Oxfordshire, and Shottisham in Norfolk. Wace calls the name " Oillie," and in the arrondissement of Falaise there are several communes called " Ouillie," but Auguste Le Prevost is of opinion that these barons came from Ailly, near to Coulibœuf.

Vassy is a small village three leagues from Vire, and the name of the Barons of Vassy still continues in that district. Some antiquarians have supposed that they descended from the Dukes of Normandy, through Archbishop Robert, son of Richard the First. But it is objected to that lineage that the chroniclers, who have spoken of Raoul, the second son of that archbishop, do not speak of a Vassy, but of a Gacé, and his posterity became extinct, at the first generation. It is, however, certain that Robert and Ives de Vassy, in English orthography Vescy, were present at the conquest. The former received from William the lordship of Baulebrook, in Northamptonshire, with several others. The latter Ives married the heiress of the baronies of Alnwick, in Northumberland, and Malton, in Yorkshire. His son-in-law, Stephen, assumed his name, and founded the abbey of Alnwick, in the reign of King Stephen. He and his descendants made a distinguished figure in the courts of the English sovereigns down to the reign of Edward the First, when the family became extinct, and their possessions passed into the house of Clifford. There is a Viscount Vescy, in Ireland, but neither connected with an English or Norman stock.

Colombières and Asnières are both in the arrondissement of Bayeux. The two barons of these names mentioned by Wace are cited in a charter of 1082, made in favour of the Abbaye-aux-Dames, at Caen, though the Lord of Asnières is there styled Raoul, while our author calls him Robert. In Domesday-book we meet with Ranulph de Columbels, as proprietor of several manors in Kent. There are no traces of the family of Asnières, in England.

The Lords of Cahagnes, and Tournières came, the former from the arrondissement of Vire, the latter from the arrondissement of Bayeux. The former figure among the benefactors of the abbey of Lewes, in Sussex, and the latter, styled Richard de Turneriis, is mentioned in the foundation charter of the priory of Kenilworth, in the reign of Henry the First.

Hugh de Bolbec was one of the vassals of Walter Giffard, Lord of Bolbec and Longueville. He received thirteen manors from the Conqueror. The elder branch of this family terminated with a daughter, in the second generation. The younger, which founded the abbey of Blanchelande, in Northumberland, existed to the reign of Henry the Third.

Richard de Bienfaite, son of Gislebert, Earl of Brionne, and eldest brother of Baldwin de Meules, received Orbec, and Bienfaite from William, in compensation for a part of his patrimonial inheritance, which had been alienated during his minority. This baron espoused Rohais, daughter of the first Walter Giffard. He was grand justiciary of England, conjointly with Walter de Warenne, and contributed powerfully, in 1073, to quell the dangerous revolt of the Earls of Hereford and Norfolk. He was created Earl of Clare, in the county of Suffolk, and possessed, in addition to other lordships, the castle of Tunbridge, in Kent, which was his chief residence. This powerful lord died in 1090. His descendants, in different branches, were the Earls of Clare, Hereford, Gloucester, and Pembroke.

Trégoz is in the arrondissement of Saint-Lo. The ruins of the old castle are still visible at the confluence of the Vire and the rivulet of Marqueran. The lord of this district, who fought at Hastings, is mentioned in the list furnished by the Brompton Chronicle, under the name of Traygod. His successors were among the benefactors of the abbey of Hambye, one of whom signed the charter of its foundation, in 1145. Their chief residence in England was Ledyard-Trégoze, in Wiltshire. Robert de Trégoz was sheriff of that county in the reign of Cœur de Lion, and one of the bravest warriors of that warlike age.

Montfiquet is a commune on the road from Saint-Lo to Bayeux, near Cerisy. The ruins of the old castle are yet visible. Gilbert de Montfiquet is one of the most clearly defined characters among those who were present at Hastings. One of the fortresses erected to keep the Londoners in check was committed to his governorship, and was called by his name. His son William married a daughter of Richard de Bienfaite. He gave large donations to the abbey of Cerisy, and his family founded the

priory of Ankerwike and the abbey of Stratford. They
held a distinguished rank, and filled important offices,
down to the reign of Henry the Third, when the estates
were divided between three heiresses.

Roger Bigod, or Bigot, who accompanied the Conqueror, received large grants of land in Essex and Sussex.
When Henry the First ascended the throne, Roger became one of his four principal counsellors, and was treasurer to his household. He died in 1107, at an advanced
age, and was buried in the priory of Thetford, which he
had founded four years before his decease. Wace says,
that he held the office of senechal, but he confounds the
father with the second son, William. The eldest, Hugh,
succeeded his father as treasurer, and was created Earl of
. Norfolk, or to speak with greater accuracy, Earl of East
Anglia, by the successor of the first Henry. His successors preserved the title of Earl of Norfolk till the close of
the thirteenth century, when the family became extinct.

Haie-du-Puits is in the arrondissement of Coutances.
The lord of this barony, at the date of the conquest, was
Raoul, senechal of the Earl of Mortain, and brother of
Robert de la Haie, a cotemporary of Henry the First.
Raoul seems to have been the son of Hubert of Rye, to
whom was entrusted the castle of Nottingham, and the
governorship of that county; he is frequently mentioned
in Domesday-book. It is certain that Robert de la Haie
was nephew to Odo Dapifer, another son of Hubert of
Rye. This Odo Dapifer has been frequently confounded
with Odo au Chapeau, son of Turstin Halduc, or
Haldup, one of the founders of the abbey of Lessay.
This error may be traced back even to Ordericus Vitalis,
who wrote in the twelfth century. In addition to other
grants, Robert de la Haie received the lordship of Halnac,
in Sussex, in the reign of Henry the First, and founded
the priory of Boxgrave, a dependency on the abbey of
Lessay. The name of his wife was Muriel. They had two
sons, Richard and Raoul; the former had an only daughter,
who carried the estates into the family of Saint-John. In
the war between Stephen and Geoffrey Plantagenet, Richard de la Haie, who commanded at Cherbourg, for the King
of England, was seized by pirates, and his brother, Raoul,
was compelled to surrender the castles in the Cotentin to
the Earl of Anjou. These events belong to the years 1141
and 1142. Richard de la Haie, son of Raoul, founded the
abbey of Blanchelande, in Normandy.

Roger de Montbray was brother to Geoffrey, Bishop of Coutances, and father of Robert de Montbray, (Anglicè, Mowbray,) who inherited from his uncle two hundred and eighty manors, which the Conqueror had bestowed on him for his military aid ; for, as Ordericus Vitalis says of this prelate, " He was more skilful in training soldiers for battle, than clerks for the service of the church." In 1092, Robert forfeited this immense property, together with the county of Northumberland, and died, after thirty years of hard captivity. Not only did the estates, but also the name of this opulent baron and his wife, Matilda de l'Aigle, pass into the family of D'Aubigny. The site of the old castle of Montbray is near the market-town of that name, situate on the boundary which separates the departments of Calvados and La Manche.

Say is near to Argentan. The lords of this district took the name of Picot, and they are indifferently spoken of by the old chroniclers as Picot simply, and Picot de Say. In 1060, Robert Picot de Say, his wife Adelize, Robert and Henry their sons, Osmelin de Say and his wife Avita, gave large donations to the church of St. Martin of Seez. These barons were vassals of Roger de Montgomeri, holding from him both in England and Normandy. Picot de Say figures in Domesday-book as tenant to Montgomeri, for twenty manors in Shropshire. He was one of the barons summoned by Roger, in 1083, to attend at the foundation of his abbey of Shrewsbury. A Picot of Cambridge is mentioned in Domesday-book, as founder of the priory of Barnwell. The descendants of Picot de Say, branched out into several families, one of which formed an alliance with the Mandevilles, and transmitted their united successions, with the Earldom of Essex, to the Bohuns. In Normandy, William de Say married Agnes, daughter of Hugh de Grentemesnil. In 1131, Jourdain de Say founded the abbey of Aulnay, near to Caen. His heiress, Agnes, carried the estates into the family of Hommet, by her marriage with the constable Richard de Hommet, who was the protector of the rising abbey of Aulnay.

William de la Ferté is mentioned by Ordericus Vitalis, as one of the chiefs of the Norman army in Maine, in 1073. This is probably the person to whom Wace alludes, and who was Lord of Ferté Macé, for Hugh, the second of that name, took the frock in the abbey of St. Ouen, at Rouen, before the conquest, and left no issue. As to Ferté Fres-

nel, Ordericus Vitalis says positively,(lib. xii.) that it was
not founded till 1119, by Richard Fresnel.

The next baron mentioned by Wace is Botevilain, of
whom no very distinct record remains. We might, at
first glance, confound him with the Lord of Boutteville,
near Sainte-Marie-du-Mont, who certainly fought at
Hastings, but this would be an error. The name of Boutteville appears in the Battle-Abbey List, and that of Bout-
tevilain in the Brompton Chronicle. Independently of
this, it is certain that the Bouttevilles established themselves in the counties of Somerset and Bedford, whereas
the estates of the Bouttevillains were in Northamptonshire.
William Bouttevillaine founded, in 1143, the abbey of·
Pipwell, which was plundered by his grandson, Robert
Bouttevillain. William Bouttevillain, of Cotesbrook,
was one of the benefactors of the abbey of Sulby, in Northamptonshire.

The name of Trousebot, mentioned by Wace, also figures
in the Battle-Abbey list, and in the Brompton Chronicle, so
that some one of that name must have been at Hastings.

The origin of the family is, however, very obscure, and
this is to be accounted for from the fact of their being of
very low rank in the conquest, and under the two first
kings of the Norman line. We learn from Ordericus Vitalis that they were among the *novi homines* whom Henry
the First aggrandized, to the prejudice and discontent of the
ancient nobles. William Troussebot, probably the son of
the former, commanded at Bonneville-sur-Touques, for
King Stephen, in 1138, and distinguished himself by repulsing the invasion of the Earl of Anjou, who was compelled to retreat to Falaise. In 1132, Geoffrey Troussebot
had founded the monastery of Wartre, in Yorkshire. The
family are eminent in the Norman rolls, Nicolas Troussebot, descending from the earls of Montfort, and Geoffrey
the chatelains of Gavray.

It was not Hugh de Mortemer who fought at Hastings, as
Wace affirms, but his father Raoul, son of Roger, Lord of
Mortemer-sur-Eaulne, and brother of the first William de
Warenne. Wace seems to have been as ignorant of Roger
as of Raoul, for he does not mention him in his recital of
the battle of Mortemer, though Ordericus Vitalis positively
affirms that he was one of the two chiefs of the Norman army.
Although he was greatly instrumental in defeating the
French, he fell into disgrace with the duke, was exiled,

and stripped of his estates, for having set at liberty, of his own accord, Raoul de Montdidier, one of the principal barons of the hostile army.  But shortly afterwards he was restored to favour, when the duke gave him back all his property, but Mortemer; this estate, however, did not go out of the family, for the duke presented it to William de Warenne, his brother.  It was at the request of Roger de Mortemer, and through his benefactions, and those of his wife, that the priory of Saint-Victoren-Caux was raised to the rank of an abbey, in 1074.  Raoul, son of Roger, recovered the estate of Mortemer, and contributed largely, both from his English and Norman estates, to enrich the abbey of Saint-Victor.  He founded, in England, the priory of Wigmore.  In 1089 he was one of the principal barons who took part with William Rufus, against Robert Courte-Heuse.  In 1104 he joined the party of Henry the First, when he arrived in Normandy.  William the Conqueror bestowed on him large possessions, among others, the castle of Wigmore, in Herefordshire, which districts his personal efforts had mainly subdued.  From him descended the Mortemers, Earls of Marche.  In Normandy, Jane de Mortemer, about the middle of the thirteenth century, conveyed the estates of this family, and the barony of Varanguebec, into the house of Bec Crespin, by her marriage with William Crespin, fifth of the name, and a marshal of France.

There are two communes in Normandy, called Auviler, the one is situate in the arrondissement of Pont l'Eveque, the lords of which were allied to the family of Tournebu ; the other is contiguous to Mortemer-sur-Eaulne.   The person alluded to by Wace probably came from this latter district, and may have been a military vassal of Mortemer, noticed above.   In the Norman rolls, we find Henry D'Auvilliers among the knights of the Bailiwick of Rouen, in 1271.   Hugh d'Auviler was one of the vassals of Robert Malet, of Suffolk, and his name appears among the benefactors of the priory of Eye, in that county, in the reign of the Conqueror.

Asnebec is near to Vire.  We do not think that this person had any particular lordship at the date of the conquest, but that Asnebec then formed part of the domains of Robert Fitz-Haimon, whose father, Haimon-aux-Dents, was killed at the battle of Val-des-Dunes.  Margaret of Gloucester, descended from this Asnebec, conveyed the estates by marriage into the family of Harcourt, at the close of the twelfth century.

s

Saint-Clair is an arrondissement of Saint-Lo. The remains of the old baronial castle are still visible near to the church. The name of Saint-Clair figures distinctly in the Brompton Chronicle, and though greatly defaced, may be traced in the Battle-Abbey List. William Saint-Clair endowed the abbey of Savigny, in the reign of Henry the First. In 1139, the priory of Villers-Trossard was founded by a person of the same name. The Saint-Clairs formed establishments in England, but it is now changed to Sinclair.

Robert Fitz-Erneis was nephew of Raoul Tesson, the first of that name, and cousin-germane to Raoul the second, enumerated by Wace among the Norman warriors. This Robert was son of Erneis, whose name became patronymic with the junior branch of the house of Tesson, and Hacvise, sister of Fulk d'Aunou. He himself married another Hacvise, and was slain at Hastings, as is proved by a passage in a charter granted by his son.[1] The family received no lands in England, at the division after the conquest, probably in consequence of the death of their ancestor in the battle; but they afterwards acquired property there by marriage.

Robert, Earl of Mortain, was uterine brother to the Duke of Normandy. After William himself, he received the largest portion of the English spoil, there being allotted to him nine hundred and seventy-three manors, in eighteen different counties. He was present at the death of the Conqueror, and, by his entreaties, obtained the release of his brother Odo, Bishop of Bayeux. He himself died in 1090, and was buried at Grestain, an abbey founded by his father, Herlouin, and greatly enriched by his personal donations. He also founded the collegiate church of Mortain, in 1682. He married Matilda, daughter of Roger de Montgomeri.

Wace mentions Errand de Harcourt, among those who fought at Hastings. There is a noble family of this title in England, bearing the same name as that of Normandy, with the same device: "*Le bon temps viendra.*" The English genealogists have invented an apocryphal filiation, in order to fix their arrival at the date of the conquest; with this object in view, they have created a Gervase, a Geoffrey, and an Arnold de Harcourt, all three of whom they represent as having been present at the battle of Hastings. But the whole statement is untrue. La Roque

---

[1] Eodem verò patre meo in Angliâ occiso. Gallia Christiana, xl. instrum. col. 334.

says it was Raoul, second son of Robert, himself second baron of Harcourt, who, having attached himself to the party of King John, quitted France, and became the stock of the Harcourts of England.

Crevecœur-en-Auge is in the arrondissement of Lisieux. The barons of Crevecœur established themselves in England, and the family was divided into two branches in the reign of Henry the First. That of the barons of Redburn, benefactors of the priory of Bolington, lived in Lincolnshire. The other line, established in Kent, had for their chief, Robert de Crevecœur, who founded, in 1119, the priory of Leeds.

Driencourt is the modern Neufchâtel. The name was changed when Henry the First there built the castle. There exists no authentic record of the lords of Driencourt. La Roque speaks of Hugh, Lord of Neufchâtel, who, in the twelfth century, married a daughter of Robert, Earl of Meulan, but he confounds Neufchâtel in the Saônois with Neufchâtel in Bray.

There is no such name in Normandy as Briencourt, which Wace probably used to suit his rhyme. We may conjecture that he intended Brucourt, in the arrondissement of Pont l'Eveque. The first baron of this name who can be traced by any authentic documents, was Robert de Brucourt, who flourished in the middle of the twelfth century, and confirmed the foundation of the priory of Walsingham, the charter of which had been granted by Geoffrey de Fervaques. About the same epoch, Gislebert de Brucourt gave to the abbey of Val Richer large estates in the vicinity of Fervaques.

Combray is near to Harcourt Thury. Roger de Combray figures among the benefactors of the priory of Sainte-Barbe-en-Auge, and Geoffrey and Raoul de Combray among those of the abbey of Fontenay, but at a date much posterior to the conquest.

There are four communes in Normandy called Aulnay, or Aunay. We have already seen that Aulnay, near to Caen, belonged, in the twelfth century, to the lords of Say. It is difficult to decide from which of the other three came, first, Berenger de Alneto, who attested the foundation charter of the abbey of Aumale, in 1115; secondly, Herbert de Alneto, a cotemporary of Henry the First, and who witnessed two charters granted by that monarch; and, thirdly, Roger de Alneto, who seems to have been a relation of Gondrée de Gournay, wife of Néel d'Aubigny, and who became a monk at Bellaland.

There exists in Normandy nine communes of the name of Marmion. The one alluded to by Wace is that of Fontenay, near to Caen, and called, for distinction's sake, Le Marmion, from the name of its ancient lords. The Mar-. mion who fought at Hastings was called Robert, and not Roger, as Wace inaccurately states. The name of Roger Marmion does not appear before the reign of Richard Cœur de Lion, when he signed the charter in favour of the abbey of Grestain. It is certain that Robert Marmion received from William the town and castle of Tamworth, in Warwickshire. After having expelled the nuns of Pollesworth from his estates, he invited them back again, so that himself and his wife, Milisenda, were regarded as the second founders of that convent. The family of Marmion possessed, during several generations, the estate of Scrivelsby, in Lincolnshire, to which was attached the privilege of the royal championship on the day of the coronation. English genealogists date the gift of Scrivelsby from the conquest, but this is fully contradicted by Domesday-book. Robert Marmion, son or grandson of the preceding, sided with King Stephen, and his castle of Fontenay was taken and razed to the ground by Geoffrey, Earl of Anjou. He himself perished miserably, in 1143, after having desecrated the church of Coventry, by converting it into a fortress. A third Marmion founded the abbey of Barbery, in 1181. The family existed in England to the reign of Edward the Third, when the estates passed by marriage to the Ludlows, and afterwards to the Dymokes, who still hold the manor of Scrivelsby, and exercised their right to the championship at the coronation of George the Fourth.

Rebercil, the modern Rubercy, is in the arrondissement of Bayeux. The abbey of Longues was founded in 1168, by Hugh Wac, Lord of Rebercil. This Hugh Wac seems to be the person who married Emma, daughter of Baldwin, who, in 1138, founded the abbey of Brunne, in Lincolnshire. The family of Wac appears to be quite extinct in England.

William Bacon du Molay, in 1082, gave large donations to the abbey of the Holy Trinity, at Caen, in which his sister had taken the veil. The first English baron of this name on record is Richard Bacon, Earl of Chester, who founded a priory in Staffordshire. From this stock some presume

-that Lord Chancellor Bacon descended, but his own family trace themselves from a Grimbauld, a cousin of William de Warenne. They maintain that it was a grandson of this Grimbauld who took the name of Bacon, in Normandy. Jane Bacon, a very wealthy heiress, conveyed the estates of the barons de Molay into the families of Briquebec and Luxembourg, about the middle of the fourteenth century.

Alain Le Roux, son of Odo, Earl of Brittany, rendered powerful assistance to William in the conquest of England. He received, in recompense for his services, four hundred and forty-two lordships, and the title of Earl of Richmond, the castle of which name he built in Yorkshire. He died without children, and was succeeded by his brother Alain Le Noir. Wace does not mention their brother Brient, who fought at Hastings, and who, in 1068, repulsed the invasion of the two sons of Harold at Exeter. Alain Le Roux commanded the Norman army in Maine, after the departure of the king, in 1085, and died in the reign of William Rufus.

Bernard of Saint Valery-sur-Somme, was grandson of Richard the Second, through his daughter Papia, and consequently cousin-germane to Duke William. It was from the harbour of St. Valery that the fleet of the invaders set sail, for at that time Dieppe was not a port. In Domesdaybook, we find Ranulf de Saint Valery proprietor of domains in Lincolnshire, with several others of that name, and one of them, called Bernard, died at the siege of Saint Jean d'Acre. It is very singular, as Auguste Le Prevost remarks, that Wace should have omitted the name of Guilbert d'Aufay, cousin of Bernard of Saint Valery, who was, without doubt, the most disinterested soldier in the Norman army. Ordericus Vitalis thus describes his character, and we put it here on record as a specimen of virtue rarely equalled : " Consanguineus ducis, semper ei fidelis fuit, et cum illo præcipua cætibus suis stipatus in bello anglico discrimina pertulit. Verum postquam regnum pacatum est et Gulielmus regnavit, Gulbertus (rege multas in Angliâ possessiones offerente) Neustriam repetiit, legitimâque simplicitate pollens de rapinâ quicquam possidere noluit."[1]

Robert, Earl of Eu, was grandson of Richard the First, and consequently uncle of Duke William. This baron

[1] Ord. Vit. L. v. p. 606.

distinguished himself among the Norman chiefs at Mortemer. In 1059 he founded the abbey of Treport. He received a large share of the English spoils. In 1069 he was
most active in repulsing the Danish invasion. After the
death of the Conqueror, he attached himself to the party
of William Rufus, and remained faithful to his cause.

Such is the list of the principal warriors who fought at
Hastings, according to the text of the Roman de Rou. In
the "Recueil des Historiens de France, apud Duchesne,"
there are many other names, as is the case also in the
Battle-Abbey List and the Brompton Chronicle. Dumoulin
has preserved the armorial bearings of the knights and
barons.

----

### III.—THE PROPHECY OF MERLIN.

THE following curious document has been preserved by
Ordericus Vitalis, in the twelfth book of his History, which
corresponds with the fourth volume, page 415, of the
edition of M. Guizot and M. Louis du Bois. The translation of the fragment, so intimately connected with the
family of the Conqueror, cannot fail to interest the reader.

" I shall record the prophecy of Ambrose Merlin, which
he uttered in the time of Vortigern, King of England, and
which was fully accomplished in many particulars during
a period of six hundred years. For that reason I think it
right to insert in this work some passages which seem to
relate to our era. Merlin was the cotemporary of the
blessed Germain, Bishop of Auxerre. In the time of the
Emperor Valentinian he travelled twice into Brittany,
where he disputed against Pelagius and his followers, who
blasphemed against the grace of God, and he confounded
the heretics by several miracles which he performed in the
name of the Saviour. After having celebrated the festival
of Easter with devotion, he made war against the Anglo-
Saxons, who, being then pagans, were opposed to the Christian Britons. Stronger in his prayers than in his arms, he
routed the whole pagan army by simply singing *Halleluia*,
with a few newly baptized converts. If any one desires to
know these things and others more fully, he should read
the works of Gildas, a Breton historian, and the English
Bede. There shines a brilliant narrative concerning Wor-
temer, as well as his brothers, and one relating to the

brave Arthur, who made war against the English twelve
times. It is said that Merlin showed Vortigern a pond in
the middle of the path; in the pond were two vases, and
in the vases a roll of linen, and in the roll two worms, of
which one was white and the other red. Suddenly the
worms increased to a great size, and became dragons,
when they began to fight cruelly. At length the red
triumphed, and drove the white to the edge of the pond.
While the king was observing these things with the
Britons, Merlin shed tears. The prophet, interrogated by
the astonished spectators, explained, in a prophetic spirit,
that the pond in the middle of the path was a symbol of
the world; the two vases were figurative of the isles of
the ocean; the roll of linen was an emblem of the towns
and villages of Britain, in which are the habitations of men;
the two worms designate the Breton and English people,
who will, said Merlin, engage in bloody combats till the
sanguinary Saxons, typified by the red dragon, put to flight,
up to Cornwall, and the margin of the ocean, the Bretons,
denoted by the white worm, because they have been puri-
fied, or whitened in the fountain of baptism, from the time
of King Lucius and Pope Eleutherius. The prophet of
whom we speak predicted circumstantially all that would
happen in the islands of the north, and wrote down his
predictions in allegorical language. After having spoken
of the Germanic worm and the decimation of Neustria,
which took place under Alfred, brother of Edward, son of
King Ethelred, and under his companions at Guilford, he
prophesied as follows, on the revolutions of the present
time, and on the troubles which would bring about great
changes.

" A people will arrive in wood[1] and in tunics of iron;
they will take vengeance on perversity. They will restore
their dwellings to the aboriginal inhabitants, and the ruin
of the strangers will clearly be effected.[2] Their seed
shall be plucked out of the gardens, and the remnant of
their race shall be decimated. They shall bear the yoke
of eternal servitude, and strike their mother with the
pick-axe and the plough. There shall come two dragons,
one of which shall be slain by the arrows of envy,[3] and
the other shall perish under the shadow of a name.[4] Then
shall appear a lion of justice,[5] at whose roar the French
castles and the insular dragons shall tremble. In those

---

[1] That is, in ships.                    [2] Allusion to William the Conqueror.
[3] William Rufus.        [4] Duke Robert.         [5] Henry the First.

days gold shall be expressed from the lily and the nettle;
silver shall flow from the feet of lowing animals; the elegant shall cover themselves with different fleeces, and the
exterior of their dress shall show the interior of their
hearts. They shall cut the paws of animals which bark;
wild beasts shall have peace. Humanity shall be afflicted
in being given up to punishment: the form of commerce
shall be cleft, and the half shall be round. The rapacity
of hawks shall perish, and the teeth of wolves shall be
blunted; the young lions shall be changed into fishes of
the sea,[1] and the eagle shall build its nest on the mountains
of Araun.[2] Vendocia shall be reddened with maternal
blood, and the family of Corinna shall massacre six
brothers: the island shall be bathed with nocturnal tears,[3]
and each, in consequence, will be induced to hazard various
enterprises.[4] Our descendants will fly in the air, and
novelties will be esteemed. Piety on the part of the impious will injure him in possession, till he has clothed himself with paternity; armed in consequence with the teeth
of the wild boar, he will traverse the summit of mountains
and cross the shadow of him who wears a casque. Albion
will be indignant, and, summoning her neighbours, will
busy herself with spilling blood. They will put into the
jawbones a curb which shall be manufactured in the sea of
Brittany.[5] The eagle, breaking the treaty, will devour
this curb,[6] and will rejoice in building his nest for the third
time. The children of the roaring lion will awake,[7] and
disdaining the forests, will hunt within the walls of cities;
they will make a great carnage of those they may meet,
and cut the tongues of bulls; they will load with chains
the neck of those who roar, and bring back old times.
Finally, the thumb shall be bathed with oil, from the first
to the fourth, from the fourth to the third. The sixth
shall throw down the walls of Ireland, and change the
forests into plains; he shall reduce divers portions under
one; he shall crown himself with the head of a lion; his
beginnings will sink under a vague affection, but his end
shall fly to the skies. In fact, he will renew the seats of

---

1 The sons of Henry the First, who perished in the shipwreck off Barfleur.
2 Montes Araunium, the Ceraunian Mountains.
3 The death of Henry the First, whose body was carried to England and interred
at Reading.
4 The Latin note appended to this passage runs thus: "Neustria, woe to thee,
for the brains of the lion shall be scattered, and shall be thrown out of the paternal
soil, after having its members torn." The allusion is to King Stephen, raised to
the throne in preference to the daughter of Henry the First.
5 Henry the Second, born among the Angevins, near the sea of Brittany.
6 Eleonora of Aquitaine.          7 The sons of Henry the Second.

the blessed in different countries, and place pastors in suitable places. He will cover two cities with a mantle, and make a virginal present to virgins: this will obtain for him the favours of the master of the thunder, and he will be crowned among the happy. There will issue from him a contagion which will penetrate everywhere, and which will menace with ruin his own nation.[1] This contagion will cause Neustria to lose her two islands,[2] and she will be despoiled of her ancient dignity. Afterwards the citizens will return into the isle."

Such is the curious prophecy of Merlin, preserved by Ordericus Vitalis, the whole of which he professes himself able to interpret, but he neglects to do so, saying that he must proceed with his narrative. He, however, dwells on some points; for example, the death of William Rufus by the arrow, and the death of Duke Robert, who perished under the shadow of a name, that is to say, in prison, with the nominal title of duke. This indeed seems to be a literal fulfilment of the prediction, as does the drowning of the sons of Henry the First at Barfleur, (the young lions shall be changed into fishes of the sea.) The lion of justice, at whose roar the French castles and the insular dragons shall tremble, our author refers to Henry the Second, who, after his marriage with Eleonora of Aquitaine, excelled in power and territory all his predecessors, and became truly formidable to France.

The foot-notes appended to this translation are from Guizot's edition; we might add some additional explanations, but as they would merely amount to conjectures, it is perhaps best to suppress any further commentary.

[1] Richard Cœur de Lion and King John.　　　[2] England and Ireland.

THE END.

Joseph Rickerby, Printer, Sherbourn Lane.

*Works Published by Joseph Rickerby.*

In 18mo. cloth lettered, price 2s. 6d.,

# THE YOUNG NATURALIST'S BOOK OF BIRDS.

### By PERCY B. ST. JOHN.

#### With ILLUSTRATIONS from DESIGNS by LANDSEER

" This little volume is written with a simplicity and ease that cannot be too much commended."—*Athenæum.*
" This pre·ty little book is full of anecdotes collected from travels, and is both amusing and informing."—*Atlas.*

In post 8vo., price 7s., cloth elegant,

# GERALDINE, a Sequel to COLERIDGE'S CHRISTABEL,

## WITH OTHER POEMS.

### By M. F. TUPPER, Esq., Author of " PROVERBIAL PHILOSOPHY."

" Mr. Tupper takes up the tale where Coleridge broke off, and skilfully connects his own story with the original, as well as imitates its wildness of style and images with a felicity which nothing but a long and enthusiastic acquaintance with his prototype could impart."—*Spectator.*

SECOND Edition, enlarged.—Post 8vo. cloth lettered, Price 6s.

# PROVERBIAL PHILOSOPHY:

### By MARTIN FARQUHAR TUPPER, Esq., M.A.

" A book as full of sweetness as a honeycomb, of gentleness as a woman's heart; in its wisdom worthy the disciple of a Solomon, in its genius the child of a Milton."—*Court Journal.*

In demy 8vo. cloth, price 8s.; half-bound Morocco, gilt edges, 10s. 6d.; Lage Paper 16s.

# THE BOOK OF THE CARTOONS.

### By the REV. RICHARD CATTERMOLE, B.D.

A few Impressions of the Plates, India Proofs, on 4to. Colombier, with Historical Account, price 21s.

" A deep feeling of the sentiment that pervades the designs, and a nice perception and just appreciation of their peculiar excellences, joined to the taste and learning of a connoisseur, are the characteristics of this elegantly-written volume. The portrait of RAFFAELLE is exquisitely beautiful."—*Spectator.*

In foolscap 8vo., price 5s.

# SIR THOMAS BROWN'S RELIGIO MEDICI;

### To which is added,

## HYDRIOTAPHIA, OR URN-BURIAL.

#### With a Discourse and Notes, by J. A. ST. JOHN, Esq.

" These quaint and extraordinary treatises are presented in a neat and cheap volume, with the addition of an able Discourse, and copious explanatory Notes."—*Critical Notice.*

In foolscap 8vo., price 5s.

# LADY MONTAGU'S LETTERS FROM THE LEVANT.

#### With a Discourse and Notes, by J. A. ST. JOHN, Esq.

" The letters are full of fascination; and Mr. St. John has laid before the English public, for the first time, the peculiar circumstances that contributed to form her ladyship's character."—*Critical Notice.*

In foolscap 8vo., price 5s.

# UTOPIA; OR, THE HAPPY REPUBLIC;

### A PHILOSOPHICAL ROMANCE, BY SIR THOMAS MORE.

### To which is added,

# THE NEW ATLANTIS, by LORD BACON.

#### With an Analysis of PLATO'S REPUBLIC, and Notes, &c., by J. A. ST. JOHN, Esq.

CPSIA information can be obtained at www.ICGtesting.com
Printed in the USA
BVOW06s1109251015

424033BV00014B/319/P